HOW SWEET IT WAS

TELEVISION: A PICTORIAL COMMENTARY

By
Arthur Shulman
and
Roger Youman

BONANZA BOOKS, NEW YORK

Designed by Harold Franklin

TABLE OF CONTENTS

ACKNOWLEDGMENTS

WE ARE GRATEFUL to a number of persons and organizations for helping us with various aspects of this book, particularly the acquisition of photographs for it. Our thanks go to the American Broadcasting Company, the Columbia Broadcasting System, the National Broadcasting Company, National Educational Television, the International Communications Archives, the Xerox Corporation and Telsun Foundation, the Herbert Floyd Kasselle Estate, Donald C. W. Mooney, Ed Justin, and Shirley Imo. For their assistance in preparing the index, for their patience, perseverance, wisdom, and devotion, and for adding a touch of class to our lives, we thank Joan Shulman and Lily Ann Youman. Finally, our largest debt of gratitude is owed to *TV Guide* magazine, for lending us several dozen of the photographs that appear in this book and for providing the research facilities that were so useful in pinning down elusive facts. So many persons at *TV Guide* have been helpful to us, we could not begin to thank them all individually, but we would like specifically to express our appreciation to its editor, Merrill Panitt, and its publisher, James T. Quirk, for their cooperation and encouragement.

A. S. and R. Y.

To JIMMY,
NANCY,
LAURA,
KAREN,
and JOSH (who just beat the deadline).

□*"Television is the educator and the communicator, the informer, the thing that can inspire and enrich man as he makes his greatest transition from what he is today into the first genuine adult human being."* —Sylvester L. Weaver

□*"Television is a triumph of equipment over people, and the minds that control it are so small that you could put them in the navel of a flea and still have enough room beside them for a network vice-president's heart."* —Fred Allen

□*"Television is the greatest single power in the hands of mortal man."* —LeRoy Collins

□*"It is a medium of entertainment which permits millions of people to listen to the same joke at the same time, and yet remain lonesome."* —T. S. Eliot

□*"Television is now recognized everywhere as a vehicle for education and information, a force to arouse and unify developing nations, and a symbol of national status and prestige that soars above the home-grown airline."* —Robert E. Kintner

□*". . . a vast wasteland."* —Newton N. Minow

□*"Well, I'd say it's pretty good, considering it's for nothing."* —Bing Crosby

□*"Some television programs are so much chewing gum for the eyes."* —John Mason Brown

□*"We are human and, given a chance, we still might create an art form of television."* —Gilbert Seldes

How Sweet It Was

ONE CAN OBTAIN as many opinions about television as there are people with eyes. No two people see it in exactly the same way. But whatever you think of television —whether you like it or loathe it or just tolerate it; whether you are grateful for it or scornful of it; whether you watch it a lot or a little—whatever your attitude is toward it, television has become a part of you.

You may not be aware of it, but up there, in that compartment of your brain where memories are stored, all sorts of strange images are stockpiled. They are greyish rectangles, sort of, but with rounded edges, and inside them are people and places and things of every de-

scription. Some of them can be recalled merely by twisting a mental dial; others lurk there patiently, waiting for an external stimulus that will pull them out of their dusty corners and into your mind's eye. These are your memories of television past.

The purpose of this book is to coax those memories out of their hiding places and bring them front and center, where you can savor them anew. The book contains more than fourteen hundred photographs, and they are populated by thousands of people. Some of them you will recognize immediately; others will be vaguely familiar; many will be total strangers. You will find programs you remember with affection, and others you recall with distaste; programs that lasted for years, others that disappeared after a few weeks; significant events from television's history, and trivial moments; brilliantly talented performers, and inept clods. Some of the photographs will make you smile fondly, some will make you laugh derisively, some will bring back solemn recollections, some will draw a complete blank.

Although this book is intended to be a comprehensive review of television during the past twenty years—the two decades that have passed since the medium became a commercial reality—it is not meant to be just a scholarly history. The programs and people represented here were chosen not because they were "good" or "popular" or "successful," but because each contributed, in some large or small way, to the progress of television. Theirs may not necessarily have been a beneficial contribution, just as the progress of the medium has not necessarily been in the direction of higher quality. Individually many of these pictures mean little, except to a few people; but considered cumulatively and in relation to each other, they constitute a panorama of the television scene since the late forties.

For better or for worse, in sickness and in health, this is what television has been during the past twenty years.

A Bunch of Bananas

RESPLENDENT IN BAGGY PANTS and putty nose, the comedians were in the vanguard when television arrived. Although from the beginning it had been evident that comedy would be an important part of programming, no one, in the primitive and experimental days of 1946, could have foreseen the course it would take.

Most comedians came to the home screens after years of basic training in vaudeville, burlesque, the theater, or radio. And most were unprepared to meet television's peculiar and exacting demands. In burlesque or vaudeville a comedy act could be constructed and developed before live audiences in a thousand little theaters in the hinterlands; by the time a comedian became a top banana, his material had been burnished to a high gloss through years of trial and error. Television changed all that. The training grounds vanished; preparation time was telescoped from years into hours; and every appearance before the cameras was like opening at The Palace.

This posed a cruel dilemma for comedians. To maintain their stature (and market value), television exposure was a necessity, yet the medium's voracious appetite for fresh material and creative technique was simply beyond the capacity of most of the funnymen. In time, though often with great reluctance, most of them took a crack at it. One by one the giants of American comedy trooped to the stage to face the unblinking red eye, some for a few hours of guest appearances, others for a season or two with their own shows. Nearly all such attempts were abortive. As a

CHAPTER I

group, the comedians fell victim to the technological revolution in show business.

There were exceptions: Berle and Caesar and Skelton attacked the medium head on and shaped it to their own advantage; Benny and Hope made the transition by adding a visual dimension to an established radio format. But for most of the comedians television was an artificial environment, unlike any other in their experience. Though in many cases they were enormously talented performers, they could not successfully adapt to the new surroundings for any sustained period. Many found themselves relying heavily on directors, producers, and a horde of gag writers, but these efforts tended to dilute rather than enhance their comedy image, and they were quickly dismissed by a jaded and insatiable audience.

The high mortality rate among comedians forced television to reevaluate the concept of comedy as it related to the picture tube. Tradition was cast aside and what emerged were personalities, performers who, like Willy Loman, wanted only to be liked. Along with them came the situation comedies, which emphasized home, love, and family, and rarely contained more than a few legitimate chuckles. The quest was for warmth, not laughter.

Although it would still have room for an occasional attempt at something new or unusual in comedy (Jonathan Winters or *TW3*), by the mid-sixties television had relegated the comedian to guest shots on variety shows, exile in Las Vegas, or a forced retirement in which he damned the Nielsen ratings as he muttered over his scrapbooks. A bland curtain had descended, and the laughter had become muted and almost inaudible.

MILTON BERLE

was known as "Mr. Television," and with some justice. His show *The Texaco Star Theater* went on the air in 1948 and remained on (with some changes in title and sponsorship) until 1956. Tuesday night was Berle Night, and in those early days owners of television receivers could usually expect half the neighborhood to drop in for a Tuesday-night visit. Another typical scene of that era was the crowd gathered on the sidewalk outside an appliance store, watching Uncle Miltie through the plate-glass window. Berle was a major factor in establishing the popularity of the new medium, and he was undoubtedly responsible for the purchase of the first television set in many households. His shows featured brash and raucous comedy, guest stars, and lavish production. In later seasons, Berle appeared as the host of another comedy series, as a guest on both variety and dramatic programs, and, briefly, as the comedy emcee of a bowling show.

Berle's version of a vacationing Englishman, in a sketch with comedienne Gracie Fields.

With guest Bob Smith, Berle appears in a typically outlandish costume.

Ruth Gilbert played Berle's secretary, Max.

Pitchman Sid Stone, whose "I'll tell you what I'm gonna do" became a conversational fad.

Ventriloquist Jimmy Nelson and his dummy, Danny O'Day, were permanent cast members.

A typical rehearsal scene. Berle was noted for his long hours of rehearsal and his meticulous attention to every detail of his programs.

JACKIE GLEASON

has long been a performer in the theater, nightclubs, and motion pictures, but his greatest popularity and his most creative comedy efforts resulted from his work in television. With a few brief hiatuses, he has appeared regularly since 1950. In that time, he has introduced a gallery of comedy characters, each a sharply etched portrait with depth and dimension. In recent years he has made a number of dramatic appearances, most notably as Minnesota Fats in the film "The Hustler."

Gleason, costarring with Rosemary DeCamp, was the first Chester Riley in *The Life of Riley* series (1950). William Bendix later took over the role.

On *Cavalcade of Stars*, Gleason introduced "The Honeymooners," a series of sketches featuring Pert Kelton as his wife.

Reginald Van Gleason III.

Charley the Loudmouth, with Art Carney.

/ **17**

Joe the Bartender.

The Poor Soul.

first appeared on the *Admiral Broadway Revue* in 1949. The program was later entitled *Your Show of Shows* and remained on the air until the summer of 1954. Featured on the ninety-minute productions were Imogene Coca, Carl Reiner, Howard Morris, Marguerite Piazza, the Hamilton Trio, the Billy Williams Quartet, and the dance team of Bambi Linn and Rod Alexander. From the outset it was clear that Caesar possessed a comedy talent of extraordinary range, and the show constantly reflected his versatility. Ably abetted by Coca, Reiner, and Morris, he presented pantomimes, sketches, and, most memorably, savagely satirical burlesques of motion pictures and operas. When *Your Show of Shows* ended, Caesar and Coca went their separate ways. They were later reunited as a team for a single season, 1958. Caesar has since starred on Broadway in "Little Me" and has appeared as a guest star on numerous shows.

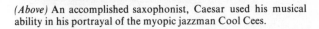

(Above) An accomplished saxophonist, Caesar used his musical ability in his portrayal of the myopic jazzman Cool Cees.

(Top, right) In a takeoff on the musical tastes of the day, Carl Reiner and Howard Morris join Caesar in a trio called The Haircuts.

(Right) In one of his most famous lampoons, Caesar became author and storyteller Somerset Winterset.

(Bottom, right) Art Carney is the director, as silent-film star Caesar enjoys his daily milk bath.

(Below) One of the Caesar-Coca trademarks was the ability to perform a sketch realistically on a bare stage, with no elaborate props or costumes.

In the course of his many shows, four stars appeared as Caesar's "wives." They were *(Right)* Imogene Coca, *(Above)* Nanette Fabray, *(Top, right)* Janet Blair, and *(Below)* Gisele MacKenzie.

(Below) In this movie satire Audrey Meadows watches intently as Caesar, a man of simple tastes, eats a meal consisting only of boiled bread. □ *(Bottom, left)* Eating scenes abounded in the Caesar shows. Here Cliff Norton looks on as Caesar, Carl Reiner, and Howard Morris attack a Chinese dinner. (During another memorable meal, the boys were served a flaming Cherries Jubilee. The flame, of course, refused to go out.)

RED SKELTON
first appeared on television in 1953, and *The Red Skelton Show* has been a fixture ever since. Over the years, Skelton has developed dozens of character vignettes, each a small gem of buffoonery. Although best known for his broad, physical comedy, Skelton often injects a note of pathos in his portrayals. In the classifications generally assigned to his trade, Skelton is considered a clown rather than a comic or comedian; as such, his fellow professionals usually rate him the master. Audiences, as interpreted by Nielsen, also award him top ratings.

With Vincent Price and Chanin Hale, Skelton appears as the scourge of the badmen, Sheriff Deadeye.

Janis Paige plays Hatti Mari, a glamorous spy, in this fantasy sketch featuring the befuddled Clem Kaddiddlehopper.

The ring veteran who has absorbed more than his share of upper-cuts, Cauliflower McPugg.

Comic Jack E. Leonard appears with the Mean Widdle Kid.

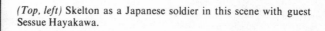

(*Top, left*) Skelton as a Japanese soldier in this scene with guest Sessue Hayakawa.

(*Bottom, left*) In a musical sketch with Helen Traubel.

(*Below*) Still in costume as a braggart politician, Skelton takes a curtain call.

BOB HOPE

cannot be ranked competitively with other show-business personalities; he stands alone as an American institution. *The Bob Hope Show* first appeared on a regular basis in 1952, although Hope had starred in a number of programs for some three years before that date. For the most part his television work has been confined to monthly specials; notable among these have been the Christmas shows for servicemen in remote areas. Hope's popularity and acceptance are such that whoops of laughter greet his barbed comments on social and political problems, comments that might, in other hands, be considered a breach of taste or manners. The basic format of Hope's comedy shows—a monologue followed by sketches with guest stars—has remained unchanged since his radio days in the thirties, but the passing years have diminished neither the polish nor the exuberance of his performance.

(Top) In an early series called *Star Spangled Revue*, Hope appears with guest Frank Sinatra.

(Above) Always known as an admirer of feminine charm, Hope appeared with Jane Russell in the premiere program of his 1954 season.

(Left) With guest star Beatrice Lillie.

(Above) Hope (shown here with Oscar-presenter Lana Turner) has been the perennial emcee of the Academy Awards telecasts. While the show itself frequently takes a critical pasting, Hope's contribution is usually outstanding.

(Above) Hope is perhaps best known, and certainly most loved, for the hundreds of shows performed for servicemen since World War II. Here he introduces a member of one of his troupes, actress Marie McDonald.

(Below) With guests Natalie Wood and the Crosby Brothers (Gary, Dennis, Philip, and Lindsay), Hope has the role of Scarface in this gangster sketch.

KEN MURRAY

first presented his show in 1950 and remained on the air for three seasons. Murray was a veteran showman with an extensive background in vaudeville and the theater, and he made the transition to television easily. His shows were a mélange of music, comedy, drama, and novelty acts. More recently Murray has turned a hobby into a profitable vocation: he has made frequent television appearances with his collection of old home movies featuring famous personalities of the entertainment world.

(*Right*) He was both star and producer of *The Ken Murray Show,* which was billed as a "variety extravaganza."

(*Below*) With Laurie Anders, who was best known for saying "Ah love the waaaahd open spaces."

(*Above*) Benny's daughter Joan, along with his wife Mary Livingstone, appeared with Jack in this 1954 program.

(*Top, left*) Eddie "Rochester" Anderson, whose gravel voice has delighted Benny audiences for some thirty years.

(*Left*) Benny conducts the Twist with Hugh Downs, Rock Hudson, and Dennis Day.

(*Bottom, left*) The musical aggregation in this 1954 program included Fred MacMurray, Tony Martin, Dick Powell, Kirk Douglas, and Dan Dailey.

(*Below*) With Marilyn Monroe, who made her television debut on Benny's show in 1953.

JACK BENNY
was first seen on television in a regular series in 1952. He brought with him the family of players long familiar to radio audiences: Don Wilson, Dennis Day, Rochester, Mary Livingstone, and Mel Blanc. Benny's radio trademarks—the long, pregnant pause and the exasperated "Well!"—were bolstered by some visual affectations: the prancing walk, the hand held to the cheek, and the look of numbed horror as he was beset by life's little tragedies. Visible too were the celebrated Maxwell, the underground bank vault, and the long-abused violin. Benny's low-pitched, underplayed situation comedy proved as attractive in television as it had in radio. His work today is largely confined to specials and infrequent guest appearances.

JIMMY DURANTE

was seen frequently on television in the early fifties on such shows as *The Colgate Comedy Hour, All Star Revue,* and *Four Star Revue.* His previous work in nightclubs, radio, vaudeville, and the theater served him well, and viewers were soon entranced by the little man with the beady eyes, the formidable schnoz, and the tortured vocabulary. In addition to his singing, dancing, and keyboard clowning, Durante's special stamp is the trace of wistful melancholy in his character. On television this was highlighted in several ways. There was the slow exit, coat slung over his shoulder, amid the beams of overhead spots. There was the inevitable goodnight to Mrs. Calabash (whom Jimmy has recently identified as his first wife). More recently there was the Durante rendition— sans comedy—of "September Song." In 1954–56, Durante starred in his own series, *The Texaco Star Theater.* Now, however, he makes only occasional appearances on television.

Eddie Jackson and Durante are the surviving members of the famed vaudeville team of Clayton, Jackson, and Durante.

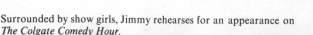

The suave Durante greets guest star Ethel Barrymore.   / 31

Surrounded by show girls, Jimmy rehearses for an appearance on *The Colgate Comedy Hour.*

DEAN MARTIN AND JERRY LEWIS made their television debut on Ed Sullivan's first *Toast of the Town* in June, 1948. From that point on, they made numerous guest appearances before appearing for six seasons, on a rotating basis, on *The Colgate Comedy Hour*. They were, in many respects, the perfect comedy team. Martin's good looks and smooth baritone balanced Lewis' impishness and frantic comedy. The team split in 1956, at a time when their popularity and earning power had reached dizzying heights. Despite some predictions to the contrary, each became enormously successful on his own. Lewis wrote, directed, and starred in a long string of motion pictures which, without exception, have been box-office bonanzas. Lewis has confined most of his television work to guest shots and specials (including telethons for victims of muscular dystrophy). In 1963 he embarked on an expensive and much-heralded Saturday-night series which ended quickly after being universally pronounced a disaster. Martin, too, turned to motion pictures, and is now considered to be a stellar box-office attraction. He got his own television series in 1965.

(Top) In a typical scene, Martin appears pained as Lewis demonstrates his vocal abilities. □ *(Above)* In their early days, at least, the team enjoyed themselves immensely as they worked. □ *(Left)* The adjectives most often used to describe Martin and Lewis were "wild," "zany," and "uninhibited." All were accurate. □ *(Below)* Rehearsing for *The Colgate Comedy Hour*, Martin attempts a song as Lewis leads the musicians astray.

(*Above*) The late Leon Errol performs his famous drunk act on *The Ed Wynn Show* in 1950. The two had appeared together in "The Ziegfeld Follies of 1914."

ED WYNN,
known to several generations of Americans as "The Fire Chief" and "The Perfect Fool," arrived on television with *The Ed Wynn Show* in 1949. The show ran for two years, after which Wynn appeared in several other comedy-revue series. His bizarre costumes and high-pitched cackle were absent from television after 1952, until his dramatic (in more ways than one) reappearance in 1956. In that year Wynn essayed a serious role in the *Playhouse 90* blockbuster "Requiem for a Heavyweight." After decades as a comedy performer, he astonished both critics and audience with his skillful adjustment to serious drama. His success paved the way to a new phase of his career; he was subsequently featured as a dramatic actor in many television shows and motion pictures. In 1958 he did a situation-comedy series.

(Above) ABBOTT AND COSTELLO: Seen here doing their famed "Who's on First?" routine, the team made many appearances on *The Colgate Comedy Hour* and other variety programs.

(Below) TALLULAH BANKHEAD: After her success in radio's "The Big Show," she became hostess of *All Star Revue* on television.

(Top) RAY BOLGER: A guest performer on comedy and variety shows, Bolger has also starred in his own series (*Washington Square* and *Where's Raymond?*). □ (Above) CLIFF NORTON: Besides stints with *Garroway at Large* and *Your Show of Shows*, Norton appeared in the syndicated *Public Life of Cliff Norton* and *Funny Manns*. □ (Below) JUDY CANOVA: In the fifties, the singer-comedienne was a frequent guest artist.

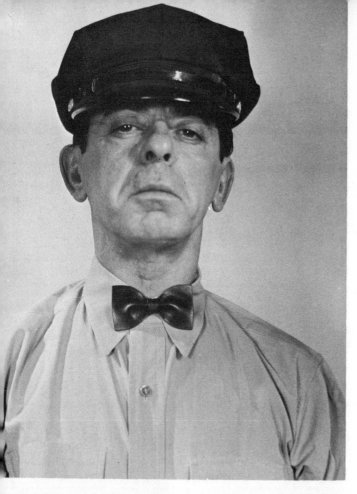

EDDIE CANTOR,
after a long and illustrious career in almost every phase of show business, came to television via *The Colgate Comedy Hour* in 1950. He was with the show for four seasons. Ill health forced him to curtail his activities thereafter, but he undertook several comedy and dramatic guest appearances during the next several years. He was the host and occasional star of a syndicated series, *The Eddie Cantor Comedy Theater,* prior to his death in 1964.

/ **35**

(Top, left) As "Maxie the Taxi," a character created on *The Colgate Comedy Hour.*

(Bottom, left) With guest star Dorothy Lamour.

(Below) The banjo eyes and outstretched hands were Cantor's identification.

SAM LEVENSON: A master storyteller, Levenson starred in his own shows in 1950 and 1951, then became a game-show panelist and guest performer. He is seen here with his son, in 1952.

AL PEARCE: In 1950 Pearce brought to television the character he had made famous in radio: Elmer Blurt, the low-pressure salesman.

JOE E. BROWN: He was the star of *The Buick Circus Hour* in 1952.

JACK CARTER: Shown here with singer Donald Richards and show girls Jackie Lockridge and Susan Stewart, Carter starred in *The Saturday Night Revue* in 1950 and 1951.

MARTHA RAYE

brought her high-decibel comedy to television in 1951 on *All Star Revue*. After two seasons, she starred in *The Martha Raye Show,* which was on the air for four years. She has been a guest star on almost every comedy and variety show of note, and was a frequent visitor to *The Steve Allen Show.*

(Left) As a torchy siren, Martha unleashes a come-hither look.

(Bottom, left) In a typical slapstick sketch, she entertains a gentleman caller (Cesar Romero).

(Below) When his ring career ended, Rocky Graziano found a new kind of fame as Martha Raye's comedy foil. They are shown here on *All Star Revue* in 1953.

JOEY ADAMS: Shown here with double-talk king Al Kelly on a 1953 quiz show called *Back That Fact*, Adams was also a comedy performer on other early variety shows.

JACKIE KANNON: He made a number of visits to Hoagy Carmichael's *Saturday Night Revue*.

ALAN YOUNG and BEN BLUE: Both talented pantomimists, Young and Blue alternated as guest stars on *The Saturday Night Revue* in 1954. The show's host at that time was Eddie Albert.

DONALD O'CONNOR: With sidekick Sid Miller (at the piano), singer-dancer-comedian O'Connor made many appearances on *The Colgate Comedy Hour*.

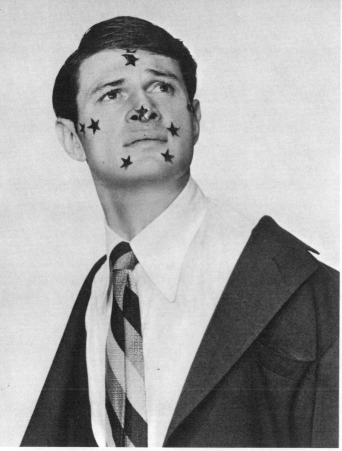

LARRY STORCH: A featured performer on *Cavalcade of Stars* (which he publicized with this photograph), he later starred in *The Larry Storch Show* (1953) and *F Troop* (beginning in 1965).

GENE SHELDON: The comedian and instrumentalist made many appearances on *The Colgate Comedy Hour*.

PHIL SILVERS: Shown here with comic Joey Faye and the chorus girls from *Showtime . . . U.S.A.* (in 1951), Silvers was seen as a guest performer numerous times prior to the introduction of his Sergeant Bilko series.

/ **39**

THE RITZ BROTHERS: The knockabout trio worked occasionally on television, but preferred to confine their activities mostly to nightclubs.

(Above) JACK HALEY: He was emcee of *The Four Star Revue* in 1951.

(Top, left) GEORGE JESSEL: With his guest, Fred Allen, on *All Star Revue* in 1953. In recent years Jessel has made numerous guest appearances on *The Tonight Show* and *The Jackie Gleason Show*.

(Left) BOB AND RAY: Bob Elliott and Ray Goulding (with cast member Audrey Meadows) on *The Bob and Ray Show* in 1953.

(Bottom, left) JACK CARSON: Shown here in a sketch from *The Four Star Revue*, Carson later turned to dramatic roles.

(Below) OLSEN AND JOHNSON: In 1949 they starred in their own show, *Fireball Fun for All*.

PINKY LEE,
an ex-burlesque comic, made his television
debut on *Those Two* in 1951. For a time it
was fashionable for other comedians to poke
fun at Lee, but *Those Two* remained on the
air for three years, and Lee's children's show
was similarly successful.

(Above) A capable dancer and storyteller, Lee used both talents
to advantage on his children's program, *The Pinky Lee Show*.

(Right) With costar Martha Stewart on *Those Two*, a variety
series. Miss Stewart was succeeded by Vivian Blaine.

HENNY AND ROCKY: Henny Youngman, Rocky Graziano, and singer Marion Colby teamed up for *The Henny and Rocky Show,* a program designed to fill the gap between the end of the Wednesday-night fights and the next program on the schedule.

WAYNE AND SHUSTER: Originally booked as an act on *The Ed Sullivan Show,* this team of Canadian comics made numerous guest appearances and later starred in their own situation-comedy series.

DOODLES WEAVER: One of television's pioneer performers (he appeared regularly in 1946), Weaver later starred on his own series, *The Doodles Weaver Show.*

DAVE KING: An English comedian and singer, King was a summer replacement for *The Perry Como Show.*

RED BUTTONS,
a former burlesque and Catskill-resorts comedian, burst into television in 1952. His show was an instantaneous hit. But after its first season *The Red Buttons Show* floundered, and despite some tinkering with the format it disappeared from view in 1954. Buttons' difficulties with writers were legendary, and there is no accurate tally of the total number who were employed by the show at one time or another. A trade joke of the time had a writer wandering into Madison Square Garden and, confronted by a screaming mob of some 18,000 fans, retreating in panic because he thought he had stumbled into a meeting of Buttons' writers. Buttons went to Hollywood, and was voted an Academy Award for his appearance in the film "Sayonara." He / **43** returned to television in 1966 with a spy-spoof series, *The Double Life of Henry Phyfe*.

(Top, left) In his nostalgic little-boy role, the Kupke Kid.

(Above) As a punch-drunk fighter, Rocky Buttons.

(Right) The cupped ear and "The Ho-Ho Song" were Buttons' trademarks.

(Below) With Phyllis Kirk, who played his wife after the show had become a situation comedy.

(Above) EDGAR BERGEN: Shown with dummies Effie Klinker, Charlie McCarthy, and Mortimer Snerd, Bergen was the comedy host of the daytime quiz show *Do You Trust Your Wife?* □ (Top, right) STAN FREBERG: Pictured with his puppet, Grover, in a 1956 guest appearance on the *NBC Comedy Hour,* Freberg is an inventive satirist who devotes much of his time to the production of radio and television commercials. □ (Right) ORSON BEAN: He is shown here with Polly Bergen when both appeared on the musical-variety series *The Blue Angel.* Bean is now most frequently seen as a panelist. □ (Bottom, right) ROGER PRICE: He conducted a comedy-panel show, *Droodles.* The droodle Price is holding pictures "a ship arriving too late to save a drowning witch." □ (Below) DAVE WILLOCK and CLIFF ARQUETT: Both comedians and hobbyists, they worked together in the comedy-hobby show *Do-It-Yourself* in 1955. Arquette, as Charley Weaver, later made many appearances on *The Jack Paar Show.*

44 /

ERNIE KOVACS

made his first national appearances on television in 1951 and 1952 in several series that originated in Philadelphia. He was the possessor of a wildly original comic mind, and he employed a casual, low-key technique in his comedy. He was especially creative in his use of cameras and technical equipment, with the result that most of his shows abounded in visual trickery. *The Ernie Kovacs Show* was on the air in 1955 and 1956, after which Kovacs starred in a number of specials and appeared as a comedy guest on other shows. His brilliant career was ended by his death, in an automobile accident, in 1962.

(Above) With his wife, singer Edie Adams, in an outer-space sketch on *The Ernie Kovacs Show* in 1956. □ *(Left)* Flourishing his ever-present cigar in the 1960 show *Take a Good Look*. □ *(Below)* As the lisping, half-soused poet, Percy Dovetonsils.

GEORGE GOBEL,
an easygoing, guitar-strumming comedian, had made several television appearances in the early fifties before his debut on *The George Gobel Show* in 1954. The cast included Jeff Donnell and singer Peggy King. The program enjoyed great popularity, and before long the country was awash with Gobelisms, the most prominent of which was "Well, I'll be a dirty bird." Along with guest appearances and nightclub work, Gobel currently performs in television commercials.

46 /

(Above) With Jeff Donnell, who appeared as his wife Alice. In 1959 the role was played by Phyllis Avery.

(Top, left) In 1957 Gobel and Eddie Fisher alternated each week as host and guest star of their program.

(Bottom, left) Gobel as a mad scientist, with singer Anita Bryant.

(Below) As a reluctant cowpoke, with Kirk Douglas.

ALLEN SHERMAN: A former television producer (*I've Got a Secret, The Steve Allen Show*), Sherman's highly successful song parodies ("My Son, the Folk Singer") have made him a much-sought-after television performer.

JONATHAN WINTERS: After more than a decade as a guest on everybody's show (and a brief stint with his own fifteen-minute show), he starred in a series of specials in 1964. More recently he has appeared in several motion pictures.

BOB NEWHART: Newhart's unique style and delivery first brought him success via comedy phonograph albums; he later starred on *The Bob Newhart Show* and *The Entertainers.*

ALAN KING: A skilled monologist, King is most frequently seen on *The Ed Sullivan Show* and *The Tonight Show.*

DANNY KAYE

was yet another product of the Catskill Mountains resorts. After a dazzling performance in the Broadway hit "Lady in the Dark," he embarked on a successful career that included radio, motion pictures, and one-man concert appearances. For many years he resisted the blandishments of television, and only in 1963 did he undertake the rigors of a regular series. Although his early acclaim derived from his ability to handle the tongue-twisting lyrics of special material (mostly written by his wife Sylvia Fine), he has now largely abandoned the "git-gat-gittle" songs and has become one of the most versatile entertainers of our day. Kaye possesses a superb ear for language and inflection (as in his classic impression of Sir Harry Lauder), is a nimble dancer and better-than-adequate singer, and owns the most expressive hands in show business.

(Top, right) In 1957, Kaye appeared in a *See It Now* program entitled "The Secret World of Danny Kaye." In it the comedian visited with children all over the world to demonstrate the work being done by UNICEF. The show had great emotional impact, and was ample proof that true artistry could overcome the problems posed by language and geographical barriers. □ *(Right)* In a special ("An Hour with Danny Kaye") which appeared on the air prior to Kaye's regular series, the comedian heckles trumpeter Louis Armstrong. □ *(Below)* With guest star Lucille Ball in a production number (choreographed by Tony Charmoli) on *The Danny Kaye Show.*

THAT WAS THE WEEK THAT WAS
originated in England and quickly became
famed for its mocking irreverence and savage
lampoons of people and events in the news.
The show's American counterpart, however,
wavered erratically between sophisticated
satire and broad comedy with mass appeal.
As a result, it never developed a large audience devoted to either brand of humor. But,
despite its shortcomings, *TW3* represented an
innovation in American television, for it often
displayed a courage and daring previously
lacking on our home screens. The program
was occasionally accused of political partisan-
ship, though it made obvious attempts to
balance its books by bludgeoning both political parties. Despite its flaws, many critics saw
in *TW3* a glimmering of hope for the future;
though the show itself might perish, a prece-
dent had been set for similar excursions in
satire. But when *TW3* expired, it left no
heirs, and television comedy continued in the
patterns and formats familiar to viewers
since 1946.

(*Above*) David Frost, who had appeared on the British version of
the show, was a frequent performer over here too.

(*Top, left*) The female stars of *TW3* were (left to right) Nancy
Ames, Phyllis Newman, and Pat Englund.

(*Left*) Nancy Ames, "The TW3 Girl," introduced each show with
a musical commentary on the happenings of the preceding week.

Personalities Plus

MANY OF TELEVISION'S GREATS had already achieved celebrity or stardom in other branches of the entertainment business before they tackled television, but one very special group can be considered only as the progeny of the picture tube. For lack of a more descriptive name, they have become known as "television personalities." Their unique talent is the ability to succeed without benefit of a unique talent, at least in the traditional sense. In terms of television, however, they possess a formidable talent, desirable above all others. They can reach out and grab an audience. They establish rapport; they blend.

The stars can sing, dance, or play the marimba. The personalities, almost to a man, would have been the also-rans on Ted Mack's *Amateur Hour* (including, of course, Ted Mack himself). But the personalities can generate from the audience feelings of love, affection, or mere tolerance (often this is sufficient), and the record clearly indicates that this accomplishment almost guarantees a long and lucrative television life. Such a consummation is devoutly to be wished, even by the world's greatest marimba player.

Personalities are usually called hosts or hostesses, a most apt description. Like the hosts of a well-planned cocktail party, they contribute to the occasion by circulating quietly through the proceedings, never intruding unnecessarily, always attempting a

smooth intermingling of their more volatile guests. They beam
and greet their guests on arrival; they chat briefly and engagingly, perhaps including a mild jest or two; they have a smile and
a handshake when the guests depart. Al Jolson might not have ap-
proved, but Perle Mesta would.

Because their careers depend on it, personalities are careful not
to upset the delicate equilibrium which has brought them viewer
love or viewer sufferance. They are, generally speaking, status-
quo people who shy away from controversy or radical innovation
lest they antagonize any considerable segment of the audience.
Thus their public image is fuzzy and ill-defined; sharper definition
might trigger sharper reaction, and personalities understand that
television longevity frequently depends not on reaction, but on
the lack of it. (Jack Paar is a notable exception to all of this. His
mercurial temperament and devastating candor were essential
ingredients of his charm, and audience acceptance of his out-
bursts is worth pondering. He was either a pioneer, blazing new
trails for the personalities, or he was television's first safety valve.)
It should be made clear, however, that detachment is not necessarily a self-imposed condition, but rather one that is considered
a requirement of the medium. Perhaps it is true that the mass
audience demands that the personality be homogenized, but it is
also true that everyone bought black automobiles until other
colors became available. Until television decides that other colors
are marketable, almost every personality will continue to con-
ceal emotion and intellect behind the sunshine of his smile.

Topo Gigio, the Italian mouse, has been a longtime favorite on the show. Speaking in heavily accented English, the mechanical rodent does comedy routines with Sullivan, who acts as straight man.

In the premiere telecast of *Toast of the Town* on June 20, 1948, the cast (left to right) included singing fireman John Kokoman, pianist Eugene List, comedian Jim Kirkwood, comedian Jerry Lewis, dancer Kathryn Lee, composers Richard Rodgers and Oscar Hammerstein 2nd, Ed Sullivan, singer Dean Martin, fight referee Ruby Goldstein, and comedian Lee Goodman. The dancing girls flanking the cast were the original "Toastettes." This show marked the television debut of Martin and Lewis.

ED SULLIVAN

is a television phenomenon. A Broadway columnist with no discernible theatrical talent, he appeared on home screens as emcee of *Toast of the Town* in 1948. He seemed, from the beginning, an unlikely selection for the job. Awkward of movement (for years, viewers would write, "What's wrong with his neck?"), thick of speech, plagued with a dozen nervous mannerisms, he did not appear destined for survival in television's competitive wars. But eighteen years later his show was still flying high in the ratings while most of his competition had disappeared without leaving a trace. Sullivan's popularity and longevity are no accidents. He is a master showman. He has an unerring instinct for selecting performers and acts most likely to pique the interest or stir the enthusiasm of an audience that has long since become jaded and blasé. He also pays top dollar and insists on an exclusivity clause which prevents his guests from appearing on competing programs for a set period of time before and after their appearance on his show. Small wonder, then, that Sullivan has presented almost every luminary in the sports and entertainment worlds, many precisely at that moment when public interest in them was at its peak (as in the case of the Beatles, Ingrid Bergman, and Elvis Presley). Sullivan is a man of considerable personal warmth, and for the most part he ignores the gibes aimed in his direction, but some of his feuds (with Walter Winchell, Jack Paar, Jackie Mason) produced some lively verbal fencing. Fred Allen once said that "Ed Sullivan will be around as long as someone else has talent." But Allen, an old vaudevillian himself, must have known that putting together a consistently fine variety program requires more than a little talent.

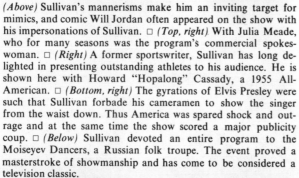

(Above) Sullivan's mannerisms make him an inviting target for mimics, and comic Will Jordan often appeared on the show with his impersonations of Sullivan. □ *(Top, right)* With Julia Meade, who for many seasons was the program's commercial spokeswoman. □ *(Right)* A former sportswriter, Sullivan has long delighted in presenting outstanding athletes to his audience. He is shown here with Howard "Hopalong" Cassady, a 1955 All-American. □ *(Bottom, right)* The gyrations of Elvis Presley were such that Sullivan forbade his cameramen to show the singer from the waist down. Thus America was spared shock and outrage and at the same time the show scored a major publicity coup. □ *(Below)* Sullivan devoted an entire program to the Moiseyev Dancers, a Russian folk troupe. The event proved a masterstroke of showmanship and has come to be considered a television classic.

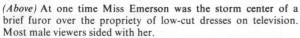

(Above) At one time Miss Emerson was the storm center of a brief furor over the propriety of low-cut dresses on television. Most male viewers sided with her.

(Top, right) With sportswriter Jimmy Cannon, who had just returned from a tour of duty as a war correspondent in Korea.

(Below) With Skitch Henderson (to whom she was married) she interviews the pride of the Brooklyn Dodgers, Jackie Robinson.

FAYE EMERSON

became one of television's most talked-about personalities. After a number of earlier appearances, she bowed with *The Faye Emerson Show* in 1949. The program was broadcast for almost three years, and during that time she made numerous appearances as a guest or panelist on other shows. Since then she has been the hostess of several programs, and for five years she was a panel member of *I've Got a Secret*.

ARTHUR GODFREY

brought to television the same easygoing manner, wry wit, and folksy warmth that had made him one of the great attractions in radio. Television rapidly succumbed to his charms. In 1948 he made his debut with *Talent Scouts,* a show that became a long-running favorite. In 1949 he added *Arthur Godfrey and His Friends,* a variety program. When delivering commercials Godfrey avoided the pompous solemnity that had traditionally surrounded the sponsor's message. As a result, he became the supersalesman of his day and his cheerful disrespect was a highlight of his shows. Godfrey was news, and his troubles with members of his staff and cast were the subject of endless speculation in magazines and newspapers. Similarly, when a plane he piloted was involved in a "buzzing" incident at the Teterboro, New Jersey, airport, the story hit the papers with screaming headlines. In 1959 Godfrey underwent major surgery for cancer. His long battle with the disease and subsequent triumph over it won him renewed respect and admiration.

With his longtime announcer, Tony Marvin.

With singer Julius La Rosa, whose on-the-air firing (for "lack of humility") caused a major sensation in television.

(Above) With his trusty ukulele Godfrey accompanies another cast member, Haleloke.

(Top, left) Singers Frank Parker and Marion Marlowe, whose supposed "romance" was long the subject of excited fan gossip.

(Bottom, left) The McGuire Sisters, winners of a 1952 *Talent Scouts* show, became Godfrey regulars in 1953.

(Below) As accompanist for singer Janette Davis.

ARLENE FRANCIS

became a *What's My Line?* panelist in 1950 and has remained with the program ever since. In 1952 she presided over *Blind Date,* the television version of a radio show in which she had starred. In 1954 she was the hostess of *Soldier Parade,* and in the same year she became "editor-in-chief" of *Home,* which was described as a women's "service magazine of the air." *Home,* the brainchild of then-NBC president Sylvester "Pat" Weaver, was indeed a programming innovation, both in scope and in maturity of approach. It remained on the air for almost four years but was finally dropped despite the strenuous objections of a loyal audience. An accomplished actress, Miss Francis has also been the proprietress of a radio interview show for some years. She is a woman of infinite poise and charm and is undoubtedly the leading female personality in the entire history of television.

(Top, right) With Hugh Downs on *Home.*

(Bottom, right) As hostess of *Blind Date,* with contestant "Reds" Bagnell, a University of Pennsylvania football star.

(Below) Surrounded by the Fort Dix Soldiers' Chorus on *Soldier Parade.*

/ **59**

GARRY MOORE

made his television debut in 1950 with a daytime variety show which remained on the air until 1958. Titled *The Garry Moore Show,* it first ran as a daily offering, and in its last four years on a three-times-a-week basis. Moore finally abandoned the show voluntarily, with the words "I'm tired." In 1952 he became moderator of one of Goodson-Todman's most durable properties, *I've Got a Secret,* and did not relinquish this post until 1964. In 1958 he embarked on a new series, as host of a nighttime variety program again titled *The Garry Moore Show.* This program featured a young comedienne, Carol Burnett, and served as her springboard to eventual stardom. Moore took leave of television completely in 1964, then reappeared in a new series in 1966. An ingratiating, relaxed performer, Moore's popularity derives from the sense of friendly rapport he maintains with a family audience.

(Above) With a pogo-cello, a gift from an admiring viewer.

(Top, right) In a program finale (left to right): Marion Lorne, Durward Kirby, Mahalia Jackson, Moore, Marge and Gower Champion, Carol Burnett.

(Center, right) Singers Denise Lor and Ken Carson were regulars on the daytime *Garry Moore Show.*

(Right) Moore, Durward Kirby, and guest Gwen Verdon in a sketch on the nighttime *Garry Moore Show* in 1962.

(Below) ANITA COLBY: A model and actress dubbed "The Face," she was hostess (in 1954) of *Pepsi-Cola Playhouse*.

(Above) VIRGINIA GRAHAM: A veteran radio and television personality, she survived a serious illness and now moderates the provocative chatter show *Girl Talk*.

(Below) BETTY FURNESS: A former Powers model, she has had several radio and television shows of her own, but achieved lasting fame as she stood by a refrigerator uttering the immortal words, "You can be sure if it's Westinghouse."

(Above) WENDY BARRIE: *The Wendy Barrie Show* was first broadcast in 1948 and Miss Barrie was among the first performers to become known as television "personalities." She is shown here with guest Juan Carlos Thorez, an Argentine radio and movie star.

(Below) ROBIN CHANDLER: In 1951 she was hostess of *Meet Your Cover Girl* and *Vanity Fair*.

(Above) CARMEL MYERS: A former star of the silent screen (shown here with composer Richard Rodgers, the guest on her premiere show), she was hostess of one of television's early interview programs, *The Carmel Myers Show*.

(Above) ROBERT Q. LEWIS: Shown here as star of a 1950 program called *Robert Q.'s Matinee,* Lewis has since been host, guest, and panelist on dozens of television offerings.

(Below) JAMES MELTON: Known best as a singer, he was also the host (in 1951) of *Ford Festival.* Melton is shown here with tiny Billy Barty, another member of the show's cast.

(Above) RENZO CESANA: He was "The Continental," suave, sophisticated, reeking of manly allure. At his candlelit table for two, his husky voice and perfect manners were supposed to cause female viewers to swoon with ecstasy. Perhaps some did.

(Below) REX MARSHALL: Later to become known as a commercial spokesman ("Hi there, I'm Rex Marshall"), he was host (with actress Sondra Deel) of an early DuMont show, *A Date with Rex.*

(*Above*) NEIL HAMILTON: Pictured here with guests Rita Gam and Hurd Hatfield, he was host of *Hollywood Screen Test* in 1949.

(*Top, left*) ROBERT L. RIPLEY: The cartoonist-creator of *Believe It or Not* adapted the series for television after it had become a national byword as a newspaper feature.

(*Left*) GALEN DRAKE: His show, *This Is Galen Drake,* came to television after he had developed a large and loyal following as a radio performer.

 / **65**

(*Bottom, left*) JOHN NESBITT: His *Passing Parade* was a perennial favorite as a movie short and then became a television series. He was later host of *Telephone Time.*

(*Below*) MORTON DOWNEY: The renowned Irish tenor was host of an early interview show, *Star of the Family.* Here he talks with Mrs. Fiorello La Guardia.

ART LINKLETTER

moved from radio to television with his *House Party* in 1952. A glib master of ceremonies, Linkletter kept the mixture of interviews, chatter, and features moving at a brisk pace, and the show rapidly became a daytime favorite with housewives. In 1954 *People Are Funny* made its television debut. It was a show which called upon contestants to perform some unusual stunts, which they always did, surprisingly without protest. While the contents of his shows are usually something less than momentous, Linkletter is especially adept at tying the proceedings together into a bright and cheerful package.

66 /

(Top, right) As host of a special, "The Beverly Hills Story," Linkletter chats with Mr. and Mrs. James Stewart.

(Bottom, right) A publicity shot commemorating the start of the second season (1955) of *People Are Funny*.

(Below) On *House Party* Linkletter's interviews with children were a recurring highlight.

(Above) KATHI NORRIS: One of television's first hostesses, she is shown here on *The Kathi Norris Show* in 1952.

(Above) LILLI PALMER: *The Lilli Palmer Show* was described as an "informal, at home, personality" program.

(Below) ILKA CHASE: In 1950 she was hostess of both *Fashion Magic* and *Glamour-Go-Round*. She was later a panelist on several shows, most notably *Masquerade Party*.

(Below) KATHY GODFREY: Sister of Arthur Godfrey, she was mistress of ceremonies of the 1954 quiz show *On Your Way*.

TED MACK

brought radio's *Original Amateur Hour* to television in 1948. The successor to the late Major Bowes, Mack has maintained the show's format, although the famed gong which announced the untimely end of a disastrous performance has now disappeared. Over the years the general quality of the performers seems to have improved. Gone are the days when each program seemed to have at least one contestant prepared to render "Sweet Adeline" on a bicycle pump. Mack, a gentle, patient man, is adept at calming the skittish amateurs. During the program's long run, he has traveled hundreds of thousands of miles with the show in search of new contestants.

(Top) With announcer Dennis James.

(Above) A three-time winner was Liber Frenkel, an Israeli who imitated Al Jolson.

(Left) Mack is shown here with a group of three-time winners. They are (left to right): The Four Peanuts, a barbershop quartet; baritone Robert Hamilton; violinist Norma Ferris; accordionist Patrick O'Brien; tenor Michael McCarthy; and Myrna and Carolos Camara, Castilian dancers.

(Above) DUNNINGER: The master mentalist demonstrated his mind-reading act on his own show in 1955. Earlier (1948) he had costarred on *The Bigelow Show* with ventriloquist Paul Winchell.

(Top, right) VINCENT PRICE: In 1958 Price was host of *ESP*, a show designed to demonstrate the existence of extrasensory perception. The show was short-lived, a situation which some attributed to a singular lack of perception on the part of its producers.

(Right) KUDA BUX: *The Kuda Bux Show*, featuring the Indian mentalist, was seen in 1950. He has since made numerous guest appearances, reading sealed messages while his eyes were swathed in blindfolds and several yards of tape and bandages.

(Above) JACK LA LANNE: His is one of the most popular of the exercise-and-keep-fit shows, which have become a staple programming feature on many stations.

(Below) JULIA CHILD: Her program *The French Chef* is distributed widely by educational stations. Her refreshing personality along with her extraordinary talent as a gourmet chef make this show a standout. As a rule, however, the cooking shows which once flourished on almost every station's schedule are now a dying breed.

(Above) ERN WESTMORE: One of Hollywood's famed Westmore brothers, the beauty-and-makeup consultant presented his own *Ern Westmore Show* in 1953. He is shown here with one audience participant; his wife Betty stands behind him.

(Below) NORMAN BROKENSHIRE: The ex-radio announcer was featured in *Handyman,* a program aimed at the home-workshop addicts.

TENNESSEE ERNIE FORD,
the peapicker's pal, made his television debut
in 1954, heading the old Kay Kyser quiz
show *College of Musical Knowledge*. The following year he was at the helm of his own
daily variety series, and in 1956 he added
a weekly nighttime show. A singer-comedian
(his recording of "Sixteen Tons" was one of
the top sellers of the decade), Ford specializes
in rural-flavored witticisms and has been
called a "cracker-barrel Socrates." A daily
highlight of his programs is the closing hymn.

(Above) The cast of the daytime *Tennessee Ernie Ford Show* in
1955 included (left to right) singer-announcer Skip Farrell, songstress Doris Drew, Ford, and fifteen-year-old singer Molly Bee.

(Left) On the nighttime variety presentation, *The Ford Show,*
in 1958.

(Below) As host (1954) of *College of Musical Knowledge*. Cheer-
leaders are (left to right) Donna Brown, Spring Mitchell, and
Maureen Cassidy.

(Left) ART BAKER: As host of *You Asked for It,* he presented a wide assortment of guests who performed unlikely stunts. Baker is shown here with escape artist Leo Irby ("The Great LeRoy").

(Bottom, left) SHERMAN BILLINGSLEY: *The Stork Club,* which made its debut in 1950, was an attempt to re-create the atmosphere of the then famous (now defunct) cafe. As host, Billingsley moved among the tables, pausing to chat with show-business celebrities and the cream of Cafe Society. The show remained on the air for more than three years.

(Below) DON MCNEILL: *Don McNeill's TV Club* was the video version of "The Breakfast Club," a long-running radio success. Although the cast of the television program was the same as that of the radio show (Fran Allison, right, portrayed "Aunt Fanny"), the television version never achieved a similar popularity.

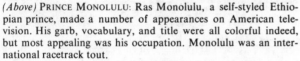

(*Above*) PRINCE MONOLULU: Ras Monolulu, a self-styled Ethiopian prince, made a number of appearances on American television. His garb, vocabulary, and title were all colorful indeed, but most appealing was his occupation. Monolulu was an international racetrack tout.

(*Top, right*) ZACHERLEY: For a period of time in the late fifties a prevailing rage was the local stations' use of live "monsters" to introduce late night movies. Zacherley was an Eastern representative of the genre (first in Philadelphia and then in New York), and differed from many of the others in that he was often deliberately funny. One of his west coast counterparts was a weird young lady who called herself Vampira.

(*Right*) JOE INTERLIGGI: One of television's most endearing traits is its habit of unearthing strange and wondrous guests. Ranking high in this group was Joe "Iron Jaw" Interliggi, a young vegetarian blessed with a set of powerful mandibles. Interliggi made a number of appearances on Steve Allen's *Tonight* show, and is shown here as a contestant on Groucho Marx's *You Bet Your Life*.

(Above) CANDID CAMERA: Host Allen Funt (shown here with guest Laraine Day) first brought *Candid Camera* to television in 1949; that particular incarnation of the series was broadcast until 1952. *Candid Camera* was the visual version of Funt's radio success "Candid Mike." Its premise is the entrapment of unsuspecting subjects in ludicrous situations. At one time critics regularly lambasted Funt for involving people in embarrassing or humiliating episodes, but such criticism is rarely voiced nowadays. The current rendition of the show regularly includes some charming interviews with young children as well as some beautifully photographed pictorial essays.

(Left) THE HOLLYWOOD PALACE: As its name implies, this is a lavish, gaudy, star-studded re-creation of the great days of vaudeville. Emceed each week by big-name stars (here, Maurice Chevalier), the show rivals Ed Sullivan's with its profusion of acts, many of them well-known and high-priced. The show's list of star-hosts has included Bing Crosby, George Burns, Judy Garland, and Martha Raye.

DAVE GARROWAY

made his first major television contribution with the Chicago-based *Garroway at Large* in 1949. One of the earliest variety programs, its unhurried, low-pitched manner—which reflected Garroway's personality—set the tone for what was to become known as "the Chicago school" of broadcasting. The show ended in 1951 and the following year Garroway came to New York to serve as host of a new concept in television broadcasting, *Today. Today* was received coolly by the critics (it suffered, initially, from an overdose of gadgetry), but settled down to become one of the most commercially successful programs in the history of the medium. A potpourri of news, interviews, time-and-weather checks, guest performances, and conversation, the show has beaten back all competitive efforts to curb its dominance of the early-morning hours. For three years (1955–58) Garroway also was host of *Wide Wide World,* which, like *Today,* was one of Sylvester L. "Pat" Weaver's many programming innovations. Since leaving *Today,* Garroway's occasional broadcasting chores have included a series for educational television.

(*Above*) In 1958 the *Today* lineup of performers looked like this (left to right): sports editor Jack Lescoulie, features editor Charles Van Doren, women's editor Betsy Palmer, news editor Frank Blair, Garroway.

(*Top, right*) On *Today*'s fifth birthday (in 1956) Garroway celebrates with J. Fred Muggs, the chimp that often upstaged him on the show. Muggs was later dropped from the cast amid insinuations (vehemently denied by his owner-trainer) that he occasionally bit some of the human members of the troupe.

(*Right*) With Pat Weaver, the innovative NBC executive.

(*Bottom, right*) The familiar Garroway sign-off—an upraised palm and the single word "Peace."

(*Below*) The *Garroway at Large* cast included (left to right) Jack Haskell, Cliff Norton, Connie Russell, Garroway, and some members of the show's dancing ensemble.

JOHN CHANCELLOR: Newsman Chancellor was Dave Garroway's successor on *Today*. He later left the show and became director of the Voice of America. Shown here with Chancellor are Frank Blair and Louise O'Brien.

HUGH DOWNS: Chancellor's successor as key man on *Today* was Hugh Downs, who had formerly served as Jack Paar's sidekick on the *Tonight* show. Pictured here are Jack Lescoulie, Downs, Barbara Walters, and Frank Blair.

(Right) WALTER CRONKITE: Among the various shows and hosts which CBS scheduled opposite NBC's *Today* was *The Morning Show* with Walter Cronkite. On this two-hour mélange of music, news, and entertainment, newsman Cronkite was supported by the Bil and Cora Baird puppets, including (right) a lion named Charlemane.

(Bottom, right) WILL ROGERS, JR.: In 1956 *The Morning Show* became *Good Morning!* and featured as host the son of America's most revered humorist.

(Below) MIKE DOUGLAS: *The Mike Douglas Show* attained widespread popularity although it defied television tradition in doing so. Based in Cleveland, it presented a variety format on a much more lavish and creative scale than is usually seen on local stations. In a short time it was being picked up by other stations, and it soon boasted a small network of its own. Starring singer-emcee Douglas, the show features a varied array of guest performers (below, comedian Dick Gregory). In 1966 the show moved to Philadelphia and now has a fresh transfusion of guests shuttling in from the canyons of Manhattan, one hundred miles away.

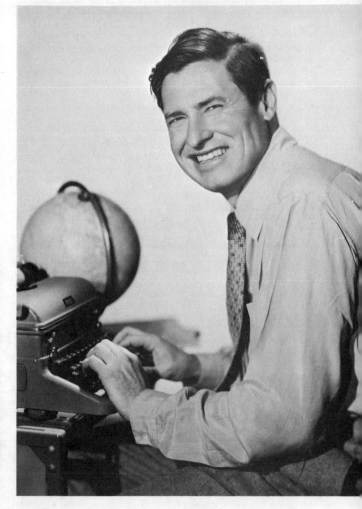

Broadway Open House was the pioneer late-night variety show. It first appeared in 1950 with Morey Amsterdam as the comedy emcee. A short time later Jerry Lester took over. Featured cast members included Milton Delugg, David Street, Ray Malone, Dagmar, and Wayne Howell. The off-the-cuff, ad-lib nature of *Broadway Open House* gave it a sparkle and spontaneity that were to be emulated by subsequent late-night variety programs. Lester's pixieish humor and his Beanbag Club are still fondly remembered by the show's loyal viewers. *Broadway Open House* departed in 1951 amid rumors of a feud between Lester and Dagmar.

(Above) In a getup reminiscent of Milton Berle, Jerry Lester wields a mop.

(Top, left) In a sketch with Wayne Howell.

(Center, left) Accordionist Milton Delugg (composer of "Orange Colored Sky") was the show's musical director.

(Left) Dagmar, a statuesque blonde whose deadpan poetry renditions were an *Open House* highlight, does a reading with Lester.

made his debut in 1954 as host of the *Tonight* show, which had begun as a local program a year earlier. It was a wild and woolly variety package which leaned heavily on the multiple talents of its star. The show was a sometimes scripted, sometimes impromptu affair consisting of songs, sketches, interviews, guest stars, and an abundance of offbeat features.

Allen remained with the show until 1957 (during the period he also served for two years as a panelist on *What's My Line?*). In 1956 he became the host of the weekly *Steve Allen Show*. More recently he replaced Garry Moore as moderator of *I've Got a Secret*, after serving for several years as host of a non-network variety program based in Holly-

80 /

wood. In addition to his comedy work, Allen is a pianist, composer, author of published works of prose and poetry, and political activist. Many of his former cast members (notably Bill Dana, Don Knotts, Steve Lawrence, Eydie Gormé, and Andy Williams) have gone on to establish themselves as stars in their own right.

(Top, right) Cast members of *The Steve Allen Show* (left to right): Dayton Allen, Bill Dana, Louis Nye, Steve Allen, Don Knotts, Pat Harrington, Jr., Gabe Dell. Not shown: Tom Poston, Skitch Henderson.

(Right) "The Question Man" was Allen's answer to a once-popular radio show, "The Answer Man." In this feature Allen provided wacky questions for previously supplied answers.

(Bottom, right) Members of the *Tonight* cast included (left to right) announcer Gene Rayburn, Allen, and singers Eydie Gormé and Steve Lawrence. Singers Andy Williams and Pat Kirby were also show regulars.

(Below) A familiar face in the *Tonight* audience was Mrs. Sterling. She was present at every performance and was a frequent recipient of both gags and gifts (especially some huge salamis, an Allen trademark). Mrs. Sterling's able successor was a Miss Miller, who attended all of Jack Paar's *Tonight* shows.

JACK PAAR

took over the *Tonight* show in 1957; the following year it was retitled *The Jack Paar Show*. He had previously been the star of four network daytime shows, but was still largely unknown to the television audience. He became a national celebrity through his work on this late-night opus. An emotional man who admitted that he wore his heart on his sleeve, Paar gave a full public airing to all his feuds and friendships, triumphs and disasters. As audiences cheered him on, he lashed out at those he considered unfair to him, notably columnists Walter Winchell and Dorothy Kilgallen. At one point he walked off the stage in mid-show, declaring that the network was censoring him (a questionable joke about a water closet had been blipped from the tape). After a hurried trip to Hong Kong, he was persuaded to return. Paar's forte was conversation, and his programs included hundreds of hilarious chats with Hermione Gingold, Alexander King, Zsa Zsa Gabor, Hans Conried, Cliff Arquette, Peter Ustinov, and many others. There was also one highly charged encounter with Mickey Rooney. Paar left the nightly grind to do a weekly one-hour variety show. This series, too, had its moments (on one occasion, Richard Nixon played the piano); among the features were Paar's own films of his trips to remote areas of the world. Paar now does occasional specials and is active in the management of a television station he owns in Maine.

(Left) For a brief period in 1953 Paar served as quizmaster of *Bank on the Stars*. He is shown here with two contestants.

(Bottom, left) As host of *The Morning Show* in 1954.

(Below) The cast of *The Jack Paar Show* (morning version): Paar, Edie Adams, Richard Hayes, bandleader Pupi Campo.

/ **83**

(Bottom, right) A year later, in 1955, an afternoon version of *The Jack Paar Show* was presented. In the cast were Paar, Jack **Haskell, Jose Melis, and Edie Adams.**

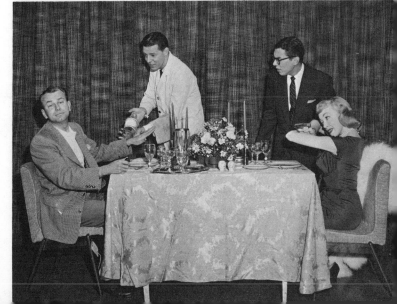

(Right) Two frequent visitors to the *Tonight* show were comedienne Dody Goodman and chanteuse Genevieve. Paar and Miss Goodman later parted ways; the cause of the split was the subject of much speculation in the press.

84 /

(Bottom, right) With singer Trish Dwelley. A minor brouhaha followed Miss Dwelley's appearance on the *Tonight* show. Paar's emotional introduction and misty-eyed reaction to Miss Dwelley's singing was based on the premise that this was her first television performance. It later developed that Miss Dwelley had sung on *The Perry Como Show* and Paar was visibly and publicly upset by the news.

(Below) With a favorite guest, the late Elsa Maxwell.

(Above) LES CRANE: ABC's entry in the late-night sweepstakes was a coltish ex-disc jockey named Les Crane. He strenuously sought controversy on his shows, as well as entertainment. Despite a spankingly modernistic set and such gadgets as a shotgun microphone (see photo), *The Les Crane Show* was canceled in 1965, after only a few months on the air.

(Top, left) TONIGHT: AMERICA AFTER DARK: In January, 1957, after Steve Allen's departure, *Tonight* adopted a new format and a longer title. Jack Lescoulie (right, with Judy Johnson) was the anchor man for the show, which featured newspaper columnists *(center, left),* including (left to right) Hy Gardner, Earl Wilson, Vernon Scott, Irv Kupcinet, Bob Considine, and Paul Coates. The program was mercilessly drubbed by the columnists' critical brethren and died seven months later.

(Bottom, left) MERV GRIFFIN: An actor and singer ("I've Got a Lovely Bunch of Coconuts") who had emceed several game shows, Griffin substituted occasionally as host on *Tonight* and was favorably received by both audience and critics. The result was *The Merv Griffin Show,* a nightly program owned and distributed (to a large lineup of stations) by Group W (Westinghouse Broadcasting). Like its competitors, the show features talk punctuated by occasional songs and stand-up comedy routines—and every once in a while by an unexpected incident like the moment from a 1966 show pictured here: Broadway producer David Merrick (far right) vehemently states his case to Griffin before walking off the show. Looking on are Renee Taylor, Phil Foster, and Beatrice Lillie.

JOHNNY CARSON, a young comedian with a great deal of previous television experience, took over as host of *The Tonight Show* in 1962. Unlike Steve Allen, who maintained a frenetic pace, or Jack Paar, who seemed to thrive on moments of emotional crisis, Carson's strong point is his cool, controlled sense of comedy, best evidenced in his conversations with his guests. He is particularly adept at "takes" (comic facial reactions), a technique he uses with devastating results when he finds himself trapped in a piece of especially dreadful comedy material. The show is generally oriented toward entertainment, and most of the guests are show-business personalities. Other program regulars are announcer Ed McMahon, who had served with Carson on *Who Do You Trust?*, and orchestra leader Skitch Henderson, who had occupied the same position when Steve Allen was the show's host.

(*Above*) With guest William Bendix on the daytime *Johnny Carson Show* in 1955.

(*Top, left*) In 1954 Carson (right, with Jackie Loughery) hosted a quiz show called *Earn Your Vacation.*

(*Bottom, left*) As host of the afternoon quiz show *Who Do You Trust?*

(*Below*) On the set of *The Tonight Show* with Skitch Henderson and Ed McMahon.

The Sounds of Music

A TELEVISION SET is a picture box. Television is something you look at, or watch, or view. It is a visual medium. What the sets sound like has been of little concern to their designers or engineers, or to the members of the public, who are referred to as "viewers," not "listeners."

All of this may explain why television, on the whole, has not been kind to people who are supposed to be heard but not necessarily seen. Men and women of music—those who sing it and those who play it—have battled hard to win acceptance on television. Very few of them have scored notable successes.

Among the singers, Perry Como, Dinah Shore, and Andy Williams have fared the best of those who have tried to carry weekly series. And Julie Andrews, Barbra Streisand, Mary Martin, and few more have done well with specials. But Bing Crosby, Frank Sinatra, Judy Garland, Sammy Davis, Jr., and dozens of others whose records and personal appearances have lifted them to the top of the entertainment business have been taken down a peg by that finicky audience out there in television land.

On the other hand, that audience has taken to its bosom a diverse assortment of musical exponents, ranging from Liberace to Dick Clark, from Lawrence Welk to Leonard Bernstein.

Bernstein has managed to break through television's serious-music barrier, but he is the only longhair (with the exception of those who carry electric guitars) who has found anything ap-

CHAPTER III

proaching steady employment on commercial television. Educational television has been a bit more hospitable to serious musicians, but there appears to be no danger that television will undermine concert halls, opera houses, or hi-fi the way it has the movie industry.

Nor has the jazz musician found a congenial outlet for his wares in television. Some of America's finest jazzmen manage to make a buck by playing in television studio orchestras, but the sound of real freewheeling jazz rarely emanates from television-set speakers.

If music is your game, how do you make the grade in television? It's the old story: You gotta have a gimmick. Como didn't just stand around singing—he worked strenuously at acting relaxed while reading words written for him by a platoon of *comedy* writers. Dinah? She got into everybody's act, displayed a magnificent wardrobe, and struggled through intricate production numbers. Bernstein? His shows are more talk than music. Mitch Miller? The name of the game is "Sing Along." Liberace? Well . . .

In other words, showmanship is the key to success. How much of a showman can you be with a violin attached to your chin? Florian ZaBach answered that question. Heifetz couldn't compete.

People simply do not buy their television sets for the purpose of staring at other people singing lieder or blues or rock 'n' roll, or playing harpsichords or banjos or tenor saxes. Those images on the screen have to *move*. If a man stands in one place for too long, or if the camera dwells on him too lingeringly—click!, all over America channels are switched.

Music may have charms, but they have yet to tame television.

Bing Crosby was a guest on several of Como's shows.

PERRY COMO,
Bing Crosby, and Frank Sinatra were the three male pop singers considered most likely to succeed when the newfangled medium of television came along. As it turned out, it was the dark horse of the three, Como, who became the most successful. In fact, no male singer yet has matched the long and prosperous career this ex-barber from Canonsburg, Pennsylvania, has had on television. His relaxed singing style became the butt of comedians' jibes ("Wake up, Perry!"), but it proved to be ideally suited to the intimate, casual atmosphere of television viewing in the home. His easygoing disposition earned him the title "Mr. Nice Guy." He started out in 1948 with *The Chesterfield Supper Club,* which became *The Perry Como Show* in 1950 and ran through 1955, mostly as a thrice-weekly, fifteen-minute series. In 1955 he began a weekly hour-long NBC series which became Saturday night's top-rated show, drove Jackie Gleason (his CBS competition) off the air, and ran until 1963 (in its latter years, on weekday nights, as *The Kraft Music Hall*). The supporting cast included announcer Frank Gallop, Mitch Ayres' orchestra, the Ray Charles Singers, and, at various times, Joey Heatherton, Kaye Ballard, Don Adams, Sandy Stewart, and Milt Kamen. Goodman Ace supervised the scripts. Como quit the weekly grind in 1963 and settled down with a half-dozen specials a year.

The finale of a 1960 Como show (left to right): Bert Lahr, Kay Starr, Como, Anne Brancroft, and the Mills Brothers.

DINAH SHORE'S

television career paralleled Como's in many ways. Of all the ladies of song, only she managed to achieve huge success with a weekly musical series. She began on television in 1951, with early-evening songfests twice a week, alternating with Como's show. In 1956 she tried a couple of hour-long specials masterminded by producer Bob Banner, written by Bob Wells and Johnny Bradford, and choreographed by Tony Charmoli. They were so well received that Miss Shore was given an hour-long weekly show a few months later, with the same production team in charge. The show became one of the most popular on the air—and also one of the most imaginative. Miss Shore's talents and those of her guests were exploited to maximum advantage, camera work was ingenious, and the production numbers were brilliantly conceived and executed. But by 1962 the show's popularity had faded—as had that of musical-variety shows in general—and Miss Shore changed from weekly programs to occasional specials. Through it all, she performed with infectious enthusiasm and an unfailing smile, ending every show with a "Mwah!"—a kiss thrown to the audience (see picture on right).

(*Above*) UKULELE IKE: Cliff Edwards strummed and sang in his short-lived early show.

94 /

(*Below*) BOB HOWARD: Perry Como and Dinah Shore were the exceptions: pop music on television has, in reality, been one long parade of singers hoping to make a lasting impression on viewers but, in most cases, basking in the television spotlight only briefly. Bob Howard and his show, *Sing It Again,* are remembered only by the owners of the earliest television sets.

(*Above*) JOHN CONTE: His *Little Show* was big in the early days. Conte later became the non-singing host of *Matinee Theatre*.

(*Below*) VAUGHN MONROE: His *Camel Caravan* was on the air in 1950 and 1951, and Monroe had another series in the summer of 1954. But his most profitable television venture was his stint delivering commercials for RCA.

(Left) KATE SMITH: For many years a radio star, Kate Smith started on television with a daily late-afternoon show in 1950, then added a weekly evening hour in 1951. Her shows had run their course by 1954. Miss Smith returned briefly in 1960 with a new weekly series, but has appeared on television infrequently since then.

(Center, left) ROSEMARY CLOONEY: Her first big television break came on *Songs for Sale* in 1950. A few months later she joined the cast of *The Robert Q. Lewis Matinee*. In 1956 she did *The Rosemary Clooney Show*, a syndicated series (she is shown here in one episode, with The Hi-Lo's). In 1957–58 it was *The Lux Show Starring Rosemary Clooney*, a network series. She has been much in demand for guest appearances ever since.

(Bottom, left) ROBERTA QUINLAN: She became television's most familiar songstress in 1949.

(Below) KYLE MACDONNELL: Most of the women singers, too, have had only brief flings on television. Kyle MacDonnell was one of the first to be "discovered" and turned into a celebrity by television. Her shows, *Girl About Town* and *Celebrity Time*, were viewers' favorites in 1948 and 1949.

(Above) PEGGY LEE and MEL TORME: These two jazz-oriented singers worked together early in the game and have appeared separately on numerous shows since then.

(Below) BILLY DANIELS: The "Old Black Magic" man had his own network series on Sunday evenings in 1952.

(Above) JOHNNY DUGAN: The daytime Johnny Dugan Show (1952) featured songs by Dugan and Barbara Logan, and audience-participation stunts.

(Below) JOHNNY JOHNSTON: In 1951 he had his own daytime show as well as singing weekly on The Ken Murray Show. Later on he branched out and became a Masquerade Party panelist, a regular on Home, and host of Make That Spare, a bowling show that filled time after boxing telecasts.

(Above) MARTHA WRIGHT: Her fifteen-minute *Packard Showroom* was seen Sunday nights in 1954. Bobby Hackett's cornet played behind her. In 1956 Miss Wright was a featured vocalist on Jack Paar's daytime show. □ (Below) BETTY CLOONEY: She substituted for her older sister, Rosemary, on *The Robert Q. Lewis Matinee* in 1950. Jack Paar hired her for his early-morning show in 1954, but fired her and bandleader Pupi Campo in 1955, for reasons which were never explained but which reportedly stemmed from the romance between Miss Clooney and Campo (they subsequently married). After leaving Paar, she hooked on again with *The Robert Q. Lewis Matinee.* □ (Bottom) PATTI PAGE: In the early fifties she made a series of syndicated films and appeared on *The Scott Music Hall.* In 1957 she became hostess of *The Big Record,* and a year later was the star of *The Oldsmobile Show,* a low-key, high-quality musical series.

(Top) DOTTY MACK: She performed pantomimes to other people's records, first on a local Cincinnati series, then on network shows. □ (Above) JO STAFFORD: She has had a few television flings—most recently a series of stylish specials filmed in London and syndicated to quite a few U.S. stations—and has made many guest appearances. □ (Below) MINDY CARSON: In 1949 it was *Mindy Carson Sings;* in 1950, a thirteen-week stay as Perry Como's guest; in 1951, *The Ford Star Revue,* with Jack Haley; and in 1952, *Club Embassy.*

FRANK SINATRA

has left an indelible mark through his performances on records, in nightclubs, in concerts, and in movies, but for some reason television success eluded him for years. He tried and failed twice with his own weekly series (1950–52 and 1957–58). He did guest shots on other people's shows. He headlined specials of his own. But it was not until recently that he found the right television setting for those talents which show to such advantage in other media. In the winter of 1965 he offered an hour-long television concert, "Frank Sinatra—A Man and His Music" —just Sinatra alone, singing as nobody else can. This was a Sinatra who had never been seen on television, free from the gimmicks, the inside jokes, the fawning of cronies, and the studied indifference that had previously erected a barrier between him and the television audience. He was, as he should have been all along, Frank Sinatra, singer.

(Top, right) The early days.

(Below) His own show in 1957.

(Bottom, right) As Dean Martin's guest on *Ford Startime* in 1959.

(Above) ERIN O'BRIEN: She was a television discovery, introduced by Steve Allen in 1956. She later worked with Liberace, Frank Sinatra, and Eddie Fisher, as well as in straight acting roles.

(Top, left) GEORGIA GIBBS: Billed as "Her Nibs, Miss Georgia Gibbs," she had a fifteen-minute weekly series called *Georgia Gibbs' Million Record Show* in 1957.

(Center) JAYE P. MORGAN: She sang on *Stop the Music* and with Robert Q. Lewis and was the summer replacement for Eddie Fisher's *Coke Time* in 1956.

(Bottom, left) INA RAY HUTTON: During the summer of 1956, she sang and led her all-girl band as star of a weekly show.

(Below) JILL COREY: She started with Dave Garroway in 1953, moved on to Johnny Carson's weekly series in 1955, *The Robert Q. Lewis Show* the following year, and *Your Hit Parade* in 1957.

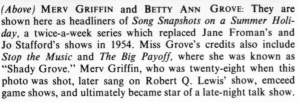

(Above) MERV GRIFFIN and BETTY ANN GROVE: They are shown here as headliners of *Song Snapshots on a Summer Holiday*, a twice-a-week series which replaced Jane Froman's and Jo Stafford's shows in 1954. Miss Grove's credits also include *Stop the Music* and *The Big Payoff*, where she was known as "Shady Grove." Merv Griffin, who was twenty-eight when this photo was shot, later sang on Robert Q. Lewis' show, emceed game shows, and ultimately became star of a late-night talk show.

(Top, right) TONY MARTIN: He had his own weekly show from 1954 to 1956.

(Right) DENNIS DAY: He never could make up his mind whether to concentrate on singing or comedy. His 1952–54 series had a little of each, plus visits from people like Ann Blyth (shown here). Day, of course, also appeared frequently on Jack Benny's show.

(Bottom, right) FRANKIE LAINE: He also had a weekly show in the mid-fifties, and he served as Arthur Godfrey's summer replacement in 1955.

(Below) HOAGY CARMICHAEL: The songwriter-singer was star and host of the ninety-minute *Saturday Night Revue* in 1953. He turned up later in a western, *Laramie*.

Judy Garland

arrived on television in 1955, starring in the opening episode of *Ford Star Jubilee*. For ninety minutes she sang, danced, and swapped small talk with David Wayne, while the largest audience ever to watch a spectacular (as the big shows were called in those days) looked on. Her next show was scheduled for 1957, but she walked out on it and a CBS contract after what was described as a dispute over the format. It was not until 1962 that Miss Garland patched up her differences with CBS and returned to television in a special (with Frank Sinatra and Dean Martin as guests) that won raves from the reviewers. She did another special in 1963, then went for broke in September of that year with a weekly Sunday-night series telecast opposite television's top-rated show, *Bonanza*. Her show was in trouble from the outset—producers came and went, the format kept changing, CBS's panicky masterminds shuttled back and forth between the Garland set in Los Angeles and network headquarters in New York—while *Bonanza* rode blithely on, trampling Garland in the ratings. In the spring of 1964, Judy Garland gave up her attempt to tame television and went back to concert halls and nightclubs, where her unique talents found a more appreciative audience.

(Below) Rehearsing for her television debut in 1955.

(Top, left) Rehearsing again in 1957 for the show that never came off.

(Left) On the air in 1964.

(*Above*) JULIUS LA ROSA: After Arthur Godfrey bounced him in 1953, La Rosa turned up on a pair of summer shows in 1955—a thrice-weekly fifteen-minute series and *TV's Top Tunes,* a weekly half-hour show on which Kitty Kallen (shown here) was one of his guests. He did another summer stint a couple of seasons later.

(*Below*) BING CROSBY: Like many performers who were on top of the movie and radio heaps, Crosby has never quite reached the same heights in television. He has done just about everything: situation comedy *(The Bing Crosby Show),* a musical play ("High Tor"), emcee chores *(The Hollywood Palace),* sports (the Bing Crosby Golf Tournament, telecast annually), several specials, and guest appearances on virtually every variety series. Here he is, insouciant as always, accompanied by Buddy Cole.

EDDIE FISHER: He made some guest appearances on television before he was drafted in 1951. During his two years in the army he managed to get onto television occasionally, making periodic appearances on *Jane Froman's U.S.A. Canteen* (top). After his discharge he starred on *Coke Time* (above) twice a week from 1953 to 1957. In the fall of 1957 he began a new series of hour-long shows, alternating as star with George Gobel. Debbie Reynolds, his wife at that time, joined him on the air occasionally (below).

(Above) EDIE ADAMS: Her first television appearances were on the local Philadelphia and New York shows conducted by Ernie Kovacs, who later became her husband. In 1955 she sang for Jack Paar on *The Morning Show,* then rejoined Kovacs in 1956 on his network morning show. She branched out into specials and, in 1962, after Kovacs' death, had her own weekly series, *Here's Edie,* on which, among other things, she performed a Kabuki sketch with Maury Wills of the Los Angeles Dodgers.

(Below) GISELE MacKENZIE: An alumna of *Your Hit Parade,* she too had her own show in 1957–58. She also played Sid Caesar's wife for a season.

(Above) PATRICE MUNSEL: She had a weekly show during the 1957–58 season.

(Below) JOHN RAITT and JANET BLAIR: In 1958 and 1959, this duo served together as Dinah Shore's summer replacement. Each of them, separately, has done many guest shots and specials. Miss Blair, too, played Sid Caesar's wife for a while.

(Above) NAT KING COLE: His network show in 1957–58 became a cause celebre. No sponsor was willing to underwrite the show nationally, and it was dropped, despite attempts of many high-priced stars to keep it going by offering to appear on it without remuneration.

(Below) GORDON MACRAE: He was the singing host of *The Colgate Comedy Hour* in 1954 (as pictured) and had his own series two years later.

(Top) CHARLIE APPLEWHITE: Milton Berle discovered this young Texan in 1953. But an army hitch, beginning in 1956, interrupted his promising career, and he never regained the momentum. He faded from sight until he hit the comeback trail in 1966.

(Above) GUY MITCHELL: He was the star of a 1957 musical series.

(Below) TONY BENNETT: His biggest opportunity came in 1958, when he replaced Perry Como for part of the summer.

DEAN MARTIN

was on his own after his split with Jerry Lewis in 1956, and for quite some time the going was rough. He did a few television specials and appeared on various variety shows. An acting role in a movie, "The Young Lions," gave his career a strong push. By 1965 he was a big enough star to dictate terms to the network that wanted him for a weekly vaudeville series. The terms include freedom to do the show with a minimum of preparation. Martin does not show up until the day of the taping, then wanders lackadaisically and engagingly through the show.

/ 105

(Left) A 1957 appearance on *Club Oasis*.

(Bottom, left) With Robert Goulet, who during the mid-sixties sang on everybody's show and starred in a spy series, *Blue Light*.

(Below) Martin on his own show in 1965, with Louis Armstrong.

(Above) ROY ROGERS: Although he has not had a regular series since the early sixties, Rogers still gets bookings (usually with his wife Dale Evans) on variety shows. During the summer of 1959, when this photo was shot, he appeared on *The Chevy Show* with Eddy Arnold (left) and Audie Murphy.

(Top, right) EDDY ARNOLD: One of the leading western troubadors, he has had his own network series on two occasions.

(Right) GRAND OLE OPRY: Country-and-western music has always found an audience—in more sections of the country than most people realize. The capital of country music is Nashville, Tennessee, where *Grand Ole Opry* was born and is still making money for people like Minnie Pearl (shown here). *Opry* was a national television fixture for years.

(Bottom, right) OZARK JUBILEE: A leading practitioner of this musical genre is Red Foley (left, with Marvin Rainwater), whose *Ozark Jubilee* (it was later called *Country Music Jubilee* and *Jubilee U.S.A.*) had a long network run.

(Below) PEE WEE KING: He presided weekly over ninety minutes of country music and comedy from Cleveland. Singer Goldie Hill (shown here with King) was a guest performer.

(Below) PAT BOONE: The kid in the white-buck shoes got his first exposure on *Arthur Godfrey's Talent Scouts,* became a member of Godfrey's television "family," then went off on his own in 1957. *The Pat Boone Show* ran for several seasons. When it ended, Boone went on to movies, though he continued to make guest appearances on television.

(Above) JIMMY DEAN: He succeeded in striking a happy medium between western music and pop—his show had the flavor of corn, but was seasoned with enough sophistication to make it palatable to its intensely loyal viewers. As a result, the hour-long *Jimmy Dean Show* survived many threats of cancellation before it finally perished in 1966. Dean, a Texan, got his start in Washington, D.C., then went network in 1957. This photo was taken in 1959, when he had a daytime series (The Noteworthies and Jeri Miyazaki are singing along with him).

YOUR HIT PARADE

was a phenomenon of television all through the fifties. It began in 1950 with the top seven tunes of the week plus some old-time "Lucky Strike Extras." As the years passed, the show did fewer and fewer current tunes and more and more extras. All through its run, *Your Hit Parade* featured inventive production numbers, staged first by Tony Charmoli and later by Ernie Flatt and Peter Gennaro. They *had* to be inventive because the same tuneless hits stayed on top of the charts for long periods, and new gimmicks were needed week after week to illustrate these tired songs. The original cast included Eileen Wilson, Snooky Lanson, and Dorothy Collins. In 1952 the personnel were as pictured here (from left): Russell Arms (in sweater), June Valli, Snooky Lanson, Dorothy Collins, and Raymond Scott (musical director and Miss Collins' husband). Gisele MacKenzie replaced Miss Valli in 1953. In 1957, as ratings sagged, the entire cast was purged and Tommy Leonetti, Jill Corey, Alan Copeland, and Virginia Gibson were brought in. In 1958 a $200,000 mystery-tune contest was introduced as an added inducement to viewers. Neither of these moves worked. The show went off, but returned under new management in 1959, with Dorothy Collins and Johnny Desmond starred. On April 24, 1959, it breathed its last. The three top tunes that night were "Come Softly to Me," "Venus," and "Pink Shoelaces," typical of the type of music that had stomped *Your Hit Parade* to death—rock 'n' roll.

DICK CLARK: The Robespierre of the music revolution that over-threw shows like *Your Hit Parade* was a clean-cut, well-spoken young chap named Dick Clark, who rose from the obscurity of Philadelphia disc-jockeydom to the position of national arbiter of popular-music fashions. It was never quite clear whether he knew instinctively what teen-agers would like or whether they mindlessly liked whatever he told them to, but Clark had the power to make stars of the likes of Fabian, Frankie Avalon, Paul Anka, and (shown here, on right, with Clark) Chubby Checker. Clark's platform was *American Bandstand,* a daily dance party which began in 1957 and was soon joined by a weekly nighttime version. By 1963 *Bandstand* had been reduced to a once-a-week show and Clark, by now an elder statesman of the Pepsi Generation, moved on to more dignified pursuits, such as emceeing game shows.

THE ARTHUR MURRAY PARTY: A different type of dance party had an extraordinary run through the fifties and into the sixties. Its hostess was a rank amateur (she admitted it freely), Kathryn Murray, who advised viewers to "Put a little fun in your life—try dancing." Her husband Arthur seconded the motion, while impassively enduring barrages of insults from comedians. *The Arthur Murray Party* started in 1950, with skits, dancing lessons, and contests. It was on and off the air countless times, usually as a summer series, until it really came into its own in the 1958–59 season, when, defying all rational analysis, it became one of the most popular programs on the air. Soon afterward it was can-celed, as it had been so many times before. But only the most foolhardy prophet would predict that television has seen the last of this remarkably resilient show.

ANDY WILLIAMS,
an unprepossessing crooner from Wall Lake,
Iowa, has, more successfully than any of his
television contemporaries, managed to with-
stand the rapid changes in musical tastes. In
alpaca sweater and sporty hat, he has kept
rolling along, singing a song, and proving that
the much-beleaguered musical-variety format
is not dead. Steve Allen introduced him to
television audiences in 1954 on the *Tonight*
show. In 1957 he did the twice-a-week bit,
costarring with June Valli. He became a
much-sought-after summer replacement, sub-
stituting for Pat Boone in 1958 and for Garry
Moore in 1959. His day came in 1962, when
he got his own weekly series. It was cut back
to twelve shows a year in 1963, but in 1964
Williams went weekly again, settling down
for what looked like a long stay.

(Left) The Andy Williams Show is a relaxed, low-pressure hour.

(Bottom, left) In 1957 it was *The Andy Williams-June Valli Show.*

(Below) The next summer he replaced Pat Boone on *The Chevy Showroom.* (The blonde is Gail Kuhr, the brunette Jayne Turner.)

LIBERACE

(full name: Wladziu Valentino Liberace) had a mouthful of luminescent teeth, a scalp full of wavy blond hair, a silky voice, sequin-festooned costumes, and a flamboyant piano style which placed as much emphasis on how the pianist looked as on how he sounded. He also had, throughout the fifties, an idolatrous audience consisting mostly of older women who apparently felt the urge to mother him (many of them, for some reason, felt the same way about the wrestler Gorgeous George, whom in some ways Liberace resembled). He started with a Los Angeles television show in 1951, went national in 1952, and began filming a syndicated series in 1953, making more than one hundred episodes, which were shown by stations all over the country. An imitation Louis XIV candelabra always graced Liberace's piano, and his brother George, a violinist, led the orchestra which accompanied him. All celebrities are subjected to ridicule, but none more vicious than that which was directed at Liberace. He accepted most of it with good grace (though he did sue a British columnist, Cassandra, for libel). Indeed, he seemed to thrive on it. His favorite answer to his critics was: "I cried all the way to the bank."

/ 111

(Below) FLORIAN ZABACH: He called himself "the poet of the violin." When it came to speed, he was unexcelled—he could play the 1,280 notes of "Hora Staccato" in one hundred seconds. Since fiddling has never been recognized as an Olympic event, he had to content himself with a television career, making guest appearances with Milton Berle, Ken Murray, and Steve Allen, then launching his own series in 1954. He was assisted on his show by the "pixie ballerina," Mary Ellen Terry.

(*Above*) PAUL WHITEMAN: Some orchestra leaders have ventured into television too. One of the pioneers was Paul Whiteman, who not only conducted several television series (a talent contest called *On the Boardwalk* when this photo was shot), but also served as ABC's vice president in charge of music.

(*Above*) EDDIE CONDON: A different brand of music was dished out by jazzman Eddie Condon and assorted sidemen on *Floor Show* when television was young. Pictured here are Wild Bill Davison on cornet and Cutty Cuttshall on trombone.

(*Below*) FRED WARING: For five years, beginning in 1949, *The Fred Waring Show* was a Sunday-night television staple. Waring did some specials during the 1954–55 season and had a daytime series during the summer of 1957.

(*Below*) KAY KYSER: His *College of Musical Knowledge* was around in the early fifties, with Ish Kabbible providing the comic relief. Ernie Ford took over the show after Kyser retired.

(Above) BOB CROSBY: This bandleader gave up the band and became the singing host of *The Bob Crosby Show*, a daytime musical series.

(Top, left) THE DORSEY BROTHERS: Jimmy (left) and Tommy Dorsey were brought to television by Jackie Gleason. They replaced Gleason's show for a couple of weeks during the summer of 1954. In the fall of 1955 they took to the air regularly, as co-hosts of *Stage Show*, which shared an hour-long time slot with Gleason's *The Honeymooners*. Elvis Presley made his television debut on *Stage Show*.

(Left) SAMMY KAYE: He starred in *So You Want to Lead a Band* in 1954 (Jeffrey Clay is the vocalist here) and *Sammy Kaye's Music from Manhattan* in 1958.

(Bottom, left) SPIKE JONES: He played it for laughs on several shows and his wife, Helen Grayco, sang along with the gags.

(Below) HORACE HEIDT: This show was called *Swift Show Wagon with Horace Heidt and the American Way*. On the air in 1954 and 1955, it featured a talent contest and a salute to a different state every week.

(*Above*) XAVIER CUGAT: His Latin rhythms have been heard often on television, in his own shows and in appearances with Ed Sullivan, Steve Allen, and others. When he was married to Abbe Lane (shown here), she always worked with him.

(*Below*) GUY LOMBARDO: He was joined by his brothers in various television ventures, including, in 1956, *Guy Lombardo's Diamond Jubilee,* featuring a letter-writing contest; and annual New Year's Eve telecasts. The Lombardos (left to right) are Lebert, Carmen, Victor, and Guy.

(*Above*) RAY ANTHONY: He had a summer series in 1956. Here he rehearses with Molly Bee, who had been a regular on Ernie Ford's show and later sang frequently on Jimmy Dean's.

(*Below*) BUDDY BREGMAN: *The Music Shop Starring Buddy Bregman* was a network show in 1959. Bregman subsequently became a major figure in British television.

(*Bottom*) RUSS MORGAN: He put on a summer show in 1956, aided by singer Helen O'Connell. Miss O'Connell also spent some time as a regular on the *Today* show.

LAWRENCE WELK

is the only orchestra leader who has had a long-lived success on television. His "Champagne Music" has been burping along since 1955 and appears to have become a permanent part of the television scene. Critics have derided the show for years, musicians have knocked the music, comedians have mocked the tongue-tied maestro's "a-one and a-two" song introductions, but the show and its leader have continued to please a substantial portion of the population. Welk's explanation: "Mother likes our music."

/ 115

(Left) Jazzman Pete Fountain remained relatively subdued when he was a member of Welk's orchestra.

(Bottom, left) Welk's singing group was The Lennon Sisters. Here are three of the five: Kathy, Peggy, and Janet.

(Below) Here he dances with the original "Champagne Lady," Alice Lon. Welk later fired her, because, said Miss Lon, her knees had been visible to the television audience once too often.

MITCH MILLER

exhorted viewers at home to "sing along," and for half a decade they did just that, by the millions. It all started in 1960 when a *Ford Startime* hour was turned over to Miller, whose "Sing Along" record albums were best sellers. After the show NBC was besieged with requests for more of Mitch. In January of 1961 the network found a spot for him, and he did seven shows. Viewer enthusiasm was stronger than ever, and Miller got a weekly series the next fall. Its main components were an all-male, mostly middle-aged chorus, chosen for sound, not for sex appeal; girl vocalists such as Leslie Uggams, Diana Trask, and Gloria Lambert, chosen for both; the simplest, most familiar melodies in ASCAP's catalogues; and Miller's beard, effervescence, and herky-jerky conducting. By 1964, however, the novelty had worn off, and Mitch and his bouncing ball left the air. But not for good—reruns of some of the shows were broadcast in 1966.

116 /

LEONARD BERNSTEIN

did not ask viewers to sing along, but rather to listen, learn, and enjoy. Though he did not hesitate to delve into popular music, his subject was more likely to be a symphony, a sonata, a concerto, or an opera. Bernstein, who had achieved mastery over the piano, orchestra conducting, composition, and musical comedy before his hair turned gray, has dominated the presentation of serious music on television. He has made his mark as much with words as with music. An extraordinarily articulate and lucid lecturer, he arrived on the television scene in November of 1954, when *Omnibus* gave the thirty-six-year-old Bernstein half an hour to explain Beethoven's "Fifth Symphony." He did it so effectively that he was asked to lecture on other aspects of music, and he has done so—with the aid of the New York Philharmonic, various soloists, and his piano—ever since, several times a year. His *Young People's Concerts* began in 1958, and most seasons he has conducted an adult series of specials as well.

(Above) On *Omnibus* in 1956.

(Below) He traveled to Tokyo in 1962 and filmed a performance of gagaku—the symphonic music of ancient Japan—played by the Imperial Court Musicians.

(Bottom, right) In 1959 Bernstein did a Christmas special with England's celebrated St. Paul's Cathedral Boys' Choir.

(Above) VOICE OF FIRESTONE: Outside of Bernstein's programs, there has been little room for serious music on television. *Voice of Firestone* survived for fourteen years on television (after twenty-one years on radio), presenting classics and semiclassics to a small but fervent segment of the television audience. In 1963, despite protests from viewers and some government officials, *Firestone* was canceled. The show's longtime conductor was Howard Barlow (right), here greeting baritone Thomas L. Thomas.

(Below) THE BELL TELEPHONE HOUR: Classical music has been offered by this series too—it has been on the air in one form or another since 1959—but pop, show, folk, and jazz tunes are usually sprinkled liberally among the more serious musical pieces. Here is one show's cast: violinist Zino Francescatti, ballerina Nina Novak, musical-comedy star Alfred Drake, jazz trumpeter Red Nichols, Broadway star Sally Ann Howes, and, at the piano, pop vocalist Connee Boswell. Their 1959 show also featured a folk-singing group, the Kingston Trio. A typical *Telephone Hour* mixture.

(Above) OSCAR LEVANT: Many of the world's finest musicians have been seen on television. Oscar Levant, however, became known to television audiences not as a pianist but as a talk-show host and guest and as a devout neurotic. Before that he spent a summer starring on a panel-variety show, *General Electric Guest House,* shown here.

(Below) ARTUR RUBINSTEIN: He performed on *Meet the Masters* in television's early days.

(Bottom) MISCHA ELMAN: He played on *Saturday Night Revue.*

(Top) MARIAN ANDERSON: The great contralto has made a number of appearances on television. Here she rehearses for 1953's *Ford 50th Anniversary Show.* She was also the subject of a memorable *See It Now* documentary.

(Above) IGOR STRAVINSKY: He has appeared with Bernstein and as conductor of a Stravinsky-Balanchine ballet depicting Noah and the Flood and, here, conducting a concert shown on educational television.

(Below) JOAN SUTHERLAND: She gave a recital on educational television in the mid-sixties.

(Above) THE LIVELY ONES: Popular music has adopted various guises in recent years. This was a brightly original summer series in 1962 and 1963. Vic Damone was its star, and he was accompanied by two girls called Tiger (Joan Staley) and Charley (Shirley Yelm). They were upstaged by first-class singers and musicians, who performed in odd settings or amid offbeat visual effects devised by director Barry Shear. Here is Benny Goodman and his sextet swinging at the Capitol in Washington.

(Top, right) SAMMY DAVIS, JR.: The versatile performer was given his own weekly show in 1966, but it got off to an unfortunate start with a pointless show in which Elizabeth Taylor and Richard Burton joined Davis, and the series lasted only a few months before reruns of *Sing Along with Mitch* replaced it. Trini Lopez sang along with Sammy on one of his shows.

(Right) MAX MORATH: What Leonard Bernstein did for classical music, Morath did for *The Ragtime Era* in his educational-television series.

(Bottom, right) THE KING FAMILY: There were thirty-six of them, all singing at the top of their lungs. A guest shot on *The Hollywood Palace* in 1964 led to their own weekly show, which ran until January, 1966. These are the six King Sisters: Donna, Alyce, Luise, Maxine, Yvonne, and Marilyn.

(Below) HOOTENANNY: College campuses provided the settings for this series, which emphasized folk music but also presented acts like Stan Rubin's Tigertown Five (shown here).

HULLABALOO: The arrival of the discothèque, the Frug, and "a go-go" was celebrated by television primarily in two shows which debuted during the 1964–65 season. One was *Hullabaloo*, which lasted into 1966. Emanating from New York, it featured various bizarre guest performers and (pictured here) the Hullabaloo Dancers. On the far left is Lada Edmund, Jr., whose tremors as the show's "Girl in the Cage" made her a favorite of many viewers. (It was reported that a popular pastime of college students was watching the *Hullabaloo* girls wriggle and writhe, in color—with the sound turned off.)

SHINDIG: Like *Hullabaloo, Shindig* was a frenetic item populated by assorted wailers and twangers, a kicky chorus line, and a screamy audience. It originated in Hollywood. The archives contain no documentation of this, but it may well be that the gentlemen pictured here were the only male performers on *Shindig* who had ever been inside a barber shop. These are four singing members of the Los Angeles Rams' defensive platoon in 1964: Roosevelt Grier (seated), and (from left) Merlin Olsen, David Jones, and Lamar Lundy. Like so many other manifestations of passing musical fancies, *Hullabaloo* and *Shindig* did not survive for long in the mass medium of television.

Custom-Made Comedy

IN THE EARLY YEARS OF TELEVISION, the situation comedy was typified by a single quality: believability. It did not matter whether the accent was on situation (as in *Mama* or *The Goldbergs*) or on comedy (as in *I Love Lucy* or *The Phil Silvers Show*). Nor did it matter that the characters might behave in a bizarre or outlandish fashion; there was a central core of truth and credibility which was easily identified by the audience. It was as though the screen were a mirror, and the viewer could always catch a glimpse —often slightly distorted—of himself. Even a caricature like Chester A. Riley contained a shred of believability; the awe-inspiring, authoritarian figure of the American father *had* eroded, even if it had not become the lump of helpless stupidity Riley portrayed.

In later years, situation comedies came to dominate television programming, representing as they did an excellent means to keep viewers occupied, if not mentally engaged. And if viewers were not necessarily amused, the ratings showed that they were not mutinous either. And so hour after hour, day after day, situation comedies came and went, endless rows of them, spawned of expediency and nourished by apathy. They were the sand dunes in Newton Minow's vast wasteland. Most of the personnel in television found themselves involved in the process of cranking out new situation comedies, and as the pace accelerated, believability all but vanished. The characters became pasteboard figures, with only their dress and speech to identify them as members of the human race. Plots had little inherent value except as a means to move the program toward the closing commercial. Creativity seemed to end once an occupation had been chosen for the major character in the series. (Only a few choice occupations remain unplumbed. If a way is ever found to rid us of our squeamishness about skin blemishes, we can surely expect a situation comedy about a dermatologist.)

No audience is present during the production of most situation comedies, with the result that no natural audience reaction appears on the finished film or tape. Instead, a laugh track is dubbed in. Thus a contemporary situation comedy consists of artificial characters in artificial situations being egged on by artificial laughter. From time to time, letters appear in magazines and newspapers complaining that some viewers resent maniacal laughter unaccompanied by anything even remotely funny. These complaints probably represent a minority viewpoint; presumably the cast, the producer, and most of the audience welcome the faked hysteria on the grounds that it provides reassurance that what is being perpetrated is indeed comedy.

An occasional rose blooms in the wasteland. A show appears, peopled with recognizable humans who do or say recognizably funny things. They are evidence that all is not irretrievably lost. It is still possible to create a situation comedy inhabited by humans, or reasonable facsimiles thereof, who can evoke genuine laughter. Though the industry relies on assembly lines, the craftsman still survives.

I LOVE LUCY,
starring Lucille Ball and her husband Desi
Arnaz, made its debut in 1951. The program
was destined to become the most popular in
the history of American television. Arnaz, a
Cuban bandleader, played Ricky Ricardo, a
Cuban bandleader; Miss Ball portrayed a
loving wife with a habit of getting involved
in all sorts of difficulties and misunderstand-
ings. Their neighbors, Fred and Ethel Mertz,
were played by William Frawley and Vivian
Vance. Although it was immensely successful, the show lost its first sponsor, a cigarette
company, apparently because the program
was not helping the sale of the product. *I Love
Lucy* had no difficulty in finding other sponsors, none of whom had any complaints about
the show's value as a commercial vehicle. The
show was produced by Desilu, a company
jointly owned by Miss Ball and Arnaz. Following their divorce, Miss Ball retained sole
ownership of Desilu, which had become a
large and profitable Hollywood production
organization. In recent years, Miss Ball has
been starring in *The Lucy Show* (with Vivian
Vance), but films of the classic *I Love Lucy*
series are still rerun endlessly on stations
throughout the world.

(Above) The cast of *I Love Lucy* in 1955 during the show's fourth
season included (left to right) Vivian Vance, William Frawley,
Desi Arnaz, and Lucille Ball.

(Bottom, left) Lucy and her son, Desiderio Alberto Arnaz IV,
who was born in 1953. The baby's counterpart on the show,
Ricky, Jr., joined the cast at exactly the same time as Lucy's
real son was born.

/ **125**

(Below) Crossed eyes and putty nose are Lucy's disguise in this
sequence with William Holden in 1955.

(Above) As Cleopatra (in this segment Caesar was portrayed by Hans Conried).

(Top, right) With Orson Welles, who played a magician in this 1956 show.

(Bottom, right) In this 1964 scene from *The Lucy Show* Vivian Vance aids in the search for a contact lens lost in the icing of a chocolate cake.

(Below) Lucy joins a symphony orchestra.

MAMA: Based on a successful play (which, in turn, had been based on a book), this family series featured (left to right) Robin Morgan as Dagmar, Peggy Wood as Mama, Dick Van Patten as Nels, Rosemary Rice as Katrin, and Judson Laire as Papa. *Mama* made its debut in 1949 and remained on the air for eight years. It set the style for many other domestic comedies which followed.

LIFE WITH FATHER: This family comedy came to television in 1953 as an adaptation of a hit play and best-selling book by Clarence Day. The Day family on television were Leon Ames as Clarence Day, Sr.; Lurene Tuttle as his wife Vinnie; and their sons (standing, left to right) Ralph Reed as Clarence, Jr., Ronald Keith as Whitney, Freddie Leiston as John, and (bottom) Harvey Grant as Harlan.

MAKE ROOM FOR DADDY

appeared on television in 1953 with Danny Thomas starring as Danny Williams, a nightclub entertainer who often had to spend long periods of time away from home. Thomas played the leading role with warmth and understanding, since the show's basic premise paralleled his own life. Jean Hagen left the cast in 1957 and was replaced by Marjorie Lord. The show's title was also changed, to *The Danny Thomas Show.*

(*Top, right*) The first Danny Williams family: Jean Hagen as his wife, Rusty Hamer and Sherry Jackson as his children, Jesse White as his friend and agent, and Danny Thomas as Danny Williams.

(*Right*) Thomas and Jean Hagen in a scene from an early show in the *Make Room for Daddy* series.

(*Below*) The second Danny Williams family: Rusty Hamer, Angela Cartwright, Sherry Jackson, Danny Thomas, and Marjorie Lord.

FATHER KNOWS BEST

first appeared on television in 1954. It was the saga of the Anderson family, with Robert Young and Jane Wyatt as parents Jim and Margaret Anderson, and Billy Gray, Elinor Donahue, and Lauren Chapin as children Bud, Betty, and Kathy. Unlike so many other family comedies in which the father was portrayed as a near idiot, *Father Knows Best* showed its leading character as a mature and responsible parent. The program's humor was incidental to its depiction of middle-class American family life. After the show had completed its run, Robert Young returned to television with a program called *Window on Main Street*, which was broadcast for a single season. *Father Knows Best* is currently being rerun on local stations.

(Above) Robert Young celebrates Valentine's Day with a kiss for his youngest daughter, played by Lauren Chapin.

(Right) In this scene of domestic bliss, Young is flanked by his son (Billy Gray) and wife (Jane Wyatt).

(Above) THE STU ERWIN SHOW: Erwin played a mild-mannered high-school principal, with June Collyer as his wife. Earlier this show had been called *The Trouble with Father;* later it was titled *The New Stu Erwin Show.* This series (circa 1953) was one of the first to feature a lovable but bumbling father.

(Above) PRIDE OF THE FAMILY: Paul Hartman was the father, Fay Wray was Momma, and the children were Bobby Hyatt and Natalie Wood in this show, which debuted in 1953. The leading character, Albie Morrison, was, of course, lovable but bumbling.

(Left) THE LIFE OF RILEY: Television's classic lovable bumbler, Chester Riley, was played by William Bendix. Marjorie Reynolds portrayed his wife Peg, and Wesley Morgan was Junior. The program first appeared in 1949, with Jackie Gleason and Rosemary De Camp in the leading roles, and was on for two seasons. Bendix started the new series in 1953, and it remained on the air for five years before going into syndication.

THE GOLDBERGS

made its debut on television in 1949, after having achieved the status of a radio classic. Created and written by Gertrude Berg, it mirrored the trials and joys of a Jewish family in the Bronx. Though the show found both humor and warmth in its ethnic background, its major virtue was its perceptive analysis of individuals and their relationships within the family.

In her best-known pose, Gertrude Berg leans from her window before calling out, "Yoo hoo, Mrs. Bloom!"

(Below) The Goldberg family consisted of (left to right) Robert H. Harris as Jake, Arlene McQuade as Rosalie, Tom Taylor as Sammy, Eli Mintz as Uncle David, and Gertrude Berg as Molly. In another television version of the family, Philip Loeb played Jake, and Larry Robinson was Sammy.

(Above) THE DONNA REED SHOW: A motion-picture actress ("From Here to Eternity"), Miss Reed starred in this extra-wholesome situation comedy from 1958 to 1966.

(Top, right) PLEASE DON'T EAT THE DAISIES: Mark Miller and Patricia Crowley (right) played the parents in the Nash family in this adaptation of Jean Kerr's best seller. The show made its debut in 1965.

(Right) OZZIE AND HARRIET: This family-comedy series arrived in 1952. Its principals were actually members of the same family: Ozzie Nelson, his wife Harriet, and their two sons Ricky and David. Though both remained with the show as they grew older, Ricky and David embarked on show-business careers of their own.

(Below) WONDERFUL JOHN ACTON: The saga of an Irish-American family living in the Ohio River Valley shortly after World War I, the show featured (left to right) Harry Holcombe, Virginia Dwyer, Ronnie Walken, and Ian Martin. It made its debut in 1953.

(Above) GUESTWARD HO!: Based on a book about a couple who run an inn in the Southwest, this 1960 show included in its cast Mark Miller, J. Carrol Naish, Joanne Dru, and Earle Hodgins.

(Below) THE HATHAWAYS: The story of a couple who have a house full of monkeys, this program was first telecast in 1961 and starred Peggy Cass and the Marquis Chimps.

(Top) NORBY: David Wayne appeared as Pearson Norby and Joan Lorring portrayed his wife Helen in this comedy about a household in Pearl River. The show was first broadcast in 1954.

(Above) THE ALDRICH FAMILY: The television version of the radio series, the show featured (left to right) Bobby Ellis, Barbara Robbins, House Jameson, and June Dayton. It made its first video appearance in 1949. Jameson was a member of the original Aldrich family, which began on radio in 1939.

(Below) DECEMBER BRIDE: In this "family portrait" are Frances Rafferty and Dean Miller in the roles of the daughter and son-in-law; Spring Byington starring as Lily Ruskin; Harry Morgan as Pete, the next-door neighbor; and Verna Felton as Hilda, Lily's friend and comedy accomplice. The program debuted in 1954.

(Above) THE ED WYNN SHOW: Wynn played a grandfather, and Sherri Alberoni portrayed his granddaughter, in this 1958 family comedy. □ *(Top, left)* THE WORLD OF MR. SWEENEY: Charles Ruggles was Sweeney and Glenn Walker was his grandson in this series which began in 1953 as a weekly feature on *The Kate Smith Hour.* □ *(Top, right)* LEAVE IT TO BEAVER: The Cleaver family included Hugh Beaumont and Barbara Billingsley as the mother and father, Jerry Mathers as Beaver, and Tony Dow as his older brother Wally. *Beaver,* which made its debut in 1957, was one of the best of the situation comedies because of its sensitivity in both writing and acting. □ *(Second from top, right)* THE DENNIS O'KEEFE SHOW: Hope Emerson and Rickey Kelman were starred with O'Keefe in this 1959 situation comedy. □ *(Right)* ROOM FOR ONE MORE: Timothy Rooney (Mickey's son) played an adopted child and Andrew Duggan was his father in this show, which first appeared in 1962. □ *(Bottom, right)* PECK'S BAD GIRL: Marsha Hunt and Wendell Corey were the parents, with Patty McCormack as their daughter in this 1959 program. □ *(Below)* MY THREE SONS: Fred MacMurray played the widowed father, William Frawley was the grandfather, and the boys (left to right) were Tim Considine, Stanley Livingston, and Don Grady when this long-running series started in 1959.

(Above) GIDGET: Sally Field starred as a surfing teen-ager in this 1965–66 situation comedy. □ *(Top, left)* YOUNG MR. BOBBIN: Jackie Kelk played an eager-beaver young businessman; Jane Seymour (left) and Nydia Westman were his maiden aunts in the 1951 comedy. □ *(Left)* LEAVE IT TO LARRY: Eddie Albert was a befuddled shoe clerk in this 1952 comedy. □ *(Second from bottom, left)* THE MANY LOVES OF DOBIE GILLIS: Dwayne Hickman (as Dobie) is surrounded by some of his many loves in this scene from the Max Shulman comedy series, which was first telecast in 1959. □ *(Bottom, left)* JAMIE: David Susskind produced this series, which featured (left to right) Polly Rowles, Ernest Truex, Brandon deWilde (as Jamie), and Kathy Nolan. The program was first seen in 1954. □ *(Below)* HAPPY: Happy, a baby who could think out loud, was portrayed alternately by twins David and Steven Born. The show made its debut in 1960. □ *(Bottom, right)* THE PATTY DUKE SHOW: Miss Duke played look-alike, teen-age cousins in a series first broadcast in 1963.

/ **135**

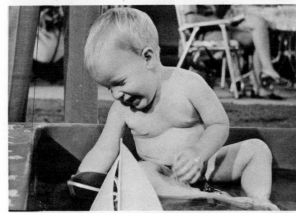

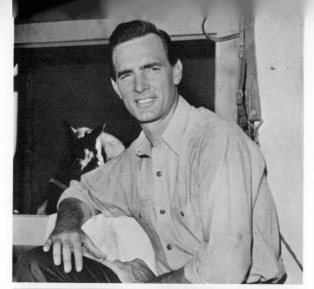

(Above) MY SON JEEP: Anne Sargent provided the romantic interest, Martin Huston (center) was Jeep, and Jeffrey Lynn was Doc Allison, a widower practicing medicine in a small town, in the 1953 series. □ (Top, right) KENTUCKY JONES: Dennis Weaver, who limped through *Gunsmoke* for many seasons, was a veterinarian in this 1964 series, which also featured young Rickey Der as a Chinese refugee. □ (Right) THE BING CROSBY SHOW: The Old Groaner with Diane Sherry, who played his precocious daughter in a show which premiered in 1964. □ (Second from bottom, right) THAT'S MY BOY: This 1954 comedy starred Eddie Mayehoff as ex-football player Jarrin' Jack Jackson and Gil Stratton, Jr. as his bookworm son. □ (Bottom, right) BACHELOR FATHER: John Forsythe was the "bachelor father," and Noreen Corcoran played Kelly, his teen-aged niece, in this 1957 series. □ (Below) TOO YOUNG TO GO STEADY: Brigid Bazlen was Pam, the fourteen-year-old daughter of a lawyer, in this comedy which arrived in 1959. □ (Bottom, left) A DATE WITH JUDY: Mary Linn Beller was Judy, Peter Avramo (center) played her brother Randolph, and Jimmie Sommer was her boyfriend Oogie in a show first seen in 1951.

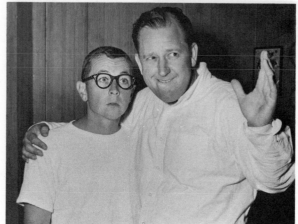

MY FAVORITE HUSBAND: Barry Nelson was starred as George Cooper, and Joan Caulfield portrayed his wife Liz (below) in a series which debuted in 1953. Miss Caulfield was later replaced by Vanessa Brown (above).

(Above) BLONDIE: Arthur Lake was Dagwood and Pamela Britton played Blondie in the television version of the Chic Young comic strip, first broadcast in 1954.

(Top, right) THE BURNS AND ALLEN SHOW: George and Gracie were first seen in this comedy series in 1950. Also featured in the cast were Bea Benaderet and Larry Keating as Blanche and Harry Morton. The show changed its format somewhat in 1958, when Gracie left the series.

(Left) FIBBER McGEE AND MOLLY: Another adaptation, this one of a famed radio show, starred Bob Sweeney as Fibber and Cathy Lewis as Molly. This version of the series had its premiere in 1959.

(Bottom, left) EASY ACES: In 1949 Goodman Ace and his wife Jane did a video adaptation of the radio favorite.

(Below) HEAVEN FOR BETSY: Jack Lemmon and Cynthia Stone (Mrs. Lemmon at that time) costarred in a twice-a-week domestic comedy in 1952.

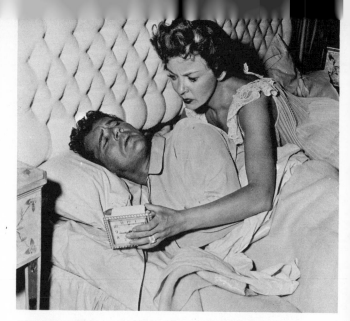

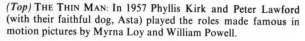

(Above) MR. ADAMS AND EVE: Howard Duff and Ida Lupino were a pair of married movie stars in this 1957 situation comedy.

(Below) THE RAY BOLGER SHOW: Marjie Millar was Bolger's girl friend in this comedy, which began in 1953 under the title *Where's Raymond?*

(Bottom) ETHEL AND ALBERT: Peg Lynch was Ethel and Alan Bunce played Albert in the 1953 series.

(Top) THE THIN MAN: In 1957 Phyllis Kirk and Peter Lawford (with their faithful dog, Asta) played the roles made famous in motion pictures by Myrna Loy and William Powell.

(Above) LIFE WITH ELIZABETH: Del Moore was Alvin and Betty White was Elizabeth in a syndicated domestic-comedy series. Miss White also starred (in 1957–58) in a series titled *A Date with the Angels.*

(Below) JOE AND MABEL: Joe (Larry Blyden) loved Mabel (Nita Talbot) in a comedy which also featured Luella Gear. It debuted in 1956.

(Above) ANGEL: Marshall Thompson and Annie Fargé starred in this 1960 comedy about a young man and his French bride.

(Below) THE MARGE AND GOWER CHAMPION SHOW: Jack Whiting was featured in this 1957 series, which boasted music and dancing as well as comedy.

(Bottom) MARGIE: Cynthia Pepper played the teen-age heroine and Dick Gering was the high-school hero. The show debuted in 1961.

(Top) I MARRIED JOAN: Jim Backus played a judge, and comedienne Joan Davis was his wife in this long-running series first aired in 1952.

(Above) DICK AND THE DUCHESS: Hazel Court was starred in a detective comedy which debuted in 1957. Dick was played by Patrick O'Neal.

(Below) THE CARA WILLIAMS SHOW: Frank Aletter costarred with Cara Williams in a 1964 comedy about a husband and wife who have to keep their marriage a secret.

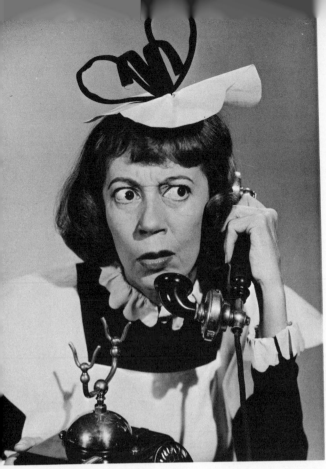

(Above) GRINDL: She was a comedy maid, played by Imogene Coca, in 1963.

(Above) OUR MAN HIGGINS: Stanley Holloway was a butler in this 1962 series.

(Below) HAZEL: In 1961 Shirley Booth debuted in a series about a maid based on the "Saturday Evening Post" cartoons by Ted Key.

(Below) BEULAH: The central role of this comedy series, that of a Negro domestic, was originally played by Ethel Waters in 1950. It was later performed by both Hattie McDaniel and Louise Beavers (below).

MR. PEEPERS

was the shy science teacher at Jefferson Junior High, often beleaguered but never outwitted. The series was a gem of quiet, underplayed comedy, and Wally Cox, in the title role, was one of those classic examples of perfect casting. *Mr. Peepers* went on the air in 1952 and continued for three seasons.

(Above) Pat Benoit portrayed the school nurse, Nancy Remington, who wed Peepers a year before the series ended in 1955.

(Top, left) Randall played Harvey Weskit, Peepers' know-it-all faculty colleague.

(Below) The *Mr. Peepers* cast: Wally Cox, Tony Randall, Marion Lorne, and Patricia Benoit.

/ **141**

(*Above*) OUR MISS BROOKS: Eve Arden was the wisecracking English teacher and Gale Gordon the apoplectic principal in the popular comedy which bowed in 1952.

(*Top, right*) MRS. G. GOES TO COLLEGE: Gertrude Berg was the mature student and Sir Cedric Hardwicke her instructor in this 1961 situation comedy.

142 /

(*Bottom, right*) HANK: Dick Kallman played Hank in this 1965 comedy about a student who attends college classes even though he is not registered.

(*Below*) HALLS OF IVY: Ronald Colman starred as Dr. William Todhunter Hall, president of Ivy College, and his wife Benita Hume played Mrs. Hall. The series premiered in 1954.

THE PHIL SILVERS SHOW

(originally titled *You'll Never Get Rich*) made its debut in 1955. Silvers was Ernie Bilko, master sergeant and master schemer, who devoted all his waking hours to the pursuit of loose cash. Stationed in Kansas in an obscure army camp which had long been forgotten by the Pentagon brass, Bilko and his buddies conjured up new money-making ventures in each episode. The series, created by Nat Hiken, continued until 1959.

(Above) Bilko with members of his platoon, which included Allan Melvin and Harvey Lembeck (seated on either side of Silvers), Herbie Faye and Billy Sands (both standing, right).

(Top, left) Phil Silvers as the army's greatest con artist.

(Left) Elisabeth Fraser was Bilko's WAC girl friend, and Paul Ford was the always-outfoxed Colonel Hall.

(Below) Maurice Gosfield as Private Doberman, platoon patsy.

(Above) NO TIME FOR SERGEANTS: Based on Mac Hyman's best-selling book and hit play, this story of a good-natured hillbilly dogface starred Sammy Jackson. This series was first broadcast in 1964; some years before, Andy Griffith had been featured in the *U. S. Steel Hour* presentation of the comedy.

(Below) BROADSIDE: Another attempt at service humor, this one featured (left to right) Kathy Nolan, Joan Staley, Lois Roberts, and Sheila James as WAVE mechanics assigned to a South Pacific island during World War II. It debuted in 1964.

(Top) HENNESEY: Jackie Cooper played a navy doctor in this 1959 service comedy. Also in the cast were Abby Dalton and Roscoe Karns.

(Above) MONA McCLUSKEY: Denny Miller was an air force sergeant and Juliet Prowse the wife (and Hollywood star) who vows they will live on his service salary. The show was first aired in 1965.

(Below) THE SOLDIERS: Hal March and Tom D'Andrea were the hapless GI's in this series about the humorous side of barracks life, first telecast in 1955.

(Above) MR. ROBERTS: A hit play and a movie, both based on Thomas Heggen's book, preceded this version of life aboard a navy supply ship during World War II. It was first telecast in 1965 and starred Roger Smith (left) in the title role, with Richard Sinatra as D'Angelo.

(Top, left) F TROOP: Larry Storch and Forrest Tucker were cavalrymen, and Edward Everett Horton played an Indian called Roaring Chicken in this slapstick portrayal of army life on the Old Frontier. It debuted in 1965.

(Left) GOMER PYLE, USMC: Another good-natured recruit, this one a marine, is played by Jim Nabors. Nabors was a graduate of the Danny Thomas production complex (he had previously appeared on *The Andy Griffith Show*) when this series began in 1964. He is shown here with Margaret Ann Peterson.

(Bottom, left) McHALE'S NAVY: Ernest Borgnine's movie roles had seen him cast as a shy butcher ("Marty") and a hissable villain ("From Here to Eternity" and "Bad Day at Black Rock"). In 1962 he tried farce as Commander McHale, skipper of a PT boat with the most lackadaisical crew in the navy. Here, he is flanked by Joe Flynn (left) and Tim Conway.

(Below) HOGAN'S HEROES: A novel twist on service comedies is this one, set in a German POW camp during World War II. When it was first telecast in 1965, it was well received by most critics, although some noted that it was difficult to laugh at any situation involving Nazi prisoners. Featured were Werner Klemperer as Commandant Klink, John Banner as Schultz, and Bob Crane as Hogan.

(Above) THE JOEY BISHOP SHOW: Bishop was assisted by Corbett Monica in this series about life in the entertainment world. It went on the air in 1961 and underwent numerous changes in cast, format, and network before it disappeared in 1965.

(Top, right) LOVE AND MARRIAGE: Another comedy about the ups and downs of show biz, this one featured William Demarest (left) as a music publisher and Stubby Kaye as his song-plugger. It debuted in 1959.

(Right) SO THIS IS HOLLYWOOD: Virginia Gibson (bottom), Jimmy Lydon, and Mitzi Green were featured in a 1954 series about two girls trying to make good in Movietown.

(Bottom, right) HARRY'S GIRLS: Larry Blyden was Harry, manager of a troupe of show girls on a tour of European nightclubs. It was telecast in 1963.

(Below) IT'S ALWAYS JAN: Janis Paige starred as a nightclub singer in this 1956 show.

THE DICK VAN DYKE SHOW
was first shown in 1961 and continued on the air through the 1966 season. It starred Dick Van Dyke as comedy writer Rob Petrie; Mary Tyler Moore as his wife Laura; Morey Amsterdam and Rose Marie as Buddy and Sally, the other two members of the writing team; Richard Deacon as Mel, the producer; and, occasionally, Carl Reiner as Alan Brady, the tyrannical star of a mythical television show. Reiner also wrote and directed some episodes, and ex-movie heavy Sheldon Leonard supervised the production of the series. *The Dick Van Dyke Show* got off to a slow start in the ratings race and faced cancellation, but it won a reprieve from its sponsor and went on to become one of the most popular and successful shows on the air. Usually well-written, and always well-played, the series differed from many of its contemporaries in the situation-comedy field in that it was often genuinely funny.

/ **147**

(Above) Buddy (Morey Amsterdam) and Rob (Dick Van Dyke) compare pipes in this early (1962) episode of the show.

(Below) Rob and Laura (Mary Tyler Moore) re-create an incident from Rob's army days in this 1964 scene.

(Below) The cast: (top, left to right) Richard Deacon, Rose Marie, Morey Amsterdam; (bottom) Mary Tyler Moore, Dick Van Dyke.

(Above) BEWITCHED: Agnes Moorehead (left) is Endora, and Elizabeth Montgomery her daughter Samantha, television's prettiest witch, in the series which first appeared in 1964. Also featured in the cast: Dick York and the late Alice Pearce.

(Top, right) MY FAVORITE MARTIAN: Ray Walston (left) was the Martian and Bill Bixby was Tim O'Hara in this 1963 fable of a visitor from another planet.

(Right) THE MUNSTERS: 1964 was the year for comedy monsters, and prominent among them was a family of creeps called the Munsters, Fred Gwynne (shown here with Paul Lynde) was Herman, Yvonne DeCarlo was his wife Lily, and Al Lewis was Grandpa.

(Bottom, right) THE ADDAMS FAMILY: Another spooky clan to emerge in 1964 were the video versions of Charles Addams' cartoon creatures. Carolyn Jones (shown) played Morticia, John Astin was Gomez, Jackie Coogan was Uncle Fester, and Ted Cassidy was Lurch.

(Below) I DREAM OF JEANNIE: Barbara Eden played a genie in this 1965 comedy, which also starred Larry Hagman and Hayden Rorke.

(Above) MY MOTHER, THE CAR: A car that talked! Jerry Van Dyke (Dick's brother) was the owner of the car in this 1965 series; Ann Sothern supplied Mother's voice.

(Left) MY LIVING DOLL: Julie Newmar was a robot named Rhoda (here, with guest Michael Jackson), which startled those who visualized robots as more clanky and less cuddly. Robert Cummings costarred in this series, which debuted in 1964.

(Bottom, left) MISTER ED: A horse that talked! This was the premise of the 1961 comedy which starred Alan Young, Connie Hines, and a horse named Ed.

(Below) TOPPER: Leo G. Carroll played Cosmo Topper, Anne Jeffreys and Robert Sterling the charming ghosts in this adaptation of the Thorne Smith novels. The show debuted in 1953 and was the forerunner of the many spirits and nonhumans who materialized on television in the middle sixties.

MICKEY: A swank California motel was the scene of the action in this 1964 series. Mickey Rooney was a Midwesterner who had inherited the place and all the comic difficulties that went with it.

IT'S A MAN'S WORLD: A houseboat was the setting for this imaginative 1963 comedy. In the cast were Glenn Corbett (left), Jan Norris, and Randy Boone.

GILLIGAN'S ISLAND: An exotic island is the setting for this series, which debuted in 1964. Stranded there was Gilligan (Bob Denver), shown here with Mary Foran. When this show came on the air it was almost unanimously condemned by the critics, who attacked it with unparalleled ferocity. Viewers, however, seem to feel differently, and *Gilligan* has scored consistently well in the ratings.

(Above) DUFFY'S TAVERN: "Where the elite meet to eat," manager Archie (Ed Gardner) used to say. First telecast in 1954, *Duffy's* also featured (above) Pattee Chapman as Miss Duffy and Alan Reed as Charlie the waiter. □ *(Top)* THE CHARLIE FARRELL SHOW: The locale for this one, first broadcast in 1956, was the Racquet Club in Palm Springs. Ann Lee (left) and Marie Windsor aided Farrell. □ *(Below)* STUDS' PLACE: This Chicago-based show won loyal support from local fans, then went on the network in 1950. It took place in a restaurant, and featured (left to right) Win Stracke, Studs Terkel, Beverly Younger, and Chet Roble. □ *(Bottom)* CAMP RUNAMUCK: A children's summer camp was the backdrop for this 1965 situation comedy. Some of the grownups were (left to right) Nina Wayne, Arch Johnson, Alice Nunn, and Dave Ketchum.

(Above) STANLEY: Buddy Hackett was Stanley, the manager of a newsstand in a hotel lobby, and Carol Burnett played his girl friend. Max Liebman *(Your Show of Shows)* produced it, but it ran for only one year after its 1956 debut.

(Top, left) BOB CUMMINGS SHOW: The featured role was that of a commercial photographer (Cummings) who always seemed to be surrounded by a horde of beautiful girls. One of them (right) was Joi Lansing. This series was first seen in 1955, and Cummings used the same formula in several subsequent television comedies.

(Left) DOC CORKLE: Eddie Mayehoff was a dentist and Connie Marshall was his daughter in this 1952 comedy. Not shown, but also featured in the cast, were Arnold Stang, Hope Emerson, Billie Burke, and Chester Conklin.

(Bottom, left) THE PEOPLE'S CHOICE: Jackie Cooper was the mayor of a small town in this 1955 series which featured a basset hound named Cleo.

(Below) DEAR PHOEBE: Another 1955 comedy, this one costarred Peter Lawford and Marcia Henderson as colleagues on a newspaper staff.

(Above) THE JIM BACKUS SHOW: Backus was editor John Michael O'Toole, and Bobs Watson (left) was Sidney the office boy in a series first seen in 1960.

(Top, right) THE TYCOON: Walter Brennan was a wheeler-dealer and Van Williams played his aide. The show premiered in 1964.

(Right) THE DUKE: Paul Gilbert was a retired prizefighter with a penchant for the arts in this 1954 series.

152 /

(Bottom, right) ICHABOD AND ME: Robert Sterling (left) played a small-town newspaper editor. He is shown here with writer Rod Serling, who turned performer for this episode in the series. It went on the air in 1962.

(Below) THE RAY MILLAND SHOW: This one took place on a college campus. Shown with Milland is guest star Miriam Hopkins. An earlier version of this 1955 show was entitled *Meet Mr. McNutley*, then *Meet Mr. McNulty*.

(Above) THE GREAT GILDERSLEEVE: In this 1955 adaptation of a popular radio program, Gildy was played by Willard Waterman and his nephew Leroy was enacted by Ronald Keith.
(Below) IT'S A GREAT LIFE: A comedy of domestic strife, it featured (left to right) James Dunn, William Bishop, and Michael O'Shea. It was first seen in 1954.
(Bottom) HARRIGAN & SON: Father and son were law partners in a comedy courtroom series first seen in 1960. Harrigan, Sr. was Pat O'Brien (left); Junior was Roger Perry.

(Top) I'M DICKENS . . . HE'S FENSTER: John Astin was Dickens and Marty Ingels (shown) was Fenster in a 1962 series about two not-so-handymen.
(Above) THE MICKEY ROONEY SHOW: Rooney was "the irrepressible Mickey Mulligan" in this 1954 show.
(Below) THE ADVENTURES OF HIRAM HOLLIDAY: In 1956 Wally Cox returned to television in the unlikely role of an international adventurer. He is shown here with Angela Greene.

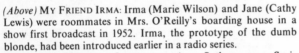

(Above) MY FRIEND IRMA: Irma (Marie Wilson) and Jane (Cathy Lewis) were roommates in Mrs. O'Reilly's boarding house in a show first broadcast in 1952. Irma, the prototype of the dumb blonde, had been introduced earlier in a radio series.

(Top, right) PRIVATE SECRETARY: Ann Sothern was Susie McNamara, secretary to a theatrical agent. The show was first telecast in 1954.

(Right) THOSE WHITING GIRLS: Margaret (left) and Barbara Whiting costarred in the 1955 series in which they played themselves.

(Bottom, right) WILLY: June Havoc played a lawyer in this situation comedy which appeared in 1954.

(Below) OH! SUSANNA: Gale Storm (right) was Susanna, the social director on a luxury liner, in this 1956 production which was but one of several Gale Storm comedy series. Her sidekick in the *Oh! Susanna* series was ZaSu Pitts.

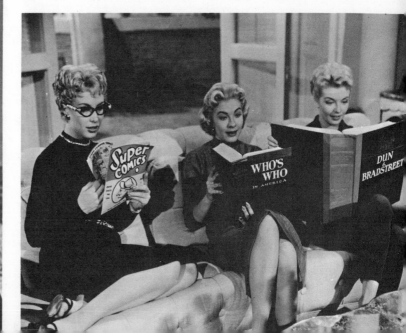

(Above) HONESTLY, CELESTE!: Celeste Holm starred as a small-town girl working on a big-town newspaper in this 1954 comedy.

(Top, left) SALLY: Joan Caulfield and Johnny Desmond were the costars of this series, first seen in 1957. Marion Lorne was also in the cast.

/ **155**

(Left) GLYNIS: Glynis Johns (shown here trying to revive Eddie Foy, Jr.) was a writer of mystery stories in this 1963 spoof. Keith Andes was her private-eye husband.

(Below) HOW TO MARRY A MILLIONAIRE: The three man-hunting females in this 1958 comedy series were (left to right) Barbara Eden, Merry Anders, and Lori Nelson.

(Above) THE FARMER'S DAUGHTER: Inger Stevens had the starring role as the Swedish farm girl who marries a Congressman. The program premiered in 1963.

(Top, right) MEET MILLIE: In this 1952 comedy Elena Verdugo starred as a typical Manhattan secretary, while Ross Ford played the boss's son. Florence Halop was featured as Millie's mother.

(Right) LOVE THAT JILL: Anne Jeffreys and Robert Sterling were rival owners of model agencies in this 1958 show.

(Below) TUGBOAT ANNIE: Minerva Urecal was the skipper of the tugboat Narcissus in this syndicated 1958 series. The show was based on the movie of the same name, which had starred Marie Dressler.

(Above) HEY, JEANNIE!: Jeannie Carson played a Scottish miss just off the boat and caught up in the excitement and adventure of the big city. Her friend the cabbie was Allen Jenkins. The program premiered in 1956.

(Below) OH, THOSE BELLS!: This 1962 slapstick series starred the Wiere Brothers as custodians of props in a theatrical warehouse. Pictured below are Herbert (left) and Harry Wiere. Missing: Sylvester.

(Bottom) MANY HAPPY RETURNS: John McGiver (right) was joined by Russell Collins (left) and Mickey Manners in a 1964 entry about the complaint bureau of a department store.

(Top) THE BROTHERS: The comedic tribulations of the bachelor Box brothers were displayed in this 1956 show with Gale Gordon (left), Nancy Hadley, and Bob Sweeney.

(Above) PETE AND GLADYS: In 1960 Cara Williams and Harry Morgan teamed up in this comedy of love and marriage, an off-shoot of *December Bride*. They are shown above with Bill Hinnant (right).

(Below) THE JOHN FORSYTHE SHOW: Forsythe, surrounded by Ann B. Davis (left) and Elsa Lanchester, was an ex-air force officer who inherited a girl's school in this 1965 series.

(Above) LIFE WITH LUIGI: J. Carrol Naish (left) was the newly arrived immigrant who settles in Chicago; Alan Reed was Pasquale, the friend who was forever trying to make a match between his sister Rosa and Luigi. This early series was first shown in 1948. Naish, a versatile character actor, later employed other accents when he was seen as Charlie Chan and as an Indian in *Guestward Ho!*

(Below) BONINO: Ezio Pinza had the leading role in this story of a retired concert singer who was the father of a large family of motherless children. Mary Wickes played Martha, the family maid. The show debuted in 1953.

(Above) THE REAL McCOYS: This long-running hillbilly comedy was first shown in 1957. Walter Brennan was Grampa, and Richard Crenna (right) was Luke.

(Below) AMOS 'N' ANDY: This was the show that became an American fixation in the dear, departed days of radio. In the television version, which first appeared in 1951, Alvin Childress (left) was Amos, Tim Moore (center) was the Kingfish, and Spencer Williams was Andy. In 1966 CBS withdrew the program from syndication and overseas sale after several civil-rights groups protested that it was a distorted portrayal of Negro life in the United States.

THE BEVERLY HILLBILLIES:

In 1962 CBS first presented this simple comedy of simple country folk who strike it rich and move into posh digs in exclusive Beverly Hills. The reaction was simply incredible. The show was an overnight sensation and quickly moved to a position high in the ratings, a status it was to maintain for several years. During that same period, those critics who were gloomiest about the state of television invariably cited *The Beverly Hillbillies* as the most flagrant example of the decadence of television comedy. Created and produced by Paul Henning, it was based on a time-honored theme: the innocent bumpkins who outwit and confound the city slickers at every turn. It starred Irene Ryan as Granny Clampett (left), Buddy Ebsen as Jed, and Donna Douglas as Elly May. Another member of the Clampett tribe (not shown) was Max Baer, son of the former heavyweight champ.

(Above) THE ANDY GRIFFITH SHOW: Andy was the sheriff of Mayberry, and Don Knotts played his deputy when this comedy series got going in 1960.

(Top, left) CAR 54, WHERE ARE YOU? Fred Gwynne (left) and Joe E. Ross were the minions of the law in this 1962 Nat Hiken concoction.

(Left) COL. FLACK: Humphrey Flack (Alan Mowbray, right) was an amiable con man with a heart of gold. His trusted aide, Frank Jenks, assisted him in fleecing the unwary. The show was first broadcast in 1953.

GET SMART!:
International agents a la James Bond ran rampant through the mid-sixties, but in 1965 a countermovement appeared—and the spy spoofs were upon us. The ultimate in this area of spoofery was *Get Smart!*, which starred Don Adams as Maxwell Smart, the most inefficient secret agent in Christendom. Smart always got his man (with the assistance of Agent 99, Barbara Feldon), by making the most of his chief assets—stupidity and incompetence. Adams had previously appeared as a house detective on *The Bill Dana Show;* Miss Feldon first attracted attention when she was seen in a series of commercials in which she reclined on a tigerskin rug. Shortly after the show went on the air, two of Smart's catch phrases were being repeated endlessly: "Sorry about that, Chief" and "Would you believe. . .?"

They Called Them Spectaculars

UNTIL 1954 "spectacular" was a perfectly respectable adjective. In that year, however, it was transformed into a noun and put to use to identify a new television phenomenon—the lavish extravaganza which began, with increasing frequency, to appear all over the television schedule in place of regularly scheduled programs.

Previously there had been isolated instances of big, one-time-only shows muscling in on the regular schedule. But in 1954 these special shows began arriving by the carload. Sylvester L. Weaver, NBC's president during that period, introduced the spectaculars. His genius for dreaming up new programming concepts was exceeded only by his talent for making them seem immensely exciting. Occasionally they lived up to expectations; more often they did not. But they broke up the monotony of television's rigidly constructed schedules, gave viewers something to stay home for, and every now and then provided a thrilling or joyous moment that made owning a television set more than worthwhile.

It was Weaver's idea to call them spectaculars, and the name caught on everywhere except at the other networks, which did not want to be caught using a term NBC had invented. Eventually NBC dropped it too, when it switched its publicity emphasis from the grandeur of its shows to the fact that increasing numbers of them were being telecast in color as the fifties progressed.

Whatever you choose to call them—and "specials" has become the generally accepted term—all three networks have presented them, and they have been the source of a great many of television's most unforgettable moments: Mary Martin and Ethel Merman singing their duet . . . Fred Astaire dancing . . . Peter Pan flying . . . "Annie Get Your Gun," "Wonderful Town," and "Kiss Me, Kate" coming to television from Broadway . . . Barbra Streisand running wild in a department store . . . Elizabeth Taylor wandering around London . . . Julie Andrews and Carol Burnett having a ball . . . Harry Belafonte, Victor Borge, Gene Kelly, Leontyne Price, Rudolph Nureyev, Art Carney—just about everybody in the world who can sing, dance, or make people laugh has turned up in television's specials. (So have many of the world's greatest plays and actors, but these will be considered in a later chapter.)

In recent years the networks have shied away from specials. Production costs have mounted to stratospheric heights. The ratings race has intensified to the point that the networks are afraid to risk the loss of Nielsen points by preempting sure-thing weekly programs. And many of the men who were responsible for the great specials have drifted away to the movies or the stage.

Still, specials will always be with us. They are the shows which add that extra dimension of surprise, of excitement, and, now and then, of true distinction to the experience of watching television.

And sometimes they are *genuinely* spectacular.

THEY CALLED THEM SPECTACULARS/*Introduction*

AMAHL AND THE NIGHT VISITORS: On Christmas Eve, 1951, an opera arrived, commissioned specifically for television, which was to become an annual television tradition. Gian Carlo Menotti's "Amahl and the Night Visitors," performed by the NBC Opera Company and produced by Samuel Chotzinoff, has been telecast every year at Christmastime (and once at Easter). In 1951 the crippled shepherd boy, Amahl, was played by Chet Allen. The next year, and for several years thereafter, Bill McIver was Amahl. He is pictured here with Rosemary Kuhlmann as his mother. Miss Kuhlmann originated the role and continued to play it in various new productions of the opera.

164 /

(Bottom, right) IRVING BERLIN'S SALUTE TO AMERICA: In a 1951 entertainment special, songwriter Berlin was joined by Tony Martin (at piano), Dinah Shore, and Margaret Truman.

(Below) OLYMPICS TELETHON: Bob Hope and Bing Crosby were the anchor men for a mammoth telethon which raised money for the 1952 U.S. Olympic team.

FORD 50TH ANNIVERSARY SHOW:
On June 15, 1953, Mary Martin and Ethel
Merman sang a duet which proved to be one
of television's most memorable events—and
a turning point in the history of television
specials. The show was a lavish anniversary
celebration produced by Leland Hayward
and telecast simultaneously on CBS and
NBC. Marian Anderson, Amos 'n' Andy,
Oscar Hammerstein 2nd, Howard Lindsay,
Dorothy Stickney, Edward R. Murrow, and
Ollie Dragon also performed in the two-hour
program, but Merman and Martin stole the
show when they sat on two swiveling stools,
on a bare stage, and belted out a song medley
in their own captivating styles. Since then
countless performers have sat on stools on
bare television sets and tried to duplicate the
excitement of that moment. On that night in
1953 the television special came into its own.

SATINS AND SPURS:

In 1954 the "spectacular" was born—sired and named by Pat Weaver of NBC, and produced by Max Liebman. The first spectacular, on September 12, 1954, was preceded by an extravagant publicity buildup. No program could have lived up to all that ballyhoo, but the ninety-minute musical comedy "Satins and Spurs" did not even come close.

Reactions of critics and viewers were so hostile that Betty Hutton, who had made her television debut in the show, decided to retire from show business (though she soon changed her mind). Her role was that of a rodeo queen who falls in love with a magazine reporter (Kevin McCarthy). Despite their disastrous beginning, spectaculars were here to stay.

(Above) BABES IN TOYLAND: Victor Herbert's operetta became Max Liebman's Christmas spectacular in both 1954 and 1955. Jack E. Leonard and Wally Cox were in it, along with Dennis Day and Dave Garroway.

(Below) ONCE UPON AN EASTERTIME: Easter specials of all sorts—some religious, some purely entertaining—sprout every spring. This was one of 1954's, with Gwen Verdon, Bobby Clark, and **Doretta Morrow.**

(Above) A CHRISTMAS CAROL: *Shower of Stars,* which displaced *Climax!* once a month, presented a musical version of Dickens' story in 1954, with Fredric March as Scrooge. Maxwell Anderson wrote the libretto.

(Below) GENERAL FOODS 25TH ANNIVERSARY SHOW: General Foods adopted Ford's formula (as a number of other companies have done since) and celebrated its anniversary on television in 1954. Rodgers and Hammerstein show tunes were performed by Yul Brynner and Patricia Morison (here doing a scene from "The King and I"), and Mary Martin, Ezio Pinza, Celeste Holm, Gordon MacRae, Tony Martin, Rosemary Clooney, and others.

(Top, left) OUR TOWN: Thornton Wilder's play was set to music by Sammy Cahn and James Van Heusen for *Producers' Showcase* in 1955. Eva Marie Saint and Paul Newman had the romantic leads, but most of the singing ("Love and Marriage," etc.) was done by Frank Sinatra, as the "Stage Manager."

(Center, left) MADAM BUTTERFLY: Operas have been produced only rarely on television, most often by the NBC Opera Company. Elaine Malbin sang the lead role in this English-language version of Puccini's opera in 1955.

(Bottom, left) THE SLEEPING BEAUTY: Full-length ballets are also television rarities. In 1955 *Producers' Showcase* imported the Sadler's Wells Ballet for a ninety-minute production starring Margot Fonteyn and Michael Somes.

(Top, right) HEIDI: Jeannie Carson starred (with Wally Cox, Elsa Lanchester, and Natalie Wood) in this 1955 musical.

(Center, right) ONE TOUCH OF VENUS: Janet Blair and Russell Nype played in the Ogden Nash-S.J. Perelman-Kurt Weill musical in 1955.

(Bottom, right) GOOD TIMES: This was 1955's first spectacular. Dick Shawn, Judy Holliday, and Steve Allen are shown here during rehearsals.

PETER PAN:
Most spectacular of all the 1955 spectaculars was this gay musical version of Barrie's fantasy. *Producers' Showcase* and Jerome Robbins transferred it from the stage to television on March 7, 1955, and it has been repeated approximately every two years since, with Mary Martin flying high (on wires) as Peter, and Cyril Ritchard getting his just deserts as Captain Hook. Its appearance is always eagerly awaited and joyously welcomed and will continue to be as long as there are children who believe in fairies and adults who relish superior entertainment.

(Above) THE MUSIC OF GERSHWIN: Cab Calloway was united with Ethel Merman, Alfred Drake, Tony Bennett, Eugene List, and Tanaquil LeClercq in this *Max Liebman Presents* show. □ (Below) MAURICE CHEVALIER: He was the star of a 1956 *Sunday Spectacular* and has shown up frequently on television through the years. □ (Bottom) BLOOMER GIRL: Evalina was played by Barbara Cook on *Producers' Showcase*.

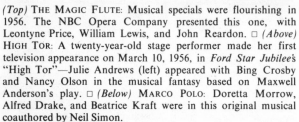

(Top) THE MAGIC FLUTE: Musical specials were flourishing in 1956. The NBC Opera Company presented this one, with Leontyne Price, William Lewis, and John Reardon. □ (Above) HIGH TOR: A twenty-year-old stage performer made her first television appearance on March 10, 1956, in *Ford Star Jubilee*'s "High Tor"—Julie Andrews (left) appeared with Bing Crosby and Nancy Olson in the musical fantasy based on Maxwell Anderson's play. □ (Below) MARCO POLO: Doretta Morrow, Alfred Drake, and Beatrice Kraft were in this original musical coauthored by Neil Simon.

(Above) VICTOR BORGE: Almost every season since 1956 has boasted at least one Borge special.

(Left) THE BACHELOR: Original musical comedies kept turning up during the mid-fifties—in this one Carol Haney and Jayne Mansfield chased Hal March. Music and lyrics were by Steve Allen.

(Bottom, left) THE LORD DON'T PLAY FAVORITES: This musical had a circus setting and a cast which included Buster Keaton and Kay Starr, plus Robert Stack, Dick Haymes, and Louis Armstrong.

(Below) HIGH BUTTON SHOES: From Broadway came this 1956 *Saturday Spectacular*. Nanette Fabray played opposite Hal March and Don Ameche.

(Above) THE WIZARD OF OZ: CBS bought the television rights to this MGM classic before the prices of such movies became prohibitive (and before movies became a major form of prime-time programming). The network's first showing of "The Wizard of Oz" (1956) was a tremendous success, and the film has been rerun every year since then, during the Christmas season. In this scene Dorothy (Judy Garland) meets the Scarecrow (Ray Bolger) on the Yellow Brick Road.

(Right) HOLIDAY ON ICE: This *Saturday Spectacular* starred Sonja Henie.

172 /

(Bottom, right) JACK AND THE BEANSTALK: Joel Gray was Jack and Billy Gilbert was Mr. Poopledoop in this *Producers' Showcase* special. Others in the cast were Celeste Holm, Cyril Ritchard, Peggy King, Dennis King, and Arnold Stang.

(Below) THE STINGIEST MAN IN TOWN: Nearly every Christmas season brings a new treatment of Dickens' "A Christmas Carol." In 1956 Basil Rathbone tried his first singing role, as Scrooge. Martyn Green was Bob Cratchit in this ninety-minute holiday special produced for *The Alcoa Hour.*

CINDERELLA:
A 1957 highlight was this ninety-minute Rodgers and Hammerstein musical, written expressly for television and emanating live from a lavishly appointed New York studio. Julie Andrews (shown here with Oscar Hammerstein 2nd, left, and Richard Rodgers) portrayed Cinderella. Jon Cypher was her prince, and the cast also included Howard Lindsay, Dorothy Stickney, Ilka Chase, Kaye Ballard, Alice Ghostley, Edith Adams, and, as one of twenty dancers in the production numbers, Joe Layton—who a few years later would stage and choreograph some outstanding television specials. Ralph Nelson directed. In 1965 a new version, with Leslie Ann Warren as Cinderella, was telecast and taped for reshowing in later years.

(Above, left) MR. BROADWAY: They stopped calling them "spectaculars" in 1957, but the big entertainment specials kept right on coming. Mickey Rooney played George M. Cohan in this one, supported by Gloria De Haven, James Dunn, Eddie Foy, Jr., and June Havoc.

(Above, center) PINOCCHIO: Six months later Rooney was back in another musical, as Pinocchio. Fran Allison was his guardian angel. The show was broadcast on radio as well as television.

(Above, right) RUGGLES OF RED GAP: Peter Lawford, Imogene Coca, and Jane Powell were in this one.

(Right) A MAN'S GAME: *Kaiser Aluminum Hour* observed the coming of the 1957 baseball season by hiring Leo Durocher and Nanette Fabray to do an original musical.

(Bottom, right) FESTIVAL OF MAGIC: Milbourne Christopher was one of several magicians in this *Producers' Showcase* special. Here Christopher works with model Eva Lynd. Ernie Kovacs was the show's host.

(Below) THE YEOMEN OF THE GUARD: A captivating version of the Gilbert and Sullivan operetta was offered by *Hallmark Hall of Fame,* with Alfred Drake, Celeste Holm, Bill Hayes, and Barbara Cook singing the lead roles.

174 /

(Below) MIKE TODD'S PARTY: The fiasco of the 1957 season was this "little party for a few chums" which Mike Todd tossed in Madison Square Garden to celebrate the first birthday of his movie "Around the World in 80 Days." Many celebrities were invited to the black-tie affair, but most had the good sense to stay home and watch the debacle on television. A few showed up—Georgie Jessel, V. K. Krishna Menon, Elizabeth Taylor (Todd's wife), Sir Cedric Hardwicke (who barely managed to keep from falling off an elephant), among others. But the Garden was packed with eighteen thousand freeloaders who turned into a mutinous mob after some chiseling vendors started charging extortionate prices for hot dogs and domestic champagne which were supposed to be free. Todd smiled happily throughout the entire shambles, very little of which was captured by the television cameras.

(Above) ANNIE GET YOUR GUN: Irving Berlin's Broadway musical became a two-hour television special in 1957, with Mary Martin as Annie Oakley, John Raitt as Frank Butler, and William O'Neal as Buffalo Bill Cody. Vincent J. Donehue directed.

(Top, left) THE PIED PIPER OF HAMELIN: Van Johnson starred with Claude Rains, Kay Starr, and Doodles Weaver.

(Below) THE STANDARD OIL COMPANY (NEW JERSEY) 75TH ANNIVERSARY SHOW: This one had the longest title of 1957 and one of the largest casts, as dozens of stars were on hand for the celebration. Eddie Mayehoff, Brandon deWilde, and Bert Lahr were three of them. The host was Kirk Douglas.

(Above) KISS ME, KATE: A 1958 *Hallmark Hall of Fame* show was this great Cole Porter musical, with (front to back) Patricia Morison, Alfred Drake, and Julie Wilson.

(Top, right) THE RED MILL: This *Du Pont Show of the Month* featured Evelyn Rudie, Shirley Jones, and Donald O'Connor, plus Nichols and May, and Harpo Marx.

176 /

(Right) HANS BRINKER OR THE SILVER SKATES: Another 1958 *Hallmark Hall of Fame* adaptation was this children's classic, starring Dick Button, Peggy King, and Tab Hunter.

(Below) HANSEL AND GRETEL: Red Buttons was Hansel (Barbara Cook, Gretel).

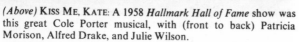

(*Above*) WONDERFUL TOWN: Another big stage musical was transferred to television in 1958, with Rosalind Russell, Jacquelyn McKeever, and Sydney Chaplin singing the Bernstein-Comden-Green score. □ (*Below, left*) THE NUTCRACKER: For its 1958 Christmas Night show *Playhouse 90* presented this Tchaikovsky-Balanchine ballet, danced by Edward Villella and other members of the New York City Ballet. Several different versions of "The Nutcracker" have subsequently been televised. □ (*Below, right*) ART CARNEY MEETS PETER AND THE WOLF: Carney and the Bil and Cora Baird Marionettes were the cast of this special, with music by Prokofiev, lyrics by Ogden Nash.

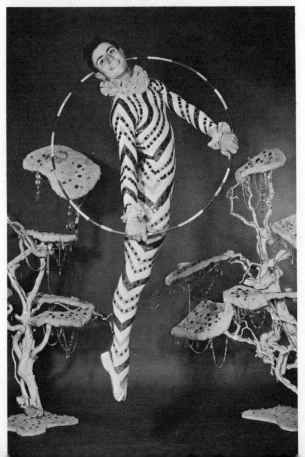

AN EVENING WITH FRED ASTAIRE:
This turned out to be the biggest television event of 1958. Astaire combined with Barrie Chase, the Jonah Jones Quartet, producer Bud Yorkin, and choreographer Hermes Pan for an hour of dancing (and a few songs) which showed how good television could be when it was put in the hands of people who knew how to use it to the performers'—and the viewers'—advantage. Astaire returned the next season with "Another Evening. . ." and later with a third dancing special. All of them were superior television divertissements.

(Above) MUSIC WITH MARY MARTIN: This was the nightcap of a day-night Easter Sunday doubleheader which Mary Martin played in 1959. The afternoon show, aimed at children, was called "Magic with Mary Martin." In the evening Miss Martin performed numbers from her various musicals.

(Top, left) FRANCES LANGFORD PRESENTS: Film was becoming a factor in entertainment specials. In this one Frances Langford appeared with Jerry Colonna (and Bob Hope, Hugh O'Brian, Julie London, Edgar Bergen, and George Sanders).

(Left) H.M.S. PINAFORE: One of several television versions of Gilbert and Sullivan's nautical operetta was this *Omnibus* production, with Cyril Ritchard as Sir Joseph Porter.

(Below) ACCENT ON LOVE: Marge and Gower Champion joined with Louis Jourdan (left), and Ginger Rogers, Mike Nichols, and Elaine May for a 1959 *Pontiac Star Parade*.

(Above) TONIGHT WITH BELAFONTE: The folk singer has limited his television bookings to a few guest appearances and fewer specials of his own, the first of which was *Tonight with Belafonte* (and with Odetta) in 1959.

(Right) STRAWBERRY BLONDE: Janet Blair played a suffragette in this 1959 musical, which also starred David Wayne and Eddie Bracken.

180 /

(Bottom, right) MEET ME IN ST. LOUIS: Tab Hunter and Jane Powell were the boy and girl next door. Walter Pidgeon, Myrna Loy, Ed Wynn, and Jeanne Crain also were in the cast.

(Below) THE GENE KELLY SHOW: Kelly has headlined a number of specials. On this one, in 1959, he performed with thirteen-year-old Liza Minnelli (this is a rehearsal shot), plus Carl Sandburg and three European ballerinas.

(*Right*) THE BIG PARTY: Specials came in big packages in 1959. *The Big Party* was supposed to be a series of fifteen, but an absurd format and sponsor interference pooped *Party* while the season was still young. Each of the ninety-minute specials was supposed to be taking place at someone's house, to which a heterogeneous assortment of celebrities had been "invited" (Eva Gabor was hostess to Carol Channing, Sir John Gielgud and the Benny Goodman Trio; Rock Hudson sprung for Tallulah Bankhead, Sammy Davis, Jr., Mort Sahl, Esther Williams, and Carlos Montoya; and so it went). They all stood around the old piano exchanging relentlessly casual banter written by Goodman Ace and his gaggle of comedy writers, and every few minutes they managed to coax one of the guests into performing his specialty, if he had one. Around this particular piano are Barbara Britton, who kept crashing the parties to recite commercial messages; soprano Patrice Munsel; and Abe Burrows, who was associated in the production of the show.

(*Below*) FORD STARTIME: This was another big series of specials. It billed itself as "TV's Finest Hour." A few times during the season *Startime* lived up to its billing, but shows like these were more typical: (*bottom, left*) "Cindy's Fella" ("Cinderella" in the Wild West), with Lois Smith, George Gobel, and James Stewart; (*bottom, center*) "Meet Cyd Charisse," a musical revue; and (*bottom, right*) "The Jazz Singer," with Jerry Lewis making like Jolson. *Startime*'s impresario was Hubbell Robinson, long an influential force in television programming. In 1966 he became producer of *ABC Stage '67*, whose prospectus read very much like *Startime*'s.

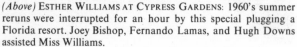

(Above) ESTHER WILLIAMS AT CYPRESS GARDENS: 1960's summer reruns were interrupted for an hour by this special plugging a Florida resort. Joey Bishop, Fernando Lamas, and Hugh Downs assisted Miss Williams.

(Top, right) HOLLYWOOD SINGS: Tammy Grimes and Eddie Albert were joined by Boris Karloff, who sang with them in this 1960 musicale.

(Right) FEATHERTOP: A 1961 musical, with Jane Powell and Hugh O'Brian.

(Below) THE FABULOUS FIFTIES: The sixties opened with a nostalgic two-hour salute to the previous decade, produced by the man they always seem to hire for television's most grandiose enterprises, Leland Hayward. He assembled an impressive cast— Rex Harrison and Julie Andrews (here simulating "My Fair Lady" rehearsals), Jackie Gleason, Dick Van Dyke, Nichols and May, Comden and Green, Shelley Berman, Suzy Parker, Eric Sevareid, and, as host, Henry Fonda.

(Top, left) HENRY FONDA AND THE FAMILY: This was "a satiric look at the American family," with Carol Lynley, Dick Van Dyke, and Cara Williams among the lookers.

(Above) THE GOOD YEARS: Fonda again, this time reminiscing about life in America from 1900 to 1914. Lucille Ball, Mort Sahl, and Margaret Hamilton were also involved in this 1961 Leland Hayward show.

(Left) YVES MONTAND ON BROADWAY: Montand was aided by Polly Bergen, John Raitt, Helen Gallagher, and Bobby Van in this musical revue.

(Below) MARINELAND CARNIVAL: These fun-with-fish spectacles are aired annually. Bill ("Jose Jimenez") Dana, Lloyd Bridges, and Rosemary Clooney were in the 1962 edition.

JULIE AND CAROL AT CARNEGIE HALL:
All it had was Carol Burnett (left) and Julie Andrews, singing, dancing, and clowning (with an occasional assist from twenty chorus boys) on the stage of Carnegie Hall. It was enough. As good as the Misses Andrews and Burnett were alone, they were even better together in this 1962 show. The result was one of television's fastest-flying hours. Producer Bob Banner, director Joe Hamilton, and writers Mike Nichols and Ken Welch gave the girls plenty to work with.

(Right) ELIZABETH TAYLOR IN LONDON: In 1963 a couple of enterprising producers found a foolproof formula for television specials: hire a movie queen, set her down in a foreign city, and let her guide a tour through the town. It worked first with Elizabeth Taylor.

(Bottom, right) SOPHIA LOREN'S ROME: A year later it scored again with Sophia Loren. (And subsequently Melina Mercouri showed us Greece, and Inger Stevens Sweden.)

(Below) THE BEATLES IN AMERICA: In 1964 they switched things around. Instead of a cinema beauty, they turned their cameras on the four hottest items on the pop-music scene. And instead of unleashing them in Europe, they imported them from there to here. The result was this chronicle of The Beatles' first visit to these shores. Here they gambol in the surf at Miami Beach.

(Left) THE JULIE ANDREWS SPECIAL: That supercalifragilistic girl was back again in 1965, joined by Gene Kelly for a zingy hour.

(Left, center) THE MIKADO: NET, the headquarters of educational television, did its share to keep sophisticated entertainment in style on the air. This is John Holmes in a *Festival of the Arts* production of the Gilbert and Sullivan classic, performed by the Sadler's Wells Opera Company and shown on educational stations throughout the United States.

(Bottom, left) DYNAMITE TONIGHT: NET also showcased domestic talent. This is a scene from a savagely satiric "actors' opera," with Eugene Troobnick and Bill Redfield.

(Below) MARY MARTIN AT EASTER TIME: The hardiest perennial of the television-specials circuit turned up again in a 1966 musicale staged by Gower Champion.

MY NAME IS BARBRA:
By 1965 Barbra Streisand had conquered
Broadway (in "Funny Girl"), and her records
were selling everywhere like bagels sell in
Brooklyn, the land of her birth twenty-two
years earlier. It took her exactly one hour to
add television to her list of conquests. She
did a one-woman show, tastefully mounted
by Joe Layton and Dwight Hemion, which
was the most generously praised special of
the 1964–65 season. The next season she did
it again, with a new solo special titled "Color
Me Barbra." These photos were shot at Berg-
dorf Goodman during the taping of a sequence for the first show.

(Left) AWARD SHOWS: Many awards are bestowed in television specials every season. The annual Oscar telecast is the biggest of the award shows. The most unpredictable, however, is the Emmy show, in which the television industry passes out statuettes to its own members—and often manages to make a fool of itself through the gaucheries of its show and the absurdities of its award categories. Sammy Davis, Jr. was co-host (with Danny Thomas) of the 1965 Emmy show, which was boycotted by two networks and was an embarrassing muddle from beginning to end.

(Below, left) PARADES: Throughout television history some types of specials have overcome the vagaries of viewers' tastes and proved popular year in and year out—parades, for example. This is Times Square during a Macy's Parade, telecast nationally every Thanksgiving Day.

(Below) TELETHONS: These grueling television marathons, which raised money for charity, were intriguing novelties during the early years. Performers like Dennis James and Jane Pickens (manning the phones and microphones here) participated in many of them, in cities all over the United States.

THE MISS AMERICA PAGEANT:
This annual competition has been making a television spectacle of itself ever since 1954, when it was telecast nationally for the first time. It always attracts one of the largest television audiences of the season. Year by year the show has become slicker—the girls better prepared, the production more polished. This has robbed the Pageant of some of its intrinsic appeal, but one vital element has remained unchanged: Bert Parks, the show's irrepressibly bouncy master of ceremonies, whose fervent rendition of "There she is, Miss America . . ." is one of the most eagerly awaited and enjoyable events of any television season. Here he serenades Marilyn Van Derbur, Miss America 1958, who went on to a television career of her own.

A Thousand and One Opening Nights

DRAMA HAS BEEN TELEVISION'S crowning glory and its Achilles heel. It brought great honor to the medium in its early days, but cast a shadow over it when television proved unable—or was it unwilling?—to continue to provide good drama. Some viewers have become scornful, others merely indifferent; many are saddened and troubled when they compare their memories of those old days with the realities of television now.

They fondly recall television's "Golden Age" of drama—the years when television was "live," when every night was opening night, when there were plays written by Paddy Chayefsky, Tad Mosel, Reginald Rose, Horton Foote, Gore Vidal; directed by Delbert Mann, Arthur Penn, George Roy Hill, John Frankenheimer, Robert Mulligan; and performed by such "unknowns" as Rod Steiger, James Dean, Grace Kelly, Jack Lemmon, Steve McQueen, Kim Stanley.

They talk of "Marty," "Twelve Angry Men," "Patterns," "Visit to a Small Planet," "Requiem for a Heavyweight," "The Miracle Worker," "Judgment at Nuremberg," "Days of Wine and Roses," all written expressly for television and later redone in other media; and of adaptations such as "A Night to Remember," "The Caine Mutiny Court-Martial," "Green Pastures," "The Turn of the Screw," "The Moon and Sixpence," and many Shakespearean productions.

But there are other men, no-nonsense types with their feet planted firmly in the 1960's, who say that nostalgia has muddled memory. Some of them are running television today. "The 'Golden Age' was perfectly dreadful," says one of broadcasting's corporate leaders. The rest of the men now in charge of television networks seem to concur. Sure there were a few superior plays, they say, but most of those live dramas were junk and were inferior to the filmed series which replaced them. If viewers could actually go back to that era, these men tell us, they would be disillusioned by what they would find.

A brief look at the program schedule of the period may help to clarify the issue. For example, we return first to the week of September 19, 1954. During those seven days one could see: "Middle of the Night," with E. G. Marshall and Eva Marie Saint; "Twelve Angry Men," with Franchot Tone; an adaptation of "Lady in the Dark," starring Ann Sothern; a play by Robert E. Sherwood, with John Cassavetes and Janice Rule; a drama by Robert Alan Aurthur; and a half-dozen others—all live, of course—with the likes of Fay Bainter, Nina Foch, Vivian Blaine, Lili Darvas, and Elizabeth Montgomery in their casts.

A year later, during the week of November 19, 1955, one could watch: "The Caine Mutiny Court-Martial," with Lloyd Nolan and Barry Sullivan; "The Devil's Disciple," with Maurice Evans, Ralph Bellamy, Teresa Wright, and Dennis King; "She Stoops to Conquer," with Michael Redgrave, Hermione Gingold, and Fritz Weaver; two original dramas by Rod Serling; and six other live plays starring Eva Gabor, Tony Randall, Elizabeth Montgomery, Don Murray, Geraldine Fitzgerald, Tom Ewell, and Lorne Greene.

Dreadful? It depends on your point of view.

The only certainty about the "Golden Age" is that it is gone forever. The men and women who gilded it have either left television or made an uneasy peace with it by doing weekly dramas about surly surgeons or incorruptible lawyers or men-on-the-run or denizens of towns like Peyton Place. Many of those who have deserted television are turning out the films, which, ironically, have now become television's dominant dramatic genre, filling the network air five nights a week, occupying time that once was enriched by television's own plays.

A THOUSAND AND ONE OPENING NIGHTS/*Introduction*

(Above) Breaking new ground: In 1948 television drama provided ample room for experiment. Producers, directors, and technicians got on-the-job training, learning how to use the new medium by presenting plays for it. This set, for a 1948 drama called "Detour" (starring James Cootes and Isabelle Robbins), was elaborate for its day.

192 /

(Bottom, right) ACTOR'S STUDIO: This was one of the earliest live drama series. Young Butch Cavell and Russell Collins played in Saroyan's "My Heart's in the Highlands" in 1949.

(Below) ANYWHERE USA: Drama had many uses. The purpose of this half-hour series was to disseminate health information painlessly. Eddie Dowling (seen here with Alan Devitt in the opening show, "Man in the Window") was the star.

(*Above*) MEDALLION THEATRE: Series like this one provided outlets for the talents of young actors like Charlton Heston, here acting in "A Day in Town."

(*Top, left*) THE MOTOROLA TV HOUR: Maria Riva and Jack Palance were two of many young actors who were almost continuously visible in early television. They appear here in "The Brandenburg Gate."

(*Below*) PULITZER PRIZE PLAYHOUSE: In addition to creating its own stars, television offered opportunities for viewers to see many of the great actors and actresses of the world's stages. Helen Hayes made her television debut in "The Late Christopher Bean," with Charles Dingle.

PHILCO-GOODYEAR TELEVISION PLAYHOUSE:
Its name changed from week to week, along
with its sponsors, but whatever it was called,
this Sunday-night series blazed a trail for
television drama, and its influence—embodied
in the writers, directors, and actors who
learned their crafts during *Playhouse*'s pioneering days—is still being felt. The show's
guiding spirit was its young producer, Fred
Coe, seen here with Jose Ferrer, who starred
in "Cyrano de Bergerac" on *Playhouse*. The
Ferrers and Cyranos had a place in Coe's
scheme of things, but new talents and original
plays were what gave the series its excitement. Coe sought and found young writers;
he encouraged them, coddled them, prodded
them, gave them freedom to write their own
way; and he produced their plays. Paddy
Chayefsky, Tad Mosel, Robert Alan Aurthur,
Horton Foote, N. Richard Nash, J. P. Miller,
Sumner Locke Elliot, David Shaw, Gore
Vidal, Calder Willingham—these men, and
others, wrote for *Philco-Goodyear,* and they
gave television some of its finest hours.

OCTOBER STORY: *Philco Television Playhouse* began on October 3,
1948. Three years later *Goodyear* started. The first *Goodyear*
production, "October Story," starred two of the busiest television
actors of that era—Julie Harris and Leslie Nielsen. The entire
show was live, of course, and for this scene a camera was placed
atop the RCA Building.

MARTY: What was the single outstanding television drama of all time? Most people would answer, "Marty." But while millions have vivid memories of the later movie version, only a handful can recall the original 1953 television drama. The stars of Paddy Chayefsky's play were Rod Steiger, as the nebbish butcher, Marty; and Nancy Marchand, as the girl who brings love into his drab life. Delbert Mann directed both television and film versions of the play.

(Above) WISH ON THE MOON: Eva Marie Saint (left) and Phyllis Kirk were among those who could be seen frequently in *Philco-Goodyear* dramas like this one.

(Top, right) MY LOST SAINTS: Lili Darvas and Eileen Heckart appeared together in this Tad Mosel play.

196 /

(Below) OLD TASSELFOOT: E. G. Marshall was virtually unknown beyond Broadway when he played a blacksmith in J. P. Miller's drama.

(Bottom, right) THE EXPENDABLE HOUSE: John Cassavetes was virtually unknown *anywhere* until he made a name for himself in early television dramas. Glenda Farrell is with him in this scene from a 1955 play by Reginald Rose.

(Above, left) THE CATERED AFFAIR: Paddy Chayefsky became television's most celebrated playwright. He followed "Marty" with "The Bachelor Party," "Middle of the Night," and this *Goodyear* production, which starred Thelma Ritter as a Jewish mother.

(Above, right) A MAN IS TEN FEET TALL: Robert Alan Aurthur wrote this prize-winning 1955 drama of the New York waterfront which starred Martin Balsam, Don Murray, and Sidney Poitier.

(Below) SHADOW OF THE CHAMP: Eli Wallach, Jack Warden, and Lee Grant had the leading roles in another 1955 *Philco* production written by Aurthur.

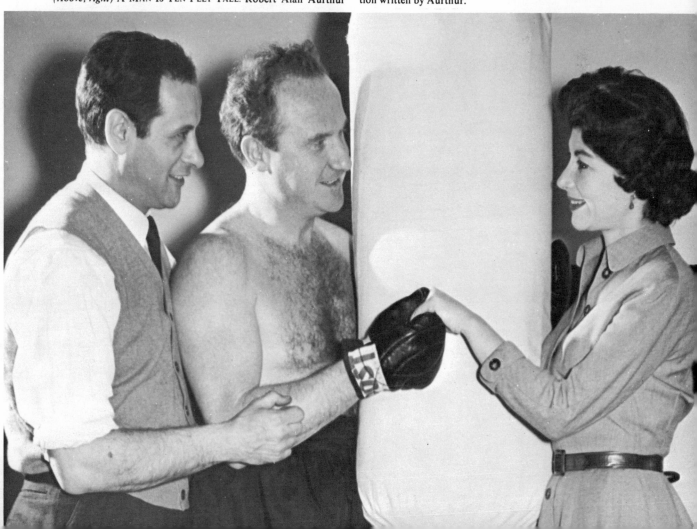

STUDIO ONE:

What *Television Playhouse* was to Sunday nights and NBC, *Studio One* was to Monday nights and CBS. And what Fred Coe was to *Playhouse*, Worthington Miner was to *Studio One*. But, whereas Coe concentrated on the writers and their scripts, Miner placed the emphasis primarily on the visual impact of his productions, on bold and imaginative camera techniques and dramatic innovations. *Studio One* premiered on November 7, 1948, with "The Storm," starring Margaret Sullavan. That was the beginning of a long run which honed the skills of such producers and directors as Felix Jackson, Gordon Duff, Alex March, Robert Herridge, Herbert Brodkin, Norman Felton, Paul Nickell, Franklin Schaffner, and Robert Mulligan. In January of 1958 *Studio One* moved to Hollywood, where the name stars and the sound-stage space were. It was the beginning of the end for *Studio One* and for live drama on television.

(Top, right) I AM JONATHAN SCRIVENER: John Forsythe and Maria Riva spent many hours perspiring under hot lights in plays like this 1952 production.

(Right) THE SCARLET LETTER: In those early days, if the leading lady was not Maria Riva, she was most likely to be Mary Sinclair. Here is Miss Sinclair in one of her most important roles, Hester Prynne.

(Right, bottom) THE KILL: Another young actress who turned up frequently on the seven-inch screen was an American beauty from Philadelphia named Grace Kelly; she appears here in a 1952 melodrama.

(Below) MRS. 'ARRIS GOES TO PARIS: Gracie Fields' performance in this Paul Gallico comedy was a highlight of the brief and mostly undistinguished career of *Studio One in Hollywood*. Janet Swanson is at left in this scene from the 1958 presentation.

(Above) MARY POPPINS: In 1949, long before Julie Andrews had been invented, *Studio One* did "Mary Poppins," with E. G. Marshall and Valerie Cossart as Mr. and Mrs. Banks, and Mary Wickes as Poppins.

(Top, right) THE REMARKABLE INCIDENT AT CARSON CORNERS: Playwright Reginald Rose gave *Studio One* some of its most distinguished plays: "Thunder on Sycamore Street," "The Death and Life of Larry Benson," "Dino," "The Defender" (a two-part drama, starring Ralph Bellamy, William Shatner, and Steve McQueen, from which the weekly series *The Defenders* was derived), and this one, which starred Harry Townes.

(Below) TWELVE ANGRY MEN: Rose's most famous play, telecast in 1954 (and subsequently done as a movie), was set in a jury room. The twelve jurors were Franchot Tone, Robert Cummings, Edward Arnold, Walter Abel, Paul Hartman, George Voskovec, John Beal, Lee Philips, Norman Fell, Joseph Sweeney, Bart Burns, and Will West. Franklin Schaffner directed.

KRAFT TELEVISION THEATRE

set all sorts of records during its eleven and one-half years on the air. It was the first full-hour drama series to hit television (May 7, 1947). It was the first drama show telecast over the coaxial cable to the Midwest (1949). It did two live one-hour plays every week for about a year (Wednesdays on NBC, Thursdays on ABC), and was the only show to accomplish this feat. Altogether it telecast 650 plays, employing some four thousand actors and actresses. A scene from its first production, "Double Door," starring John Baragrey in a cast of five, is shown on the right. The show originated in a small converted radio studio.

(Left) A LONG TIME TILL DAWN: The late James Dean starred in this 1953 *Kraft* play.

(Below) PATTERNS: This 1955 Rod Serling drama, directed by Fielder Cook, starred (left to right) Ed Begley, Everett Sloane, and Richard Kiley as the chief participants in a power struggle inside a large corporation. It is acknowledged as a television classic, was repeated (live, of course) four weeks after its first showing, and was later done as a movie.

(Above) THE EMPEROR JONES: Ossie Davis and Everett Sloane were in this 1955 version of O'Neill's play.

(Top, right) THE BLUES OF JOEY MENOTTI: In this earlier (1953) Serling drama Dan Morgan, as a honky-tonk pianist, fell in love with Constance Ford.

(Bottom, right) THE DIAMOND AS BIG AS THE RITZ: *Kraft's* five hundredth show, in 1955, was an adaptation of an F. Scott Fitzgerald fantasy. The cast included Signe Hasso and Elizabeth Montgomery (shown here), plus George Macready, Richard Franchot, and Lee Remick.

(Below) A PROFILE IN COURAGE: Senator John F. Kennedy, then thirty-eight, introduced a 1956 drama based on a chapter from his book "Profiles in Courage." It recounted the story of Senator Edmund G. Ross (James Whitmore), who cast the deciding vote against the impeachment of President Andrew Johnson. Here Senator Kennedy confers with *Kraft* floor manager Ken Lynch. Eight years later "Profiles in Courage" was transformed into a weekly drama series.

(Above) A NIGHT TO REMEMBER: When this account of the sinking of the Titanic was done in 1956, it was the most ambitious live drama that had ever been attempted—107 actors, 31 sets, 7 cameras. It was a triumph for its director, George Roy Hill, and was repeated a few weeks later.

(Top, left) THE SEA IS BOILING HOT: One of the series' last productions, in 1958, was this two-character play by Shimon Wincelberg, about a U.S. airman (Earl Holliman) and a Japanese soldier (Sessue Hayakawa) stranded on a small Pacific island during World War II.

(Bottom, left) THE SINGIN' IDOL: In 1957, when Elvis Presley was dominating pop music, *Kraft* presented this drama of a naïve country boy (Tommy Sands) who becomes a singing rage under the guidance of his ruthless manager (Fred Clark).

(Below) DRUMMER MAN: Sal Mineo, who made his first big splash as the teen-age star of a Saroyan sketch on *Omnibus,* played a jazz drummer for *Kraft* when he was eighteen.

ROBERT MONTGOMERY PRESENTS
was scheduled opposite *Studio One,* on NBC
(with a half hour's head start), beginning in
1950. Montgomery, the veteran movie actor
and director, was producer, host, and some-
time star of the series, which offered some
originals but leaned more heavily on adaptations, like this one—the opening *Montgomery
Presents* show, "Victoria Regina," starring
Helen Hayes.

204 /

(Above) AFTER ALL THESE YEARS: Claudette Colbert made a rare
television appearance in a 1956 Montgomery production entitled
"After All These Years."

(Left) SUMMER STOCK: For the summer of 1956 Montgomery
formed a stock company to perform the weekly plays. Included
were (from left): John Gibson, Mary K. Wells, Tom Middleton,
Elizabeth Montgomery (the boss's daughter), and Montgomery.

CAMERA THREE

has a minuscule budget, an impossible time slot (Sunday mornings), and little network promotion. But it also has imagination, daring, taste, and style. Drama is only one of the forms *Camera Three* employs, but its dramatic programs have a unique flavor. This is a scene from a six-part adaptation of Dostoevski's "Crime and Punishment," with the late Gerald Sarracini as Raskolnikov. Simple props (especially ladders and stools) and stark lighting became *Camera Three*'s trademark, a distinction which was mothered by necessity (the budget left no room for frills) and fathered by Robert Herridge, a gifted producer-director, who launched the series and gave it its distinctive shape. It started as a local New York show in 1953, and went network (CBS) in 1956.

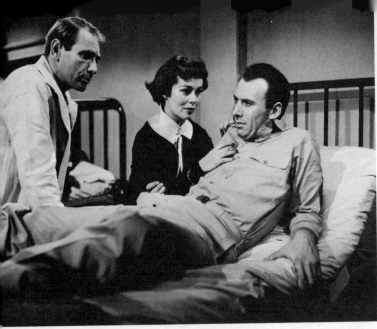

The U.S. Steel Hour

was telecast every other week from 1953 to 1963, under the aegis of the Theatre Guild.

(Above) P.O.W.: The first *Steel Hour* play, written by David Davidson, starred Gary Merrill, Phyllis Kirk, and Richard Kiley. It dealt with the brainwashing of a soldier during the Korean conflict.

(Top, right) INCIDENT IN AN ALLEY: Farley Granger was a rookie cop tortured by guilt after killing a boy who was fleeing from the scene of a crime in this play by Rod Serling.

(Bottom, right) FLINT AND FIRE: Robert Culp and Gloria Vanderbilt played young lovers in Vermont in a 1958 *Steel Hour* production.

(Below) A WIND FROM THE SOUTH: James Costigan's 1955 drama, set in Ireland, starred Julie Harris as a young spinster whose life is transformed by some Americans who stop at the inn where she works.

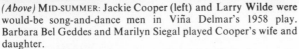

(Above) MID-SUMMER: Jackie Cooper (left) and Larry Wilde were would-be song-and-dance men in Viña Delmar's 1958 play. Barbara Bel Geddes and Marilyn Siegal played Cooper's wife and daughter.

(Top, right) NO TIME FOR SERGEANTS: Mac Hyman's comedy was presented before a live studio audience of 150 persons. Andy Griffith starred as naïve Will Stockdale (he later repeated the role on Broadway and in the movie), and Eddie LeRoy was Will's

buddy. Alex Segal, number-one director of *The U.S. Steel Hour* from the beginning, staged this show.

(Below) BEAVER PATROL: As the years passed, *Steel Hour* did fewer and fewer serious original dramas and more and more light comedies and adaptations. This play won a comedy-writing award for its author, John Vlahos. Walter Slezak starred and the kids were (from left) Thomas Tai, Seth Edwards, Johnny Borden, Luke Halpin, Jimmie Rodgers, and Johnny Towsen

LIGHTS OUT: Alongside the early hour-long drama series ran some live half-hour melodramas. An early one was *Lights Out,* the offshoot of a popular radio show, which came to television in 1949. *(Bottom, left)* For part of its run movie menace Jack La Rue was the host. *(Left)* A 1951 episode, "The House of Dust," starred Nina Foch and Anthony Quinn.

(Below) SUSPENSE: This series also moved from radio to television in 1949. Grace Kelly appeared in an episode entitled "50 Beautiful Girls."

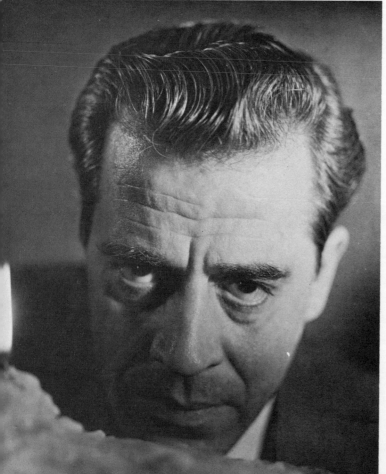

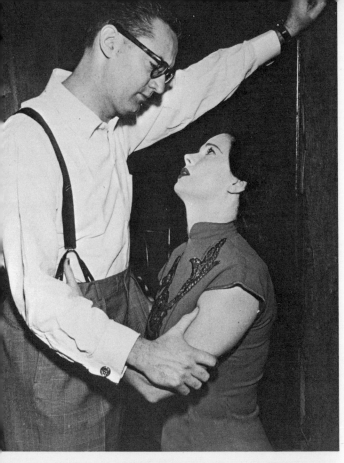

(*Above*) TALES OF TOMORROW: Science-fiction melodrama was this show's specialty. A two-part version of Jules Verne's "20,000 Leagues under the Sea" had Thomas Mitchell (as Captain Nemo), Bethel Leslie, and Leslie Nielsen in the cast.

DANGER: (*Left*) One of the best-received episodes of *Danger* (which debuted in 1950) was Mark Hellinger's "The Paper Box Kid," starring Martin Ritt (who later became a top Hollywood director) as a Broadway hood. (*Top, left*) Another *Danger* production, "Flamingo," was written by Steve Allen, who starred in it with his wife Jayne Meadows.

PLAYWRIGHTS 56: Despite the title, it actually started in 1955, on alternate Tuesdays, with Fred Coe as producer, and Delbert Mann, Arthur Penn, and Vincent Donehue among the directors. Even this array of talent could not make a ratings success of *Playwrights 56;* its competition was the immensely popular quiz show *The $64,000 Question.* Below, Kim Stanley stars in a love story entitled "Flight."

THE KAISER ALUMINUM HOUR: This was the successor to *Playwrights 56.* It started with Worthington Miner, Franklin Schaffner, Fielder Cook, and George Roy Hill in charge. Three of their outstanding productions were: *(above)* "Antigone," in a modern-dress version starring Claude Rains and Marisa Pavan; *(bottom, left)* Rod Serling's "Mr. Finchley Versus the Bomb," starring Henry Hull; and *(below)* Steven Gethers' "The Rag Jungle," which had Paul Newman fighting racketeers in the garment district. In midseason Miner & Co. were replaced by David Susskind's Talent Associates, whose mission was to give the series more mass appeal.

MATINEE THEATRE

was welcomed by housewives seeking relief from the soap operas and quiz shows that filled the afternoon air. It presented hour-long plays five days a week for three seasons, beginning in 1955. This Herculean task was accomplished with remarkable finesse by producer Albert McCleery and his hard-working assistants. John Conte was the series' host.

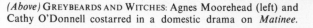

(Above) GREYBEARDS AND WITCHES: Agnes Moorehead (left) and Cathy O'Donnell costarred in a domestic drama on *Matinee*.

(Left) WUTHERING HEIGHTS: Richard Boone portrayed the distraught Heathcliff in an early *Matinee Theatre* production.

(Top, left) GEORGE HAS A BIRTHDAY: In his first serious role Eddie Cantor played a milksop.

HALLMARK HALL OF FAME

started in 1952 with half-hour dramas and
eventually shifted to ninety-minute shows,
about six of them a year. Although *Hallmark*
has done musicals, operas, and other types of
shows, its greatest success has been with serious drama, especially adaptations of classics
and, in recent years, historical plays. Producer Mildred Freed Alberg and actor-
director Maurice Evans set the tone for the
series, and producer-director George Schaefer
carried on the tradition after Mrs. Alberg
withdrew from the show.

(Above) THE GREEN PASTURES: Of all of *Hallmark's* productions,
Marc Connelly's fable-play may well be the most memorable.
It was first telecast in 1957, then repeated a year later. William
Warfield played De Lawd; Vinette Carroll (left) and Hilda
Haynes were two angels.
(Bottom, left) WINTERSET: Maxwell Anderson's verse drama
came to *Hallmark* in 1959, with George C. Scott, Piper Laurie,
Charles Bickford, and Don Murray in key roles.
(Below) THE LARK: Julie Harris starred as Joan of Arc, Boris
Karloff was Cauchon, and Eli Wallach, Basil Rathbone, Den-
holm Elliott, and Jack Warden were also in the cast. James
Costigan adapted for television Lillian Hellman's version of
Anouilh's play.

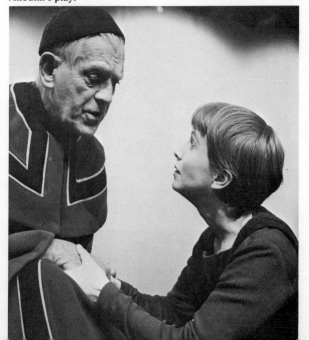

(Above) MAN AND SUPERMAN: *Hallmark* has done a number of Shaw's plays. Maurice Evans and Joan Greenwood topped the cast of this one. □ (Left) BORN YESTERDAY: Mary Martin was Billie Dawn in *Hallmark*'s version of Garson Kanin's comedy, costarring Paul Douglas and Arthur Hill. □ (Below) LITTLE MOON OF ALBAN: Among original plays, *Hallmark*'s greatest success was this 1958 drama (also repeated later) by James Costigan, set in Ireland during "the troubles." Julie Harris, a frequent performer in this series, joined Christopher Plummer (right), Barry Jones, and George Peppard (not pictured) in "Little Moon."

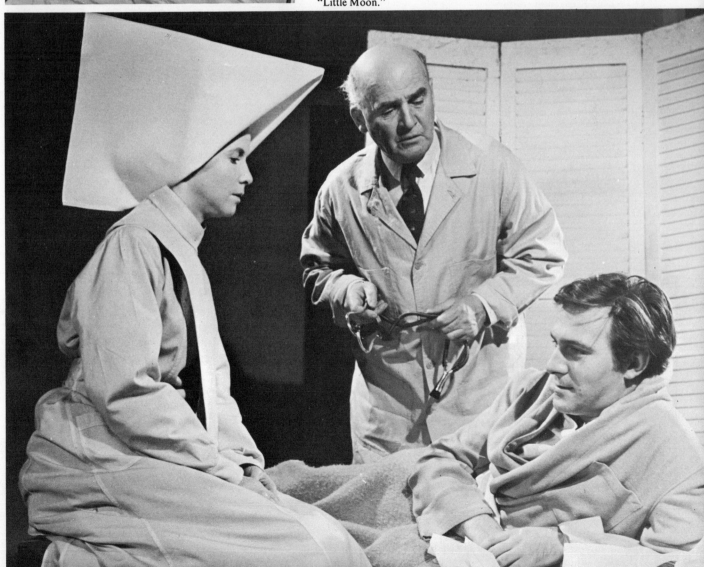

(Above) THE ROYAL FAMILY: In the fall of 1954 the networks introduced a new programming concept—lavish drama specials, scheduled monthly or fortnightly, with big-name stars in ninety- or sixty-minute productions, usually adaptations of twentieth-century stage plays. One such series of specials, *The Best of Broadway,* opened with the Kaufman-Ferber comedy "The Royal Family." Fredric March, Helen Hayes, and (not shown) Claudette Colbert starred; Martin Manulis produced; Paul Nickell directed.

(Top, right) DARKNESS AT NOON: This *Producers' Showcase* adaptation, derived from a Koestler novel and directed by Delbert Mann, starred Lee J. Cobb and Ruth Roman, plus David Wayne, Oscar Homolka, Joseph Wiseman, and Nehemiah Persoff.

(Bottom, right) THE PETRIFIED FOREST: In 1955 Humphrey Bogart repeated the role he had originated twenty years earlier on the stage—Duke Mantee in Robert E. Sherwood's drama. Henry Fonda and Lauren Bacall joined Bogart in the television cast of this *Producers' Showcase* presentation, directed by Delbert Mann.

(Below) STATE OF THE UNION: *Producers' Showcase,* supervised by Fred Coe, did this Lindsay-Crouse comedy, with Nina Foch, Joseph Cotten, and Margaret Sullavan in the cast, and Arthur Penn as director.

214 /

 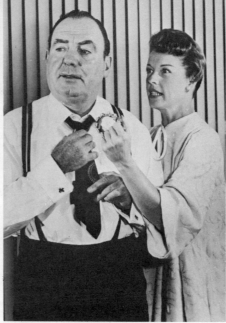 

(Top, left) THE CONSTANT HUSBAND: A novelty amid all these live 1955 productions was this English movie, shown on television (as a *Color Spread* special) before it was released to U.S. theaters. Rex Harrison and his wife, the late Kay Kendall, starred.

(Top, center) DINNER AT EIGHT: *Front Row Center* debuted in 1955 with another Kaufman-Ferber comedy. Pat O'Brien and Mary Beth Hughes were starred in this production, with Mary Astor and Everett Sloane. It was produced and directed by Fletcher Markle.

(Top, right) AH, WILDERNESS!: O'Neill's 1933 play came to *Front Row Center* with Leon Ames and Lillian Bronson featured.

(Below) THE SKIN OF OUR TEETH: Helen Hayes, Heller Hallidy, George Abbott, and Mary Martin starred in Thornton Wilder's play, presented in 1955 on *Color Spread*. Florence Reed, Don Murray, and Frank Silvera were also in the show.

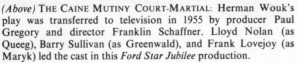

(*Above*) THE CAINE MUTINY COURT-MARTIAL: Herman Wouk's play was transferred to television in 1955 by producer Paul Gregory and director Franklin Schaffner. Lloyd Nolan (as Queeg), Barry Sullivan (as Greenwald), and Frank Lovejoy (as Maryk) led the cast in this *Ford Star Jubilee* production.

(*Top, right*) THE DAY LINCOLN WAS SHOT: Jack Lemmon was John Wilkes Booth in *Ford Star Jubilee*'s dramatization of Jim Bishop's best seller. Charles Laughton narrated, Lillian Gish played Mrs. Lincoln, and Raymond Massey was Lincoln.

(*Right*) CAESAR AND CLEOPATRA: This 1956 *Producers' Showcase* production of Shaw's play had quite a cast: Claire Bloom, Sir Cedric Hardwicke, Jack Hawkins, Judith Anderson, Cyril Ritchard, Farley Granger, Anthony Quayle, Thomas Gomez, and Patrick Macnee, among others.

(*Bottom, right*) BLITHE SPIRIT: Lauren Bacall came back to haunt Noel Coward in the *Ford Star Jubilee* version of Coward's comedy fantasy.

(*Below*) THE BARRETTS OF WIMPOLE STREET: Katharine Cornell made her television acting debut in one of her most famous roles—Elizabeth Barrett Browning—on *Producers' Showcase*. Anthony Quayle and Nancy Coleman were featured.

(Above) MAYERLING: Audrey Hepburn and Mel Ferrer were doomed lovers in Anatole Litvak's 1957 *Producers' Showcase* offering. Among others in the large cast were Raymond Massey, Diana Wynyard, and Judith Evelyn (shown here), and Basil Sydney, Isobel Elsom, Nehemiah Persoff, Lorne Greene, Ian Wolfe, David Opatoshu, Nancy Marchand, Monique Van Vooren, Peter Donat, Sorrell Booke, and Suzy Parker.

(Top, left) THIS HAPPY BREED: Noel Coward starred (with Edna Best) in another of his plays, directed by Ralph Nelson, on *Ford Star Jubilee.*

(Left) DODSWORTH: Fredric March and Claire Trevor were Sam and Fran Dodsworth in this *Producers' Showcase* presentation, directed by Alex Segal.

(Bottom, left) TWENTIETH CENTURY: Television makes strange castfellows. Betty Grable and Orson Welles clowned together in the Hecht-MacArthur farce, shown on *Ford Star Jubilee* in 1956.

(Below) THE GREAT SEBASTIANS: Alfred Lunt and Lynn Fontanne appeared on television together for the first time in 1957, in a *Producers' Showcase* adaptation of their Broadway comedy.

OMNIBUS

was true to its title—it was a vehicle for myriad passengers, heavy and light. Bernstein on music, Agnes DeMille and Gene Kelly on the dance, Frank Lloyd Wright on architecture, Joseph Welch on the law, Nichols and May on American folkways, Saroyan on Saroyan —all these, and many others, hitched rides on *Omnibus* during its somewhat erratic journey, which started on CBS in 1952, and, before it ended, meandered to each of the other two networks for brief spells. Drama figured importantly in *Omnibus'* programming. Orson Welles played Lear; Christopher Plummer, Oedipus; Peter Ustinov, Samuel Johnson; George C. Scott, Robespierre. Under the guidance of producer Robert Saudek, *Omnibus* always tried to be a bit better than anything else to be found on television. It succeeded often enough to make its ultimate demise, in the late fifties, an event that impoverished television considerably.

(Top, left) Alistair Cooke was *Omnibus'* urbane host throughout its career.

(Above) Yul Brynner donned a wig and tattered costume to portray François Villon in "A Lodging for the Night," by Robert Louis Stevenson, presented on *Omnibus* in 1953.

(Below) "Mr. Lincoln," a film written by James Agee and featuring Royal Dano in the title role, was shown biweekly in serial form during *Omnibus'* first season.

THE SEVEN LIVELY ARTS, conceptually similar to *Omnibus,* lasted only a few months. It began in 1957 with a disastrous first show, improved tremendously in subsequent weeks, but never lived down the critical pasting that first episode took. The opener, a mélange called "The Changing Ways of Love," was written by S. J. Perelman, who also appeared in it, along with Jason Robards, Jr., Piper Laurie, Rip Torn, Dick York, Mike Wallace, and the series' host, John Crosby. Crosby (above, with Perelman) was the nation's leading television critic, but he was miscast as an on-camera performer. He knew it, and his discomfort was all too apparent to viewers. The executive producer of *The Seven Lively Arts* was John Houseman.

(Top, left) Maureen Stapleton appeared in "Blast in Centralia No. 5," John Bartlow Martin's account of a mine disaster, dramatized by Loring Mandel and directed by George Roy Hill.

(Left) One of the show's dramatic successes was "The World of Nick Adams," based on Hemingway's stories, adapted by A. E. Hotchner, produced by Robert Herridge, directed by Robert Mulligan, and starring Eli Wallach, William Marshall, and Steve Hill.

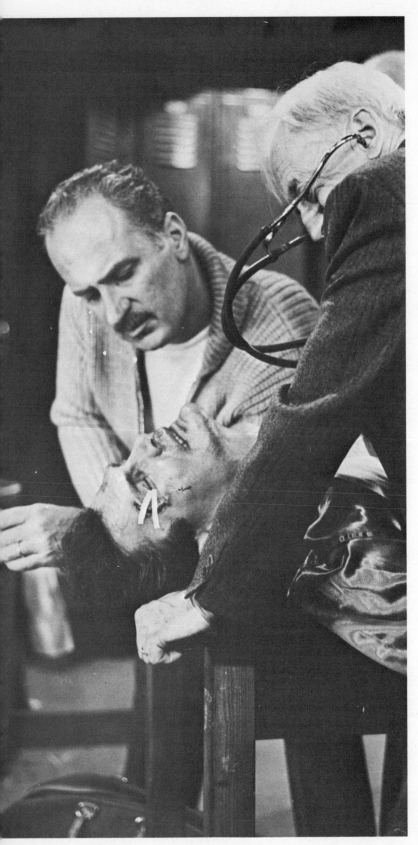

PLAYHOUSE 90

was television's most ambitious undertaking —a series of weekly ninety-minute dramas with the best casts, writers, directors, and producers that a high budget could buy. In its five years on the air it had its share of failures, particularly toward the end, when ratings considerations overrode artistic judgment; but *Playhouse 90* will be remembered for a long time to come as a show that provided some of television's most unforgettable dramas. On the left is a scene from one of them, *Playhouse 90*'s second show, telecast October 11, 1956—"Requiem for a Heavyweight," Rod Serling's story of a broken-down prizefighter. Jack Palance starred as Mountain McClintock; Keenan Wynn (shown here, with Palance), Ed Wynn, and Kim Hunter had the other principal roles, and Ralph Nelson directed. Producer Martin Manulis launched the series, which also presented "The Miracle Worker," "Judgment at Nuremberg," "The Comedian," "Journey to the Day," "A Sound of Different Drummers," "Tomorrow," and, among many other plays, those pictured on the next three pages.

OPPOSITE PAGE

(Top, left) LAST CLEAR CHANCE: Paul Muni played a distinguished lawyer who defended his son, also an attorney, in a disbarment proceeding. Muni wore what looked like a hearing aid but was really a receiver through which his lines were fed to him. Luther Adler, Dick York, and Lee Remick had featured roles in A. E. Hotchner's drama.

(Top, right) THE HELEN MORGAN STORY: Polly Bergen acted and sang in this biographical drama by Leonard Spigelgass and Paul Monash.

(Bottom, left) ELOISE: This was a highly publicized—but not so highly regarded—venture into comedy, based on Kay Thompson's book. Seven-year-old Evelyn Rudie was Eloise, and a mixed bag of bewildered grown-ups wandered through the ninety minutes. Among them were Ethel Barrymore, Louis Jourdan, Monty Woolley, Charles Ruggles, Inger Stevens, Maxie Rosenbloom, and Conrad Hilton.

(Bottom, right) THE PLOT TO KILL STALIN: Melvyn Douglas was Stalin and Eli Wallach his aide in David Karp's drama, which drew a vigorous protest from the Russians. The cast included Oscar Homolka (as Khrushchev), E. G. Marshall (Beria), Thomas Gomez (Malenkov), and Luther Adler (Molotov). Fred Coe produced and Delbert Mann directed.

(*Above*) THE DAYS OF WINE AND ROSES: On October 2, 1958, *Playhouse 90* presented this saga of a young married couple (Piper Laurie, shown here with Charles Bickford; and Cliff Robertson) who both become alcoholics. The playwright was J. P. Miller, the director John Frankenheimer.

(*Top, right*) THE TIME OF YOUR LIFE: A week later the play was Saroyan's "The Time of Your Life," starring Jackie Gleason and Betsy Palmer, with Dick York, Jack Klugman, Bobby Van, James Barton, and Dina Merrill. The play was produced by Gordon Duff and directed by Tom Donovan.

(*Right*) THE VELVET ALLEY: Rod Serling indulged in some self-psychoanalysis in this drama about a television writer, Ernie Pandish, played by Art Carney. The show was produced by Herbert Brodkin and directed by Franklin Schaffner.

(*Bottom, right*) CHILD OF OUR TIME: This searing drama was based on the autobiographical book by Michel del Castillo, who as a young boy had been cast adrift in Europe during World War II. Bobby Crawford played the title role. George Roy Hill directed Irving Gaynor Neiman's play.

(*Below*) OLD MAN: Sterling Hayden portrayed a convict, and Geraldine Page a pregnant woman he rescues during a flood in Horton Foote's adaptation of Faulkner's story, directed by John Frankenheimer.

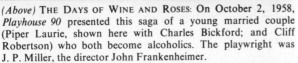

(Above) FOR WHOM THE BELL TOLLS: This was *Playhouse 90's* most ambitious production, taped in a New York studio at a cost of approximately $300,000 and shown in two ninety-minute segments, on consecutive Thursdays in 1959. Maria Schell and Jason Robards, Jr. headed a cast which included Nehemiah Persoff, Maureen Stapleton, Steve Hill, and Eli Wallach. John Frankenheimer directed A. E. Hotchner's adaptation of Hemingway's novel.

(Top, left) SEVEN AGAINST THE WALL: The St. Valentine's Day Massacre was re-created in this documentary drama in which Paul Lambert (left) played Al Capone, and Tige Andrews was Frank Nitti. John Houseman produced and Franklin Schaffner directed.

/ 223

(Bottom, left) A MARRIAGE OF STRANGERS: Diana Lynn and Red Buttons were cast as troubled newlyweds in Reginald Rose's play, directed by Alex Segal.

(Below) MISALLIANCE: *Playhouse 90* proved it could handle sophisticated comedy with style and inventiveness in this free-wheeling version of Shaw's play, directed by Robert Stevens. Siobhan McKenna and Rod Taylor were featured, along with Claire Bloom and Robert Morley.

CLIMAX!: As the fifties ended, original drama was becoming a rarity on television. "Filmed in Hollywood" was replacing "Live from New York" (or "Live from Hollywood," for that matter). *Climax!*, a Hollywood melodrama series, was telecast live when it first arrived in 1954, but it soon switched to film. *(Top, right)* Its host and hostess, Bill Lundigan and Mary Costa, made more of an impression on viewers than did most of the series' plays. (Miss Costa, of course, went on to a brilliant career on opera and concert stages.) The opening episode, Raymond Chandler's "The Long Goodbye" *(above),* had Dick Powell playing private eye Philip Marlowe; Teresa Wright was an irate suspect.

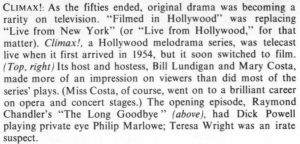

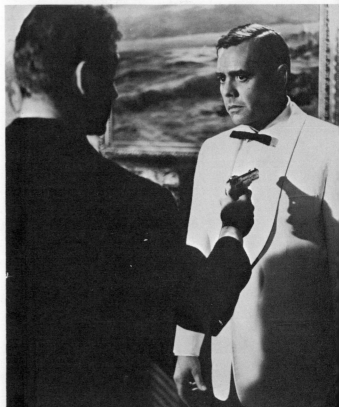

DESILU PLAYHOUSE: A later hour-long film series from Hollywood, this was the successor to *Studio One*. Desi Arnaz served as producer, host, and occasional star. Here he is in a scene from "Thunder in the Night."

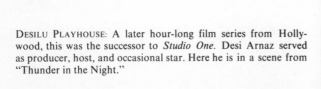

DU PONT SHOW OF THE MONTH:

Virtually the only drama left in New York was in the form of adaptations, most of them in packages of specials wrapped up by producer David Susskind. The monthly Du Pont series was Susskind's. It began in 1957 and covered a wide range of source material.

(Above) I, DON QUIXOTE: The hit musical "Man of La Mancha" is based on this 1959 *Du Pont* play written by Dale Wasserman. Lee J. Cobb played Cervantes and Quixote.
(Below) THE BROWNING VERSION: John Gielgud and Margaret Leighton costarred in Terence Rattigan's drama.
(Bottom) A TALE OF TWO CITIES: *Du Pont* tackled Dickens in 1958. The cast (left to right): Denholm Elliott, Eric Portman, James Donald, Gracie Fields, Rosemary Harris, Walter Fitzgerald; plus (not shown) Agnes Moorehead, George C. Scott, Fritz Weaver, and Alfred Ryder.

(Top) THE BRIDGE OF SAN LUIS REY: This 1958 *Du Pont Show,* based on Thornton Wilder's novel, had Hume Cronyn and Viveca Lindfors in the cast, as well as Judith Anderson, Eva LeGallienne, Theodore Bikel, and Rita Gam.
(Above) HARVEY: Art Carney starred in Mary Ellen Chase's whimsical comedy.
(Below) BODY AND SOUL: Ben Gazzara portrayed a boxer in this adaptation of a John Garfield movie. Jack Dempsey was the show's "technical advisor."

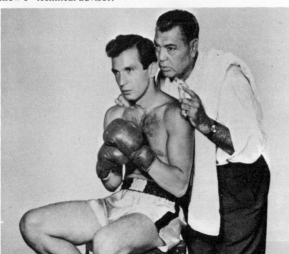

(Above) SWISS FAMILY ROBINSON: There were numerous non-*Du Pont* adaptations in the late fifties too. This one, in 1958, had Walter Pidgeon and Laraine Day as husband and wife.

(Top, right) THE BELLS OF ST. MARY'S: *Special Tonight* was the overall title for seven shows presented during the 1959-60 season. Robert Preston and Claudette Colbert started things off in this comedy.

(Right) THE HEIRESS: *Family Classics* was another series of specials. It included this adaptation of Henry James's novel, starring Julie Harris, with Farley Granger and Barry Morse.

(Right, below) THE DEVIL AND DANIEL WEBSTER: Edward G. Robinson played Webster opposite David Wayne's Devil on *Breck Golden Showcase*.

(Right, bottom) TONIGHT IN SAMARKAND: James Mason played a fortune-teller in this show, which costarred Janice Rule.

(Below) WHAT MAKES SAMMY RUN ?: Budd Schulberg's tale of a Hollywood heel was done in two parts on *Sunday Showcase* in 1959. Larry Blyden (center, between Barbara Rush and John Forsythe) was Sammy.

THE TURN OF THE SCREW: Ingrid Bergman made her television acting debut on October 20, 1959, in James Costigan's brilliantly eerie dramatization of Henry James's novella, directed by John Frankenheimer. (Alexandra Wager appears here with Miss Bergman.) "The Turn of the Screw" was part of the weekly *Ford Startime* series, which also brought Alec Guinness to American television that season in "The Wicked Scheme of Jebal Deeks."

THE MOON AND SIXPENCE: Just ten days after "The Turn of the Screw" was telecast, along came Laurence Olivier in this highly acclaimed production, supported by Judith Anderson, Hume Cronyn, Jessica Tandy, Geraldine Fitzgerald, Denholm Elliott, and Cyril Cusack. S. Lee Pogostin adapted Maugham's novel for television and Robert Mulligan directed the production.

SHAKESPEARE,
that most adaptable of playwrights, has been represented on television in all sorts of adaptations.

(Top, left) MACBETH: Charlton Heston played the Thane on *Studio One* in 1951, with Judith Evelyn as his Lady.

(Left) MACBETH: Later versions, presented by *Hallmark Hall of Fame,* starred Maurice Evans and Judith Anderson, live in 1954, and on film in 1960.

(Bottom, left) HAMLET: Maurice Evans has been television's most prolific Shakespearian actor, performing in many of the Bard's plays on *Hallmark.* He made his dramatic television debut in 1953, as Hamlet in a *Hallmark* cast that also included Ruth Chatterton, Joseph Schildkraut, Sarah Churchill, and Barry Jones.

(Right, top) KING RICHARD II: Evans starred with Sarah Churchill in 1954.

(Above) THE TAMING OF THE SHREW: Perhaps the liveliest of all Shakespearian performances seen on television was this free and fanciful adaptation, in which Evans played opposite Lilli Palmer in 1956.

(Below) TWELFTH NIGHT: Evans as Malvolio in 1957.

(Top, left) ROMEO AND JULIET: Susan Strasberg, then sixteen, and Liam Sullivan were the star-crossed lovers on *Kraft Theatre* in 1954.

(Left) ROMEO AND JULIET: Claire Bloom and John Neville played the roles in the Old Vic production telecast in 1957.

(Bottom, left) RICHARD III: In 1956 *Wide Wide World* departed from its usual format to make way for a three-hour telecast of the motion-picture version of "Richard III," starring Sir Laurence Olivier and Sir Ralph Richardson.

/ **229**

(Above) HAMLET: An Old Vic version was telecast on *Du Pont Show of the Month* in 1959. John Neville (right) was Hamlet; John Humphry, Laertes; Oliver Neville, Claudius.

(Below) AN AGE OF KINGS: This British series, comprising all of Shakespeare's chronicles of the English kings, was imported to the United States and telecast by various local stations around the country. This is a scene from "The Rabble from Kent," a portion of the seldom-performed "Henry VI, Part Two." Esmond Knight (on rostrum) played rebellious Jack Cade.

ARMSTRONG CIRCLE THEATRE: Various dramatic devices were attempted in a desperate effort to keep television drama alive in New York. "Documentary drama"—plays based on true stories —was *Circle's* technique. Above is a moment from a 1962 play, "The Man Who Refused to Die," with Alexander Scourby and Marketa Kimbrell as Polish Jews who hid from the Nazis.

THE SACCO-VANZETTI STORY: A similar technique was applied in this two-part drama written by Reginald Rose, directed by Sidney Lumet, and telecast in 1960. Martin Balsam (left) was Sacco; Steven Hill, Vanzetti. Others in the sizable cast were Peter Falk, E. G. Marshall, House Jameson, Robert Emhardt, and Ruth White.

PEOPLE KILL PEOPLE SOMETIMES: It was hoped that this highly touted poetic drama by S. Lee Pogostin would spark a revival of original plays on television. George C. Scott and Geraldine Page costarred with Jason Robards, Jr. This was the opening production of the 1959–60 *Sunday Showcase* series produced by **Robert Alan Aurthur**.

(Above) OLDSMOBILE MUSIC THEATRE: A live-drama-with-music format was tried too, in a short-lived half-hour series. Chester Morris, Hurd Hatfield, Carol Lawrence, and Roddy MacDowell performed in this two-part production, "Too Bad About Sheila Troy."

(Below) DOW HOUR OF GREAT MYSTERIES: Chilling classics were taken out of the freezer for a series of 1960 specials. This was "The Bat," starring Helen Hayes and Jason Robards, Jr., with Joseph Welch as host. With the exception of a few specials, some notable series with continuing characters, and the ever-present soap operas, New York was dead as a center of television drama when the sixties unreeled on film and on tape. Hollywood's domination of television programming was virtually complete.

(Above, top) OUR AMERICAN HERITAGE: United States history was dramatized in this series. This is a 1960 episode, "Autocrat and Son," by Ernest Kinoy, with Sir Cedric Hardwicke as Oliver Wendell Holmes, Sr., Ann Harding as his wife, and Anne Francis as the fiancée of Oliver, Jr. (Christopher Plummer).

(Above) THE SECRET OF FREEDOM: A preachy play by Archibald MacLeish was done on *Sunday Showcase* in 1960, with Thomas Mitchell, Tony Randall, and Kim Hunter acting under the direction of Alan Schneider.

(Below) THE ASSASSINATION PLOT AT TEHERAN: Historical melo-drama was attempted in this 1961 two-part special featuring (left to right) Joseph Mell, Stephen Roberts, and Billy Vincent.

(*Above, left*) BIGELOW THEATRE: Hollywood's contribution to television had been modest enough in the early days. It consisted of dozens of little half-hour playlets like this one—"The Hot Welcome," starring Gale Storm.

(*Above, right*) FIRESIDE THEATRE: A starlet named Amanda Blake turned up frequently in this series, which began in 1949.

(*Below*) YOUR JEWELER'S SHOWCASE: Jan Clayton and Dave Willock were in a gem called "Three and One-Half Musketeers."

(*Bottom*) CAVALCADE OF AMERICA: Leo G. Carroll portrayed William Penn's father in "The Splendid Dream" in 1954.

——ALL-STAR THEATRE: They left room for local stations to insert the sponsor's name in the title of this omnipresent syndicated series, which provided work for such Hollywood denizens as (top to bottom) Corinne Calvet, Robert Stack, William Eythe, and Gale Robbins; Laraine Day, Franchot Tone, and Natalie Wood; and Keefe Brasselle and Marjorie Lord.

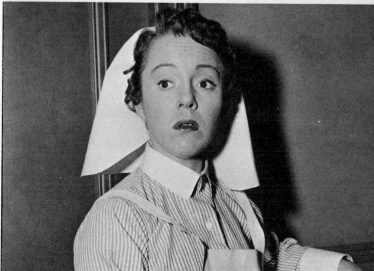

(*Above*) SCREEN DIRECTORS PLAYHOUSE: Pat Hitchcock, Alfred's daughter, first appeared on television as a nurse in "White Corridors."

(*Top, right*) STAGE 7: Alexis Smith was menaced by Dan Barton in an adaptation of Jack London's "To Kill a Man."

(*Top, left*) STAR STAGE: Greer Garson adopted Linda Bennett in "Career."

(*Center, left*) THEATRE TIME: Ricardo Montalban and Patricia Hardy were the combatants in "Rhubarb in Apartment 7."

(*Bottom, left*) O. HENRY PLAYHOUSE: Thomas Mitchell was the storyteller.

(*Below*) DAMON RUNYON THEATRE: Gene White, Robert Strauss, and Vivian Blaine were in "Pick the Winner."

FOUR STAR PLAYHOUSE: Charles Boyer, Dick Powell, Rosalind Russell, and Joel McCrea were the original foursome in this popular film series, which began in 1952. Two dropped out and the four eventually became three—(Below) Powell, Boyer, and David Niven (left to right)—who expanded into Four Star Studio, which also produced other series. (Right) Niven's "favorite role" was that of an Anglican priest imprisoned by Indians in "The Collar."

SCHLITZ PLAYHOUSE OF STARS: This show started in 1951, and was on the air for several years. Three of its stars were: (Above) Raymond Burr, as a doctor (with Marilyn Erskine); (right, center) James Dean, in "The Unlighted Road" in 1955; and (right) Rod Steiger, as Steinmetz (with Diane Brewster).

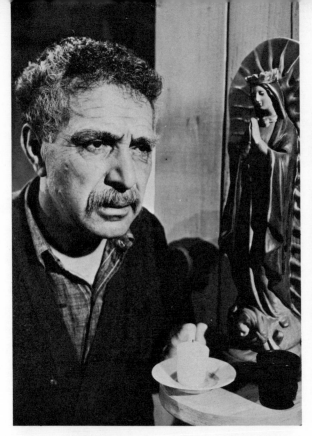

/ 235

LUX VIDEO THEATRE: *Lux* moved from radio to television in 1951. *(Left)* J. Carrol Naish starred in "A Medal for Benny"; *(below)* Teresa Wright and Dan O'Herlihy in "The Enchanted Cottage."

FORD THEATRE: This series began in 1952. *(Left)* Jack Lemmon and Ida Lupino costarred in one episode; *(bottom, left)* Bette Davis played Dolley Madison in another.

(Below) 20TH CENTURY-FOX HOUR: Like *Lux,* this was an hour-long series; it was first telecast in 1955. Joe Mantell, Fred Mac-Murray, and Arthur Farlee were featured in a 1957 episode.

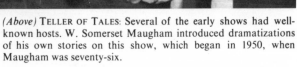

(Above) TELLER OF TALES: Several of the early shows had well-known hosts. W. Somerset Maugham introduced dramatizations of his own stories on this show, which began in 1950, when Maugham was seventy-six.

(Top, right) MY FAVORITE STORY: Adolphe Menjou was the host and, as in this picture, occasional star of this series.

(Right) GEORGE SANDERS MYSTERY THEATRE: Sanders provided typically suave introductions.

(Below) DOUGLAS FAIRBANKS PRESENTS: Fairbanks was the show's host and he also performed in this production, which costarred Robin Wheeler.

JANE WYMAN THEATER: Only a handful of actresses landed drama shows of their own, among them Jane Wyman. She comforts Penny Santon in this scene from "The Thread."

THE LORETTA YOUNG SHOW: Miss Young had a longer-lasting success than any other actress who tried to buck television with her own series. Her show began in 1953 as *A Letter to Loretta*, became *The Loretta Young Show* a year later, and enjoyed popularity for several seasons. Miss Young usually played more romantic, glamorous roles than this one (a 1954 episode entitled "The First to Ask Her"). Her trademark was her swirling entry through a door at the beginning of each show.

GENERAL ELECTRIC THEATER

ran for more than a decade, starting in 1953. It did full-hour films for a while but was a half-hour series throughout most of its tenure on the air. Many of Hollywood's biggest stars performed in *G.E. Theater* episodes.

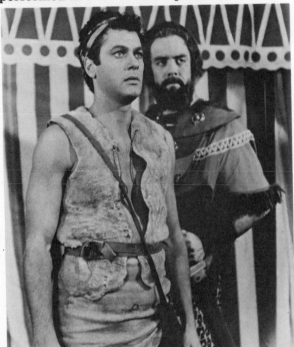

(*Top, left*) Ronald Reagan was the show's host during its last years on the air. He also starred in some of its shows, including this one, "The Lord's Dollar," in which he played a gambler.
(*Top, right*) James Stewart played a reluctant gunfighter in "The Windmill."
(*Above*) Myrna Loy shot pool in "Lady of the House."
(*Left*) Tony Curtis was David in a Biblical story, "The Stone," which also featured John Baragrey (with beard).
(*Bottom, left*) Charles Laughton managed a Little League team in "Mr. Kensington's Finest Hour."
(*Below*) Ward Bond was an Indian chief in *General Electric Theater*'s "A Turkey for the President."

ALFRED HITCHCOCK PRESENTS

had a long life, beginning in 1955 as a half-hour show and later expanding to a full hour. Hitchcock served as the show's host, delivering perversely humorous monologues in his inimitable deadpan manner. Criminals often went unpunished during the course of these dramas, but Hitchcock's closing speech always provided assurance that the malefactor had paid the proper penalty for his acts—thus Hitchcock himself evaded punishment as a violator of the Hollywood code which insists that crime must not pay.

(Top, left) The first *Hitchcock Presents* drama was "Revenge," starring Ralph Meeker and Vera Miles.

(Bottom, left) George Peppard and Peter Lorre were in a 1957 episode.

(Below) Suspense, not violence, was Hitchcock's stock in trade, in his television series as well as in his movies. This is Phyllis Thaxter looking appropriately terrified in a 1956 show.

(Above) ALCOA THEATRE: This long-running series produced a memorable half-hour drama in 1958—"Eddie," a one-character play with Mickey Rooney as a desperate small-time gambler.

(Below) ALCOA PREMIERE: Fred Astaire was host of this 1962 dramatic series. This episode, "Whatever Happened to Miss Illinois?," starred Carol Lynley.

(Above) THE DICK POWELL SHOW: As actor and producer, Powell had a hand in many television series. His last was his own show, which specialized in hour-long films of a melodramatic nature. One of the best episodes was an atypical one—a comedy called "The Troublemakers," starring Lee Marvin and Keenan Wynn.

(Below) SHIRLEY TEMPLE'S STORYBOOK: This was aimed at the kiddies, with Shirley Temple introducing one-hour dramas and acting in a few of them. Lorne Greene was an evil king in "The Little Lame Prince" in 1959. Rex Thompson played the prince.

(Above) DECISION: Television never seemed to run out of short, punchy titles for melodrama-anthology series. James Whitmore and June Lockhart played an unhappily married couple in this one.

(Below) NO WARNING: Everett Sloane grabs Alfred Toigo.

(Above) PANIC: Pamela and James Mason and their two children, Portland and Morgan, are trapped together.

(Below) THE WEB: Dan Barton played a fugitive and Robert Burton a cop.

/ 241

(Above) PURSUIT: Fernando Lamas is grilled by a prying reporter (Robert Middleton).

(Below) CONFLICT: Here are Virginia Mayo, Edmund Lowe, and Audrey Conti in one episode from *Conflict*.

(Above) DESTINY: Constance Towers and Mark Stevens were together in one episode.

(Below) SUSPICION: Warren Beatty, Barbara Turner, and David Wayne have words at the beach.

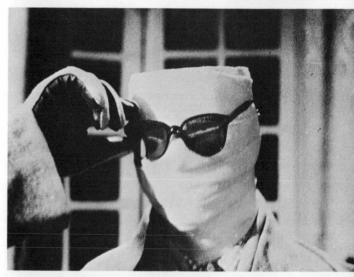

(Above) INNER SANCTUM: This converted radio serial was just one of many television series which relied on eerie effects. John Alexander and Paul Stewart are shown here in an early episode.

(Top, right) SCIENCE FICTION THEATRE: Strange things were happening in this series too. Here Zachary Scott examines a patient.

(Right) THE INVISIBLE MAN: This is a portrait of the title character in this weekly series. The identity of the actor who played the role was never revealed.

(Bottom, right) THE TWILIGHT ZONE: When television no longer had any use for his straight dramas, Rod Serling adapted readily to the change in the programming climate and in 1959 came up with this offbeat series, which was done first as a half-hour show, then as a full-hour presentation. Serling was the host and the author of many of the show's scripts.

(Below) THE OUTER LIMITS: Playwright-producer Leslie Stevens followed Serling's lead with an out-of-this-world series of his own in 1963. Jacqueline Scott and Cliff Robertson encountered a creature from another galaxy in the opening episode.

THE MILLIONAIRE: Programs with continuing characters gradually drove the anthology dramas out of business. An early example was *The Millionaire*, which was first telecast in 1955, with Marvin Miller as Michael Anthony, "ever faithful executive secretary to the mysterious billionaire John Beresford Tipton," who got his kicks by handing out million-dollar checks and waiting to see what the nouveau-riche recipients of his largesse did with the money.

BUS STOP: The continuing characters in this 1961–62 series were peripheral to much of the action. The setting was a small western town, where Marilyn Maxwell was the proprietress of a luncheonette. Guest stars wandered into town each week to play out their destinies. One visitor was Fabian, who played a psychopath in an episode called "Told by an Idiot" (based on a Tom Wicker novel) which earned national notoriety—the program was roundly denounced for sadistic excesses.

(*Above*) THEY STAND ACCUSED: As in all forms of fiction and nonfiction, the law has been the source of much of television's dramatic content. *They Stand Accused* was a DuMont-network series in which true court cases were reenacted.

(*Right*) JUSTICE: Dane Clark (right) had the lead role in this 1952 series, based on the Legal Aid Association's files. In this, the first episode, Oscar Homolka pleads with Philip Abbott while Lili Darvas and Clark watch.

(*Above*) THE COURT OF LAST RESORT: Lyle Bettger (right) investigated cases of wrongly convicted prisoners. Here he interviews John Anderson and Lorna Thayer.

(*Right*) TRAFFIC COURT: Virtually every type of municipal court became the subject of a television series. This one re-created automotive cases.

(*Above*) ON TRIAL!: Joseph Cotten starred in this series, which recalled court cases from various historical periods. Here Cotten stands by as Baynes Barron carries Marcia Sweet.

(*Below*) THE VERDICT IS YOURS: Viewer participation was an element of this daytime serial. The viewer had a chance to match his verdict against that of the real jury. Jim McKay was host.

PERRY MASON

brought to television the adventures of Erle Stanley Gardner's infallible criminal lawyer. It also brought fame and fortune to a previously obscure actor named Raymond Burr, **/ 245** who was unglamorously jowly and stocky but who evidently was the kind of man viewers liked to have on their side in courtroom duels. They rooted for him for nine years on CBS, starting in 1957. Three-dimensional characters, believable human dilemmas, and proper courtroom procedures were of scant interest to the producers and writers of this series. When Perry Mason confronted the ruthless district attorney, Hamilton Burger, across a crowded courtroom, there was no room for subtleties—nor was there any doubt that Perry would exonerate his client and nail the real killer just in time for the final commercial. Barbara Hale played Mason's devoted secretary, Della Street; William Talman was Ham Burger; William Hopper (Hedda's son) was investigator Paul Drake; and Ray Collins played Detective Lieutenant Arthur Tragg.

THE DEFENDERS,
like *Perry Mason,* hoped to entertain viewers, but it had a more serious purpose as well: to enlighten the viewer about the law and, in some cases, to persuade him to adopt a particular attitude toward it. *Mason* dealt with crimes, whereas *The Defenders* sought to come to grips with the underlying ethical questions related to what our society has branded as criminal behavior. Capital punishment, mercy killing, abortion, criminal insanity, civil liberties, even cannibalism—these were a few of the legal-moral issues debated on *The Defenders* during its four seasons on the air (1961–65). Its creator, Reginald Rose, and its producer, Herbert Brodkin, provided a haven for many refugees from the "Golden Age" of television drama. One of them, E. G. Marshall, was *The Defenders'* star, playing New York attorney Lawrence Preston, who was assisted by his lawyer son Kenneth (Robert Reed).

Viveca Lindfors, as an actress involved in a hit-and-run accident, was defended by Lawrence Preston.

Sam Jaffe, seated between Marshall and Robert Reed, played one of the Prestons' clients.

(Above) WITNESS: Famous and infamous historical figures were grilled by an investigating committee in this unusual, partly ad-lib, 1960 series. In the premiere episode Lucky Luciano (Telly Savalas) was fingered by another underworld member (Anita Dangler).

(Top, left) THE LAW AND MR. JONES: James Whitmore was impassioned Abraham Lincoln Jones, an attorney who had no patience with any form of injustice, in another 1960 series.

(Left) SAM BENEDICT: San Francisco lawyer Jake Ehrlich was the model for the bustling hero of this 1962 show, which starred Edmond O'Brien.

 / **247**

(Bottom, left) SLATTERY'S PEOPLE: A state legislator was the protagonist of this one, which arrived in 1964. Slattery (Richard Crenna) had to cope with all sorts of eccentrics like Elsa Lanchester.

(Below) TRIALS OF O'BRIEN: Peter Falk was a raffish small-time lawyer in this New York-based 1965–66 series. The girl is Joanna Pettet.

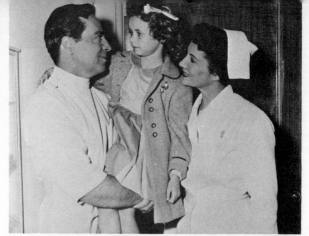

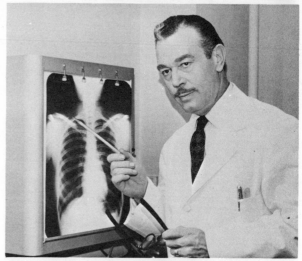

(Above) THE DOCTOR: Medical men of all descriptions have found a home in television drama, alongside the lawyers. This early series, which began in 1952, starred Warner Anderson (shown here treating Sandy Kenyon) as a G. P.

(Top, right) DR. HUDSON'S SECRET JOURNAL: John Howard (seen here with little Cheryl Calloway and Frances Mercer) was Dr. Hudson in this series based on a Lloyd C. Douglas book.

248 / (Right) CITY HOSPITAL: Melville Ruick was the star.

(Right, second from bottom) JANET DEAN, REGISTERED NURSE: Ella Raines was the first woman in white with her own series.

(Bottom, right) DR. CHRISTIAN: Macdonald Carey played the role Jean Hersholt had created on radio.

(Below) NOAH'S ARK: Vic Rodman (in wheelchair) and Paul Burke (behind him) played a pair of veterinarians in a series directed by Jack Webb.

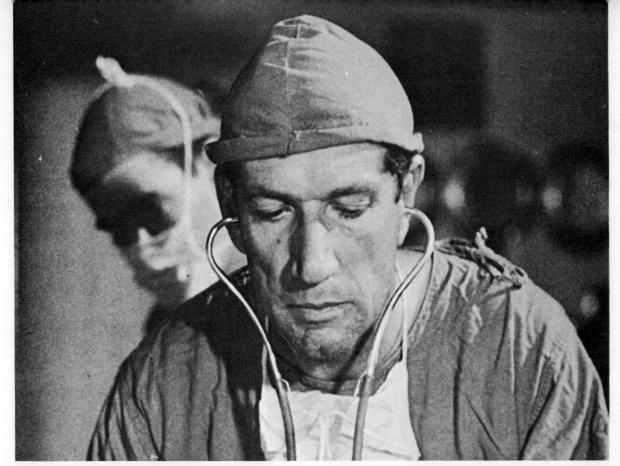

MEDIC

was a more sophisticated medical-drama show than any that had preceded it. Meticulously researched and expertly written by James Moser, it was filmed on location in Los Angeles hospitals and produced by Worthington Miner. It dealt in fictional terms with realistic medical problems and practices. Its leading role, Dr. Konrad Styner, propelled Richard Boone to fame. He narrated all episodes and acted in the first (from which these pictures were taken), in 1954. In it Dr. Styner's patient (Beverly Garland, *below*) was an expectant mother who was dying of leukemia. The birth of a baby was shown on the air.

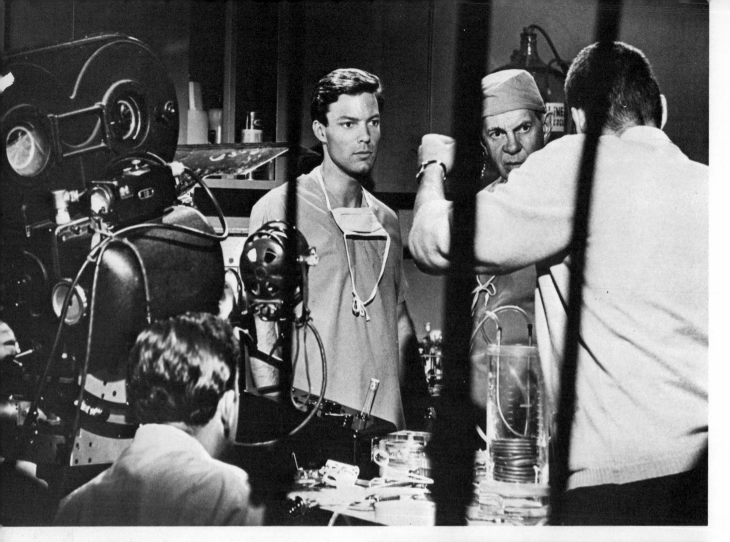

Dr. Kildare

and *Ben Casey* emerged within five days of each other during the fall of 1961. Their success spawned numerous imitators, until the epidemic of medical shows ended in 1966, when both *Kildare* and *Casey* expired. *Dr. Kildare* was based on the MGM films which starred Lew Ayres (and later Van Johnson) with Lionel Barrymore. In the television series Jim Kildare started out as a callow intern at Blair General Hospital and ended up as a self-possessed, but no less idealistic or virtuous, resident. He was played by a handsome newcomer, Richard Chamberlain, and his crusty superior, Dr. Gillespie, was depicted by Raymond Massey. Norman Felton produced the series for MGM.

250 /

(Right) THE ELEVENTH HOUR: Norman Felton followed *Kildare* with *The Eleventh Hour*, in which Wendell Corey played a psychiatrist (assisted by Jack Ging).

BEN CASEY

was chief resident in neurosurgery at County General Hospital. His prickly disposition earned him the sobriquet "The Surly Surgeon." His face usually wore a scowl, he chewed out underlings, defied overlings, bullied patients, and managed to alienate practically everyone in the hospital. But wise old Dr. Zorba stood by him because he knew that beneath that sloppily buttoned tunic beat the heart of a true humanitarian and that in Ben's hands reposed the skill of a virtuoso against whom subdural hematomas did not stand a chance. Dark, brooding Vincent Edwards was Casey; pixieish Sam Jaffe, Zorba. James Moser (the *Medic* man) created the series for Bing Crosby Productions.

(Below) THE BREAKING POINT: Bing Crosby Productions' offshoot of *Ben Casey* was *The Breaking Point*, whose psychiatrists were Paul Richards (left) and Eduard Franz.

(Bottom, right) THE NURSES: Produced in New York by Herbert Brodkin, this series was a medical counterpart of *The Defenders*, with soap-opera overtones. Shirl Conway (left) and Zina Bethune were the stars. Eventually some doctors (Joseph Campanella and Michael Tolan) were added, in hopes of improving the show's ratings, but the transfusion failed to save the show.

(*Above*) Mr. Novak: Other professions were not entirely neglected in the sixties. Schoolteachers got a hearing in this Norman Felton series, with James Franciscus as an English teacher at Jefferson High and Dean Jagger as his principal.

(*Top, right*) Channing: College professors were represented—but not for long—by Jason Evers, with Henry Jones as Channing College's dean.

252 /

(*Bottom, right*) East Side/West Side: Social work was the subject of this controversial David Susskind series. George C. Scott was the unconventional hero (or antihero), Neil Brock, and Elizabeth Wilson played his supervisor. The show won critical acclaim but was considered too downbeat for popular consumption and was canceled after a few months. Its extinction signaled the end of the cycle of problem-play series which had begun with *The Defenders*. (During 1963–64 repertory drama also was dealt a knockout punch, when *The Richard Boone Show* was replaced in mid-season.)

(*Below*) The Reporter: Several series have had newspaper-reporter heroes. This one went to press in 1964, with Harry Guardino as its leading man and Janice Rule as a guest star. Keefe Brasselle produced it, and Jerome Weidman supervised its scripts.

THE PLAY OF THE WEEK

was a series of two-hour dramas, many of them distinguished, few of them original, all of them staged and performed with great care and skill. The plays were taped in New York and offered to independent stations around the country. David Susskind and Worthington Miner both had a hand in the production of the series.

(Top, right) MEDEA: Judith Anderson (center), Aline MacMahon, and Morris Carnovsky were in *The Play of the Week's* production of Robinson Jeffers' adaptation of the Euripides tragedy.

(Top, left) DON JUAN IN HELL: Shaw's didactic fragment had a cast of four: George C. Scott, Dennis King, Siobhan McKenna, and Hurd Hatfield.

(Left) THE WALTZ OF THE TOREADORS: Hugh Griffith and Mildred Natwick gave bravura performances in Anouilh's play.

(Above) THE WORLD OF SHOLOM ALEICHEM: Several of the Jewish humorist's stories were enacted by Zero Mostel, Morris Carnovsky, Nancy Walker, and Sam Levene (plus Jack Gilford).

(*Above*) UN DRAMAS: Some corporations and foundations tried to pick up the slack in television drama. Xerox, for example, spent several million dollars to underwrite a series of plays dramatizing the work of the United Nations. Peter Sellers appeared in the first one, a parable written by Rod Serling and produced by Joseph Mankiewicz. The following season (1966) Xerox sponsored an acclaimed version of "Death of a Salesman," with Lee J. Cobb, Mildred Dunnock, and George Segal. Its success sparked a revival of network interest in drama.

254 /

EDUCATIONAL TELEVISION: Noncommercial stations also did what they could to provide dramatic sustenance for their viewers. Two outstanding examples, both shown during the 1965–66 season, were: (*right*) "The Old Glory: Benito Cereno," Robert Lowell's prize-winning play based on Melville's novella, with Roscoe Lee Browne (kneeling) and Frank Langella among the players; and (*below*) "Nur Ein Tag," a harrowing depiction of life, suffering, and death at a Nazi extermination center.

PEYTON PLACE:

Commercial television, meanwhile, was discovering that viewers would go for nighttime soap opera—and go for it twice a week. (Three times a week proved once too often when ABC tried to stretch its luck in 1965.) *Peyton Place,* whose inhabitants coupled and uncoupled with the frequency—and the subtlety—of a freight train, was an instantaneous success. It provided a handy outlet for televoyeurs and employment for the hundreds of actors and actresses who were needed to keep the plot steaming. One of them, Mia Farrow, was a girl of fragile beauty and unknown ability when *Peyton Place* began. When she left the series in 1966, she was an international celebrity. And so was *Peyton Place,* which was enthralling viewers all over the world, in dubbed versions.

Where the Action Is

"NEXT YEAR will be the year of the spy!" The whisper passes urgently through all the echelons of the television industry. It is the subject of a thousand luncheon conversations. It appears in the trade press, and perhaps in the television columns as well. A reasonably alert viewer, attuned to the history and traditions of the medium, knows what he can expect. He can expect spies, counterspies, spy spoofs, and spy cartoons; he will see spies in Pittsburgh and spies in Tangier. The theme has been sounded, and the variations will follow automatically and inevitably.

The desire to participate in a successful trend is apparent in all areas of television (as indeed it is apparent in the manufacture and distribution of any commodity), but nowhere does the copycat thrive so obviously as in the production of the action-adventure programs.

It all began with a private eye. Martin Kane struck the first responsive chord, and his spiritual offspring keep his heritage alive in a thousand dramas of law enforcement, each a chronicle of the adventures of an omniscient (or, in some variations, merely handsome) seeker of law, justice, and happy endings. Thus *Rocky King*, *Dragnet*, *The Untouchables*, and *The Man from U.N.C.L.E.* Law enforcement is a natural backdrop for these series, presenting as it does a clean framework for quick and easy portrayals of good guys and bad guys. Limited to an hour or half-hour, these programs have little time to probe the nuances of character. A hero is a hero, and a villain has a black heart. Any prolonged wrestling with conscience would subtract valuable minutes from the more important chase and showdown sequences.

In the many twists applied to the formula, the labels may change, but the central theme remains. Simple righteousness opposes simple evil. These ingredients, stirred together with a dollop of sex and a smidgeon of violence, are constant. The law-enforcement motif takes on many disguises. In the war dramas, for example, the cop becomes a dashing young American warrior; the crook is transformed into a smirking Japanese. In the jungle epics, the good guy may wear a pith helmet or a leopard skin (most fetchingly, in the case of Sheena); the bad guy may be a murderous pygmy or a rogue elephant. The crusading newspaper-man opposes corruption and venality (City Editor: "You mean the dope ring is masterminded by high officials in our state?" Reporter: "I mean exactly that!"); there have even been crusading free-lance magazine writers and, in one mind-boggling instance, a crusading public-relations man.

The cycles whirl on, but nothing essential changes. Even though a spate of comic strips had been adapted to television, it was suggested that *Batman* was revolutionary because it was camp. But it appears to have been neither, since it is merely an exaggeration of its predecessors, with a visible rather than an implied "Pow!"

No student of odds would bet against the proposition that we will witness the return of the private eyes, the intelligence agents, the insurance investigators, and the long-suffering lieutenants of the Homicide Squad. We will probably even see another crusading public-relations man. They will all come back again and again, shooting their way out of moral dilemmas.

WHERE THE ACTION IS/*Introduction*

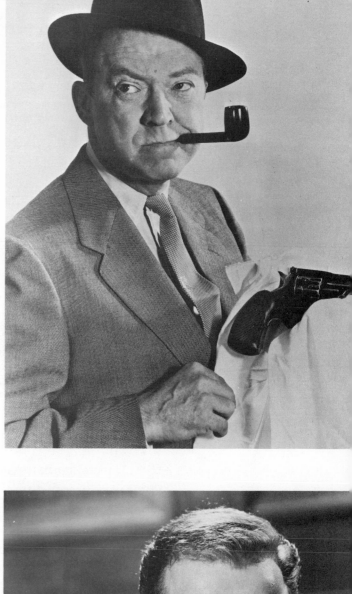

MARTIN KANE, PRIVATE EYE

was one of television's earliest cops-and-robbers series. It went on the air in 1949; during its five-year run four different men played the part of the intrepid Kane. They were Lee Tracy, Lloyd Nolan, William Gargan, and Mark Stevens. In its latter stages the show was renamed *The New Adventures of Martin Kane* and, finally, *Martin Kane*. The success of this program was probably responsible for the later flowering of many similar television efforts centering around the dogged, incorruptible private investigator.

258 /

(Above) William Gargan (left) with Marianne Brauns and Walter Gotell. □ *(Top, right)* Lee Tracy. □ *(Bottom, right)* Mark Stevens. □ *(Below)* Lloyd Nolan, with Lisa Loughlin.

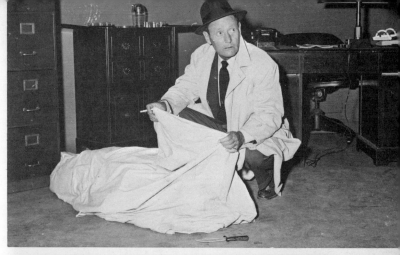

(Right) ROCKY KING, DETECTIVE: Another of the early crime-and-punishment dramas, this one starred Roscoe Karns as a police detective who relied on brains rather than brawn to solve his cases. The series began in 1950.

(Below) ELLERY QUEEN: Four men appeared, at various times, in the role of writer-sleuth Queen. They were (in chronological order) (below) Lee Bowman, who was starred when the show made its debut in 1950; (bottom, left) Hugh Marlowe, shown with Jean Willes in a 1954 scene; (right, center) George Nader, who had the part in 1958; and (bottom, right) Lee Philips, who took over in 1959.

MAN AGAINST CRIME: The "Man" was Mike Barnett, a hard-boiled private eye who sometimes refused to take yes for an answer. When the show first came on the air in 1949, Barnett was played by Ralph Bellamy *(top, left,* with Gloria McGhee). After four years, the show departed, but was reactivated in 1956 with Frank Lovejoy *(above)* in the title role.

MARK SABER: When the show began in 1951 as *Mystery Theater,* Saber, played by Tom Conway *(far left)* was with the homicide squad. His sidekick (played by James Burke) was Sergeant Maloney. In 1957 Saber was in London handling cases too tough for Scotland Yard, his sidekick's name was Barney O'Keefe (played by Michael Balfour), and the series was called *Uncovered.* In the most recent edition of the series Saber was played by Donald Gray *(left).*

NAKED CITY: Mark Hellinger once wrote, "There are eight million stories in the Naked City." He produced one of them as a movie, and that film in turn served as a model for the television series. It first appeared in 1958, with James Franciscus as the young detective and John McIntire as his mentor on the force *(below).* In 1960 the cast changed, and *(bottom, left)* Paul Burke was the tyro, Nancy Malone his girl friend, and Horace McMahon the veteran cop. Throughout its run, this second version of *Naked City* was distinguished by superior writing, acting, and photography of New York City neighborhoods and landmarks.

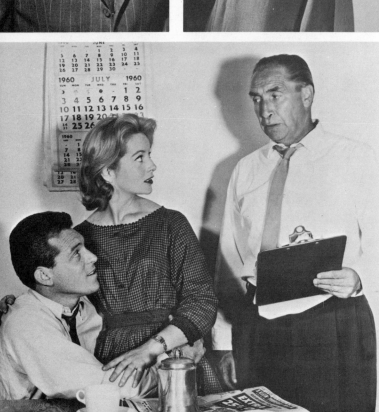

(Above) THE PLAINCLOTHESMAN: Ken Lynch was featured in this 1950 police tale. He was the "unseen Lieutenant" whose face was never shown.

(Below) THE MAN BEHIND THE BADGE: Charles Bickford was host and narrator of these tales of police derring-do. The show was first telecast in 1953.

(Bottom) WANTED: Walter McGraw introduced these sagas of desperadoes wanted by the FBI. The show was first seen in 1955.

(Top) PUBLIC DEFENDER: A 1955 entry, it starred Reed Hadley as the legal representative for indigent clients.

(Above) MANHUNT: Victor Jory (left) was the detective lieutenant and Patrick McVey played a police reporter in this syndicated series which arrived in 1959.

(Below) HARBOR COMMAND: This was billed as a series of "true-to-life stories of America's Harbor Police," and if it accomplished nothing else, it alerted America to the fact that it had police in its harbors. Wendell Corey (right) was Captain Ralph Baxter.

(Above) COLONEL MARCH OF SCOTLAND YARD: Boris Karloff played the one-eyed British crimebuster in this 1958 series.

(Top, right) FABIAN OF SCOTLAND YARD: Bruce Seton had the leading role in this 1956 show which accented scientific detection methods.

(Right) JIMMY HUGHES, ROOKIE COP: Billy Redfield starred in this early DuMont series.

262 /

(Bottom, right) DOORWAY TO DANGER: This show appeared in 1953, with Stacy Harris featured as "an agent who investigates crucial social and political situations."

(Below) THE ASPHALT JUNGLE: Jack Warden played the leading role in this 1961 series which used the title, if not the contents, of John Huston's movie.

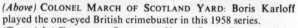

DRAGNET:

"All we want are the facts, Ma'am." Thus spake the calm and dispassionate Sergeant Joe Friday of the Los Angeles police, as he interrogated one of his quivering witnesses. Friday was played by actor-director Jack Webb, and the show was *Dragnet,* an immediate sensation when it arrived in 1952 and a constant source of pleasure to all crime buffs during its seven years on the networks. Supported by Ben Alexander (who played detective Frank Smith), Webb fashioned a show which attempted to depict police work realistically, as plodding, exhausting, dangerous, and unglamorous. An astute director, Webb was especially adept at extracting rich and colorful performances from actors in minor roles. The air of authenticity Webb sought was further heightened by the constant use of the jargon of the trade. ("What's his M.O.?" someone would invariably ask.) Joe Friday wore badge No. 714, and when *Dragnet* went into syndication, it was retitled *Badge 714.*

Friday reacts to an untidy homicide.

Smith and Friday pursue their quarry.

An unblinking Friday brings down his man.

(Above) MR. DISTRICT ATTORNEY: In 1951, when this program first came to television, the leading role was played by Jay Jostyn, the man identified with the part since radio days. The show was off the air for a year, then returned in 1954, with David Brian (above) as the legal gladiator.

(Top, right) OFFICIAL DETECTIVE: Everett Sloane was featured in this 1958 syndicated series dramatizing actual criminal cases.

(Right) BOSTON BLACKIE: Another famous radio show remodeled for television, this one starred Kent Taylor and made its network debut in 1952. In the original Boston Blackie stories, written in about 1910, Blackie was a burglar and bank robber. He changed sides for the electronic media.

(Bottom, right) CORONADO 9: The syndicated series starred Rod Cameron as a fearless detective. Cameron also starred in two other long-running favorites, *City Detective* and *State Trooper*.

(Below) THE LAWLESS YEARS: James Gregory (right) was a detective locked in combat with the underworld during the Roaring Twenties, and Robert Karnes was his colleague on the force in this show which debuted in 1959.

THE CASE OF THE DANGEROUS ROBIN: Rick Jason (he was Robin Scott) is shown here with Jean Blake in a scene from this series about an insurance negotiator. The syndicated show debuted in 1960.

BOURBON STREET BEAT: A 1959 adventure series set in New Orleans, it featured (left to right) Andrew Duggan, Richard Long, and Arlene Howell.

JOHNNY STACCATO: John Cassavetes (right) had long been a featured performer in television dramatic shows when he entered this action-adventure series in 1959. He is shown above with Eduardo Ciannelli. Cassavetes played a private eye, although when the series was first contemplated, he was to have been a jazz piano player.

THE DETECTIVES: Robert Taylor made his television debut in 1959, playing a captain of detectives. He was joined by (second from right) Adam West, who was later to soar to fame as Batman.

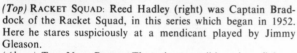

(Top) RACKET SQUAD: Reed Hadley (right) was Captain Braddock of the Racket Squad, in this series which began in 1952. Here he stares suspiciously at a mendicant played by Jimmy Gleason.
(Above) THE NEW BREED: These incorruptible crime fighters were (left to right) Leslie Nielsen, Greg Roman, John Clark, and John Beradino (a former infielder for the St. Louis Browns). The show was first telecast in 1961.
(Below) DECOY: Beverly Garland was a policewoman in this syndicated series which appeared in the fifties.
(Bottom) TREASURY MEN IN ACTION: Walter Greaza was "The Chief" in this 1953 entry about the work of the T-Men.

(Top) TARGET: THE CORRUPTERS: Steven McNally and Robert Harland (shown) were undercover agents who infiltrated secret criminal organizations in this 1961 show. □ *(Above)* HIGHWAY PATROL: "Ten-four," Broderick Crawford (left) would snap, as he signed off the radio in his squad car. There was many a chase sequence (some involving helicopters) in this syndicated series which debuted in 1956. □ *(Below)* LOCK UP: Macdonald Carey (shown) played attorney Herbert L. Maris, a fighter for those unjustly accused, in this 1959 series. □ *(Bottom)* 87TH PRECINCT: The grim, day-to-day chores of detectives in a Manhattan area were performed by (left to right) Robert Lansing, Norman Fell, and Ron Harper. The program was first telecast in 1961.

(*Above*) PETER GUNN: This program began in 1958, with Craig Stevens and Lola Albright in the leading roles and Henry Mancini providing the background jazz, which was to set a style for future shows. Gunn was more human than most of television's private eyes, and though he always came out the winner, he usually took a fearsome shellacking from the forces of evil. Herschel Bernardi, who played a detective on this show, later became the voice (in commercials) of "Charlie Tuna" and "The Jolly Green Giant."

 / 267

(*Top, left*) MEET MCGRAW: Frank Lovejoy (shown here with Ila McEvoy) was the intrepid McGraw in this 1957 private-eye series.

(*Left*) RICHARD DIAMOND, PRIVATE DETECTIVE: In 1957 David Janssen was chasing lawbreakers in this series, unaware that one day he would be on the run himself, as *The Fugitive*.

(*Bottom, left*) 21 BEACON STREET: A 1959 private-eye entry, this one starred Dennis Morgan and Joanna Barnes.

(*Below*) MR. AND MRS. NORTH: Barbara Britton and Richard Denning played the crime-solving couple in a show first seen in 1952.

(*Above*) THE LINEUP: Warner Anderson (left) was Lieutenant Ben Guthrie and Tom Tully was Inspector Matt Greb in this detective drama set in San Francisco. It was first shown in 1954.

(*Top, right*) M SQUAD: Lee Marvin was a hard-bitten detective in this 1957 series.

(*Right*) SHERLOCK HOLMES: Ronald Howard wore the deerstalker hat in this video version of the Sir Arthur Conan Doyle stories. It was first shown in 1954.

268 /

(*Right*) CHARLIE CHAN: The great Chinese sleuth (J. Carrol Naish) here performs on the bongo drums for his Number One Son, James Hong. The series was first telecast in 1957.

(*Bottom, right*) I'M THE LAW: In his films, George Raft was usually one of the bad guys, but he switched to the side of law and order in this syndicated program which was shown in 1953.

(*Below*) PARIS PRECINCT: A syndicated series about the Paris police, this program starred Louis Jourdan (shown) and Claude Dauphin. It premiered in 1955.

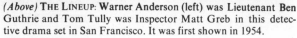

THE UNTOUCHABLES

first appeared in 1958 as two one-hour shows, on succeeding weeks, as part of the *Desilu Playhouse* series. The following year it returned, on another network, as a continuing program in its own right. Robert Stack was starred as Eliot Ness, leader of an elite squad of government agents who could not be bribed or corrupted by gangland. The action was set in the Prohibition era of the twenties and thirties and was therefore replete with hijacked beer trucks and machine-gun battles between warring factions of the crime syndicate. At one point in its run, the show was the target of protests from groups of Italian-Americans who felt that too many of the villains bore Italian-sounding names. Although *The Untouchables* broke little new ground as an action melodrama, an obvious plus for the program was the authenticity of the clothes, autos, and props of the period it depicted.

(Below) Ness gets a telephone tip as his squad looks on.

(Top, left) Neville Brand was Scarface Al Capone in the series.

(Bottom, left) Guest Joan Staley appears unperturbed during an interrogation by Ness.

(Above) MIKE HAMMER: Mickey Spillane's hard-as-nails shamus was played by Darren McGavin in a series which bowed in 1958.

(Top, right) PHILIP MARLOWE: Another tough private eye, this one originally created by Raymond Chandler, was first seen on television in 1959. Philip Carey played Marlowe.

(Right) THE D.A.'S MAN: The D.A. needed help, and so he recruited a private eye named Shannon, played by John Compton (right). The investigators from the D.A.'s office were Howard Rasmussen (left) and Frank Lavelle in this 1958 show produced by Jack Webb.

(Bottom, right) THE TELLTALE CLUE: Anthony Ross was Detective Lieutenant Richard Hale in this 1954 mystery series.

(Below) MARKHAM: Ray Milland (shown here with Cindy Robbins) played Markham, a wealthy lawyer-investigator.

(*Above*) CRIME PHOTOGRAPHER: Darren McGavin was the ubiquitous Casey, always on the scene gathering evidence for the "Morning Express" in this show, first telecast in 1952.

(*Top, left*) MAN WITH A CAMERA: In this 1958 show Charles Bronson played Mike Kovac, a "hard-hitting, adventurous, freelance photographer."

(*Left*) THE WALTER WINCHELL FILE: The Broadway columnist was both host and narrator of this action series, which made its debut in 1957. He is shown here with Jacques Aubuchon (left).

(*Bottom, left*) BIG STORY: These were dramatizations of the work of newspapermen around the country, with Ben Grauer (left) as host. He is pictured with columnist Victor Riesel, whose story was aired in 1956. The show made its debut in 1950.

(*Below*) WIRE SERVICE: The three wide-eyed newsgathering operatives in this 1956 series were (left to right) Dane Clark, Mercedes McCambridge, and George Brent.

(Above) I COVER TIMES SQUARE: Harold Huber starred as Manhattan columnist Johnny Warren in this early (1950) newspaper series.

(Top, right) FRONT PAGE DETECTIVE: The program debuted in the early fifties, and featured another newspaper columnist, this one with a nose for murder. The show starred Edmund Lowe, shown here questioning homicide suspect John Davidson (right).

(Right) BIG TOWN: Adapted from the radio series, this show was about the adventures of crusading newspaper editor Steve Wilson (played for a time by Mark Stevens, here interviewing Maxine Gates). When the show was first telecast in 1950, Patrick McVey played Steve Wilson and Jane Nigh was his girl friend Lorelei. Grace Kelly was a guest performer on the opening program.

(Right) THE BROTHERS BRANNAGAN: The brothers were a pair of private eyes, played by Steve Dunne (left) and Mark Roberts, in this show which first appeared in 1960.

(Bottom, right) TIGHTROPE!: Mike Connors (right), as an undercover agent trying to get a line on underworld activities, holds a guard (Emerson Treacy) at bay in the premiere episode in 1959.

(Below) BRENNER: Edward Binns (right) was detective Roy Brenner, and James Broderick was his son Ernie, a newcomer to police work. The show was first seen in 1959.

(Above) I SPY: This early syndicated series (1955) carried a title which was to be used again ten years later. The first version featured Raymond Massey as Anton the Spymaster and dealt with stories of notorious espionage agents.

(Top, left) FOREIGN INTRIGUE: When the show was first broadcast in 1951 under the title *Foreign Assignment*, Jerome Thor played the lead, an overseas correspondent named Michael Powers. In 1955 James Daly (shown with Ann Preville) became the star. For a time the role was also played by Gerald Mohr.

(Left) BEHIND CLOSED DOORS: Richard Webb and Ziva Rodann are shown in "The Middle East Story," one episode in this 1958 series about international hanky-panky.

 / **273**

(Below, left) THE FOUR JUST MEN: They were Jack Hawkins, Vittorio de Sica, Richard Conte, and Dan Dailey (shown here with actress Honor Blackman, who was later to become better known in a movie called "Goldfinger"). The four had different occupations (Dailey was a newspaperman), but all galloped about the globe, righting wrongs. The show debuted in the middle fifties.

(Below) THE CRUSADER: In a scene from the initial (1956) episode, Brian Keith (who starred as Matt Anders) treats the wounded Peter Bourne, while Hildegarde Christian holds the lantern.

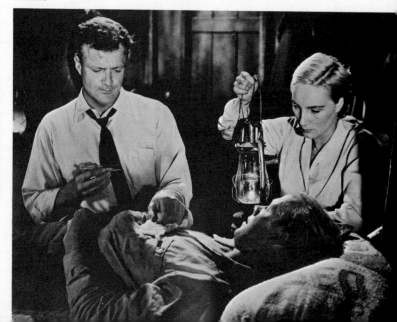

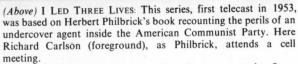

(Above) I LED THREE LIVES: This series, first telecast in 1953, was based on Herbert Philbrick's book recounting the perils of an undercover agent inside the American Communist Party. Here Richard Carlson (foreground), as Philbrick, attends a cell meeting.

(Top, right) PASSPORT TO DANGER: Cesar Romero starred as Steve McQuinn, diplomatic courier, in a 1956 series.

(Right) DANGEROUS ASSIGNMENT: Brian Donlevy coolly surveys an unfriendly warning in his role of Steve Mitchell, soldier of fortune. The show first appeared in 1952.

(Bottom, right) O.S.S.: Ron Randell had the featured role in this 1957 series about American servicemen behind enemy lines in World War II.

(Below) FIVE FINGERS: In 1959 Luciana Paluzzi and David Hedison costarred in the story of a United States counterspy (Hedison) posing as a European theatrical agent.

(Above) THE MAN CALLED X: Barry Sullivan (left) was starred in this show about international duplicity.

(Top, left) THE HUNTER: This was the story of a young American adventurer who finds trouble everywhere. Here, in the 1954 premiere episode entitled "Bucharest Express," star Barry Nelson (in disguise) talks to Rita Lynn.

 / 275

(Bottom, left) THE LONE WOLF: A 1954 syndicated series starred Louis Hayward as a globe-trotting detective named Michael Lanyard.

(Below) THE THIRD MAN: Michael Rennie (right, with Jonathan Harris) was Harry Lime in this 1960 series based—very loosely—on the movie of the same name.

THE MAN FROM U.N.C.L.E.:

Like all good espionage shows, this one, which began in 1964, has plenty of action, devious plots, and more devious counterplots. But it differs from most of the others in that it has its tongue planted firmly in its cheek. Originally the show's star was to be Robert Vaughn, as agent Napoleon Solo. But it soon developed that another member of the cast, David McCallum (playing agent Illya Kuryakin), was exciting a great deal of audience interest, and the two became costars on the program. The men from U.N.C.L.E. and their sinister opponents from THRUSH employ numerous mechanical and scientific gadgets to foil one another, but this is the show's only gesture in the direction of modern spy drama. Some of the chase and imprisonment sequences are more reminiscent of the Keystone Kops and "The Perils of Pauline." Leo G. Carroll appears as the head man at U.N.C.L.E., and a succession of guests portray the masterminds from THRUSH.

(Above) I SPY: Robert Culp (left) and Bill Cosby are American agents Kelly Robinson and Alexander Scott, posing as an international tennis player and his trainer. Sheldon Leonard produces the series, which is shot on location in such places as Hong Kong, Japan, and Mexico. Culp, who has been seen previously in television westerns and dramas, and Cosby, a nightclub comedian, work well together. This camaraderie between a white man and a Negro has provoked little or no protest from viewers in the South or elsewhere, although it was an historic bit of casting for television. The show debuted in 1965.

(Below) SECRET AGENT: Patrick McGoohan was starred as Drake, a British Intelligence operative. Filmed in England, the series first appeared in the United States as a summer replacement, then became a regular network offering in 1965.

(Above) ADVENTURES IN PARADISE: Handsome hunks of masculinity in tropical climes were on display in several of the action-adventure series during the late fifties and early sixties. In this series, created by James Michener in 1959, Gardner McKay was Adam Troy, skipper of the schooner Tiki in the South Seas. (One critic, who thought the boat was the best part of the show, wrote: "No Tiki, no watchee.")

(Top, right) HAWAIIAN EYE: A girl called Cricket (Connie Stevens) helped the eye (Robert Conrad) and sang an occasional number in this one, which premiered in 1959.

(Bottom, right) SURFSIDE 6: This 1960 show's private detectives worked out of a Florida houseboat. The cast included (left to right) Van Williams, Margarita Sierra, and Troy Donahue.

(Below) FOLLOW THE SUN: The heroes of this one were footloose magazine writers looking for material (and finding trouble) in exotic locales. Barry Coe (left) and Gary Lockwood were two of the suntanned free-lancers in the 1961 series.

77 SUNSET STRIP,
on the surface, seemed less than promising; its major characters were a pair of private eyes and their parking lot attendant. But the locale was glamorous Hollywood, there was action aplenty, and younger members of the audience were attracted to the handsome trio who were featured in the proceedings—Efrem Zimbalist, Jr., Roger Smith, and Edd "Kookie" Byrnes. (Byrnes frequently ran a comb through his locks, a mannerism familiar to many youngsters. This "shtick" eventually led to a hit rock-'n'-roll recording with a refrain that ran, "Kookie, Kookie, lend me your comb.") The program went on the air in 1958, and had a long and successful run.

(*Left to right*) Smith, Zimbalist, and Byrnes.

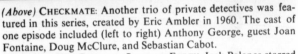

(*Above*) CHECKMATE: Another trio of private detectives was featured in this series, created by Eric Ambler in 1960. The cast of one episode included (left to right) Anthony George, guest Joan Fontaine, Doug McClure, and Sebastian Cabot.

(*Top, right*) THE GREATEST SHOW ON EARTH: Jack Palance starred as Johnny Slate in a series which used the Ringling Brothers-Barnum & Bailey Circus as a backdrop for the action. It was first seen in 1963.

(*Right*) MR. BROADWAY: Craig Stevens (shown here in a scene with Countess Christina Paolozzi) was a public-relations man with troublesome clients in this show, first telecast in 1964.

(*Bottom, right*) THE FBI: From its inception this series had the blessings of the FBI; it was, therefore, careful to be both authentic and image-enhancing. Shown here are members of the cast in the 1965 debut episode: (left to right) guest stars Jeffrey Hunter and Dina Merrill, and the series' star Efrem Zimbalist, Jr.

(*Below*) ARREST AND TRIAL: A novel idea in programming, this ninety-minute show devoted its first half to the arrest, and second half to the trial. It went on the air in 1963. Shown here (left to right) are John Larch, Chuck Connors (defending attorney John Egan), and Ben Gazzara (detective Nick Anderson, who brought in the accused criminals for Egan to defend).

(Top) HONG KONG: **Rod Taylor** was starred in a 1960 series about a "two-fisted American correspondent assigned to crowded oriental and international Hong Kong!"
(Above) CHINA SMITH: Dan Duryea (left) was the hero-adventurer in this syndicated series which has been on the air since the early fifties.
(Below) THE ISLANDERS: William Reynolds (shown here, center, with guests Wendy Barrie and Hans Conried) was one of a pair of pilots (the other was James Philbrook) who spent their time island-hopping around the Pacific.
(Bottom) CAPTAIN DAVID GRIEF: Maxwell Reed (center) was **Grief in an adaptation of the Jack London stories.**

(Top) THE ALASKANS: The Gold Rush days were relived by **Roger Moore as Silky Harris and Dorothy Provine as Rocky in this 1959 series.**
(Above) SOLDIERS OF FORTUNE: John Russell (left) and Chick Chandler were a couple of globe-trotting adventurers in this 1955 series.
(Below) CRUNCH AND DES: Philip Wylie's stories about a charter-boat service in the Bahamas were first aired in 1955, and starred Forrest Tucker as Crunch and Sandy Kenyon (not shown) as **Des.**

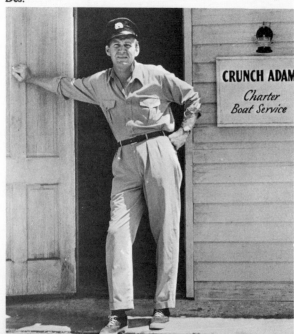

(*Above*) COMBAT: Vic Morrow is Sergeant Saunders (and Rick Jason, Lieutenant Hanley) in this tale of infantry dogfaces in action during World War II. The program was first televised in 1962.

(*Top, right*) PENTAGON CONFIDENTIAL: Addison Richards (left) was an army colonel and Edward Binns one of his secret operatives in a series described as a "dramatic documentary" and first seen in 1953.

(*Right*) NAVY LOG: Making plans to shoot down the plane carrying Japanese Admiral Yamamoto were (left to right) Mike Garrett, Morgan Jones, Robert Knapp, and Bill Allyn in the opening episode of this 1955 seafaring series.

(*Bottom, right*) WEST POINT: Donald May portrayed Cadet Charles C. Thompson, the host of these 1956 stories of the men at the United States Military Academy.

(*Below*) THE LIEUTENANT: Gary Lockwood was Lieutenant Rice, a fledgling marine officer, in 1963.

(Above) STEVE CANYON: In 1958 the comic-strip colonel was brought to life on television by Dean Fredericks. Above, Canyon palavers with two Spanish señoritas, played by Yvonne Preble (center) and Mary Moore. Miss Moore was later known as Mary Tyler Moore, when she appeared on *The Dick Van Dyke Show.*

(Top, left) TWELVE O'CLOCK HIGH: Robert Lansing was starred in this 1964 series as General Frank Savage, leader of an Eighth Air Force bombardment group in the European Theater. Though the show continued, Lansing left the cast a year later and was replaced by Paul Burke. (Viewers were advised that Savage had been shot down.)

 / **283**

(Left) THE WACKIEST SHIP IN THE ARMY: Jack Warden (left) was Major Simon Butcher and Gary Collins was Lieutenant (j.g.) Rip Riddle in this 1965 show. Both were aboard a leaky two-masted schooner called the Kiwi, which Army Intelligence believed would be an asset in winning the Pacific war.

(Bottom, left) CONVOY: Featured in the cast were (left to right) John Gavin, Linden Chiles, and John Larch. First telecast in 1965, this was the saga of merchant ships and destroyer escorts on the Atlantic run.

(Below) THE GALLANT MEN: Mala Powers played an Italian partisan in this episode of the war series. It was first telecast in 1962, with Robert McQueeney and William Reynolds featured.

(*Above*) THE 77TH BENGAL LANCERS: Warren Stevens (left) and Phil Carey (with guest Lita Milan) were starred in this saga of the British forces in India. It was first telecast in 1956.

(*Top, right*) ROBIN HOOD: Richard Greene roamed Sherwood Forest as Robin in an English-made series which was first broadcast in 1955.

284 /

(*Right*) RIVERBOAT: Darren McGavin (left) was the captain of the riverboat Enterprise, and Burt Reynolds was his pilot in this series about life on the Mississippi in the 1840's. *Riverboat* debuted in 1959 and remained afloat for several seasons.

(*Bottom, right*) FRONTIER CIRCUS: The stars of this 1961 series, Richard Jaeckel (left) and John Derek, flank Mickey Rooney in this scene.

(*Below*) SIR LANCELOT: Another 1956 costume drama, this one was about the days of yore in King Arthur's court. William Russell (right) was Lancelot; facing the sword is Garry Thorne.

(*Above*) Zorro: Guy Williams portrayed the masked swordsman (here about to impale Charles Korvin) in a galloping costume drama first seen in 1957.

(*Below*) Long John Silver: Robert Newton was Long John in this adaptation of Robert Louis Stevenson's "Treasure Island."

(*Bottom*) The Buccaneers: Robert Shaw (left) played Captain Tempest in another pirate yarn. Peter Hammond was also featured in this 1956 series, as Lieutenant Beamish.

(*Top*) Northwest Passage: Keith Larsen (left) and Buddy Ebsen advance on the enemy in this scene from a drama set in pre-Revolutionary War days. The show debuted in 1958.

(*Above*) Pete Kelly's Blues: This 1959 entry starred William Reynolds as Kelly, the trumpet-playing leader of a Kansas City jazz band in the 1920's.

(*Below*) The Roaring Twenties: Another action series set in the turbulent twenties, this one starred Dorothy Provine as Pinky Pinkham, an entertainer at the Charleston Club. The show went on the air in 1960, with Donald May and Rex Reason also in the cast.

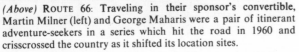

(Above) ROUTE 66: Traveling in their sponsor's convertible, Martin Milner (left) and George Maharis were a pair of itinerant adventure-seekers in a series which hit the road in 1960 and crisscrossed the country as it shifted its location sites.

(Top, right) HARBOURMASTER: Barry Sullivan was David Scott, guardian of the sea around the New England coast. The series debuted in 1957 and also featured Nina Wilcox.

(Right) THE TROUBLESHOOTERS: Former Olympic decathlon champion Bob Mathias (left) and Keenan Wynn were the leads in this 1959 series about a pair of wandering construction workers.

(Bottom, right) WHIRLYBIRDS: The 1957 syndicated show starred Craig Hill (left) and Kenneth Tobey as helicopter pilots.

(Below) WATERFRONT: Preston Foster was Captain Herrick, skipper of the tug Cheryl Ann, and Pinky Tomlin played Tip Hubbard (right) in a series first syndicated in 1953.

(*Above*) STRAIGHTAWAY: Brian Kelly was a racing-car driver in 1961.

(*Top, left*) CASEY JONES: Alan Hale, Jr. portrayed the legendary railroad engineer in this 1957 syndicated series.

(*Left*) VOYAGE TO THE BOTTOM OF THE SEA: Richard Basehart (shown) and David Hedison were featured in a futuristic 1964 series.

(*Bottom, left*) RIPCORD: Larry Pennell and Ken Curtis were sky divers in this 1961 syndicated show.

(*Below*) SEA HUNT: This became one of the most popular syndicated series, beginning in 1958. Lloyd Bridges starred as a skin diver named Mike Nelson. He and the camera crew spent a good deal of time underwater.

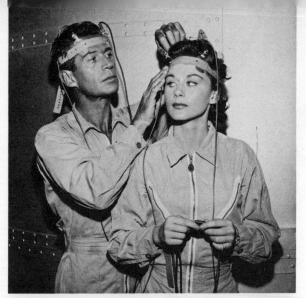

(*Above*) SHEENA, QUEEN OF THE JUNGLE: Irish McCalla was womanhood's answer to Tarzan in this syndicated series first shown in 1954.

(*Below*) RAMAR OF THE JUNGLE: Marjorie Lord and Jon Hall (Ramar) in a tense scene from this drama of the underbrush first syndicated in 1953.

(*Bottom*) JUNGLE JIM: Johnny Weissmuller, who had been one of the movie Tarzans, returned to the jungle as Jim in this television adaptation of the celebrated comic strip. It was first shown in the early fifties.

(*Top*) THE MAN AND THE CHALLENGE: In 1959 George Nader (shown here with Joyce Meadows) played a scientist assigned by the government to test the limits of human endurance.

(*Above*) MEN INTO SPACE: William Lundigan (right) starred as a spaceman who ran into difficulties like the one pictured— crossing a fissure made by a moonquake. The series went on the air in 1959.

(*Below*) LOST IN SPACE: The Robinson family got lost way out there in 1965. Featured in the cast were Marta Kristen (foreground) and (left to right) Mark Goddard, June Lockhart, Guy Williams.

(*Above*) AMOS BURKE: When this series first began, in 1963, it was entitled *Burke's Law,* and Burke (Gene Barry) was a millionaire detective captain. As the programming trend moved away from private eyes and toward spy dramas, Burke was transformed into a secret agent.

(*Top, left*) HONEY WEST: Anne Francis was a lissome but resourceful private detective in 1965.

(*Bottom, left*) RUN FOR YOUR LIFE: Told by doctors that he had only two years to live, Paul Bryan (Ben Gazzara) decided to get a lot of living done in the time left him. Pictured with Gazzara (left) is guest Macdonald Carey. The series was first broadcast in 1965.

(*Below*) THE ROGUES: They were a family of charming swindlers who constantly devised new schemes to acquire illicit boodle. Two of the brothers were Charles Boyer (left) and Gig Young; other cast members were Robert Coote, David Niven, and Gladys Cooper. The show debuted in 1964.

THE FUGITIVE:
Dr. Richard Kimble is on the run. He has escaped from custody after being unjustly convicted of the murder of his wife (she was killed by a mysterious one-armed man). Kimble is played by David Janssen, and he is relentlessly pursued each week by Inspector Gerard (Barry Morse). The show was first telecast in 1963, and its success gave rise to a number of imitative shows, all of which had heroes looking nervously over their shoulders.

BATMAN:

Bob Kane's comic strip came to life (or at least to television) in 1966. Played as broadly as the original was drawn (Zap! Pow! Bam!), it was fun for the youngsters, camp for some oldsters, and fast-moving action for anyone in between. Batman was played by Adam West, and Robin the Boy Wonder was Burt Ward (a lad given to such expressions as "Holy microbes!"). Guest stars portrayed the villains, with names like The Joker and The Riddler. In its first season the show was on twice a week, on succeeding nights, and became an immediate sensation. Entire sections of department stores were given over to the sale of Batman merchandise, and the chairman of the Federal Communications Commission attended a costume party in a **Batman** suit.

They Went Thataway

OF ALL THE FORMS of light dramatic entertainment there is one that stands alone. It has its own conventions, its own rules, its own vocabulary, its own atmosphere. Though it has been imitated all over the world, it is an uncompromisingly American phenomenon.

The western.

It began in the movies, with Bronco Billy Anderson, William S. Hart, Tom Mix, Buck Jones, Hoot Gibson, Tim McCoy; then along came Gary Cooper, Randolph Scott, Jimmy Stewart, Joel McCrea, Henry Fonda, and countless others, who added a touch of sophistication to the idiom.

When television moseyed onto the scene, the easiest thing to do was cannibalize the movies (and radio, which also had latched onto the western). So television's first cowboy heroes were Hopalong Cassidy, Gene Autry, Roy Rogers, and The Lone Ranger.

Gradually television began to create new characters, until, in 1955, it was ready to put its own unmistakable brand on the western. What appeared in 1955 were westerns, all right, but they were *television* westerns.

They came to be called "adult westerns." Previously horse operas had been aimed primarily at children and had been telecast during the day and early evening. In 1955 the object of the game was to attract the grownups in the audience. Thus, a new band of westerners began galloping across the electronic plains—Wyatt

CHAPTER VIII

Earp, Cheyenne Bodie, Matt Dillon, Paladin, Lucas McCain, Bat Masterson. By 1959 there were thirty-two different western series on television. Hour after hour television screens were filled with pounding hooves, showdowns on Dodge City streets, brawls in barrooms, grateful schoolmarms, and dauntless heroes. All over America idolatrous youngsters—and more than a few middle-agesters—were practicing their fast draws and, in an alarming number of reported cases, shooting themselves in the leg.

But the adult westerns were not all gunplay. In fact some purists complained that they did not have enough action. Too much talk. Said Gene Autry, "Television westerns drive me nuts. Too slow." And *messages,* of all things, were creeping into the westerns —sermons about brotherhood and nonviolence and togetherness.

It all used to be so simple—the white hats versus the black hats, no problems that could not be solved with a six-shooter. But in television it was different. You never knew what color hat the good guy would be wearing. As for the rest of his costume, he was likely to go sashaying down to the O.K. Corral in a ruffled shirt, silk vest, and boots and tassels. And that trusty six-shooter? Many was the week when it never even left the holster.

What was the western coming to? It was being transformed into something which suited the unique needs and purposes of television. It also seemed to suit the television audience. *Gunsmoke* kept running forever; *Bonanza* became the most popular television show on the air; and new horse operas still arrive every year, proving that in one shape or another the western will be riding on television for a long time to come.

THEY WENT THATAWAY/*Introduction*

HOPALONG CASSIDY:

In the 1940's William Boyd had the prescience to buy up the television rights to the "Hopalong Cassidy" movies he had been making ever since leaving Cecil B. DeMille's stable, where he had played leading roles in a number of sageless epics ("King of Kings," "Two Arabian Knights," "The Volga Boatman"). In 1948 *Hopalong Cassidy* rode onto television. The routine, low-budget westerns became a national sensation almost immediately. Boyd earned a fortune from the endlessly repeated telecasts of some 100 *Hopalong Cassidy* films and a merchandising campaign based on countless children's devotion to Hoppy.

A badman gets the drop—temporarily, you can be sure—on Hoppy and his sidekick, Red Connors (Edgar Buchanan). The heavy here is played by Clayton Moore, moonlighting from his more familiar television role—The Lone Ranger.

GENE AUTRY: After thirteen years as a singing cowboy in the movies, he started turning out television films by the wagonload in 1947 (with his trusty stallion Champion providing the transportation and Pat Buttram supplying the comic relief). He stayed in the saddle until the adult-western trend caught up with him in the mid-fifties.

/ 295

ROY ROGERS: A Cincinnati-born western star (real name: Leonard Slye), he became Autry's principal rival among the crooning cowpokes. Rogers hit the television trail in the early fifties, accompanied at various times by a horse (Trigger), a dog (Bullet), a wife (Dale Evans, pictured here), her horse (Buttercup), a singing group (The Sons of the Pioneers), and assorted true-blue friends and black-hearted villains.

(*Above*) In a typical closing scene from a *Lone Ranger* show, a sheriff thanks the "mysterious stranger" for his help, just before Kemo Sabay, as Tonto calls him (despite rumors to the contrary, it means "trusted scout"), rides off to his next adventure—"Hi-yo, Silver . . . Away!"

THE LONE RANGER

started his career on radio, in 1933 (created by Fran Striker). He came to television in 1948, and 130 *Lone Ranger* films were made—and played and replayed—during the show's long run on network television, which ended in 1961. Clayton Moore played "the masked man"; Jay Silverheels, a Mohawk Indian, was Tonto. Like nearly all heroes of early television westerns, The Lone Ranger never shot to kill. And he always used perfect grammar, a habit which may have pleased some parents but did not seem to make much of an impression on Tonto.

(Right) ANNIE OAKLEY: Television's first western heroine was played by Gail Davis. Featured in the series were Jimmy Hawkins (right) as Annie's kid brother Tagg Oakley, and Brad Johnson as Lofty Craig.

(Bottom, right) THE CISCO KID: This early horse opera starred Duncan Renaldo (left) as Cisco, Leo Carillo as Pancho, and Diablo as the Kid's horse.

(Below) GABBY HAYES: After playing the scruffy sidekicks of Cassidy, Autry, Rogers, John Wayne, and many other westerners, Gabby Hayes hit television in 1950 with his own show. Hayes, who was born in upstate New York, told tales of the Old West, illustrating his dissertations with film clips from various cowboy movies.

ACTION IN THE AFTERNOON
was television's first live outdoor western, originating in the wide open spaces of suburban Philadelphia *(below)* and telecast five afternoons a week.

(Left) Jack Valentine was the star of the show, supported by Blake Ritter and Mary Elaine Watts, among others.

(Above) RANGE RIDER: Another intrepid duo—Jock Mahoney (left) and Dick West.

(Below) WILD BILL HICKOK: In the early 1950's the number of filmed westerns quickly multiplied. This one starred Guy Madison (right) as United States Marshal James Butler (Wild Bill) Hickok and Andy Devine as Jingles.

/ 299

(Left) THE ADVENTURES OF KIT CARSON: Bill Williams was the famed frontiersman, Don Diamond his amigo El Toro.

(Bottom, left) BRAVE EAGLE: An Indian became the good guy in this 1955 series which starred Keith Larsen. Also in the cast were Keena Nomkeena, Kim Winona, and Bert Wheeler.

(*Above*) 26 MEN: The heroes of this western were the Arizona Rangers (limited by law to 26 men) who policed their territory during the last days of the Old West. Tris Coffin (pictured) starred as Captain Tom Rynning, Kelo Henderson as Ranger Clint Travis.

(*Right*) JUDGE ROY BEAN: He was "the law west of the Pecos," and Edgar Buchanan (elevated from sidekickdom) played him, assisted by Jack Beutel, Jackie Loughery, and Russell Hayden.

(*Bottom, right*) BUFFALO BILL JR.: Dick Jones appeared as a gun-slinging orphan who had been adopted by a kindly judge.

(*Below*) TALES OF THE TEXAS RANGERS: The costars, Willard Parker (left) and Harry Lauter, went backward and forward in time, to cover the one-hundred and twenty adventurous years of the Texas Rangers' history.

DEATH VALLEY DAYS:
Historical events were also supposed to be the source of this long-running series' stories, narrated by "The Old Ranger" (Stanley Andrews)—and later by Ronald Reagan. *Death Valley Days* has served as a launching pad for many television careers. Here are three actors who worked in *Death Valley Days* before they became stars of series of their own.

(Top) **Fess Parker** (later Davy Crockett and Daniel Boone) was virtually unknown when he played a United States marshal in an episode entitled "Kickapoo Run." The girl is Nancy Hale.

(Above) **Gardner McKay** (before embarking on *Adventures in Paradise*) was a mustachioed villain who tried to rape an Arapaho girl (Laurie Carroll) in "The Big Rendezvous."

(Right) **James Franciscus** (who would become a schoolteacher in *Mr. Novak*) was a newspaper editor in "Lady of the Press," featuring Don Beddoe.

THE LIFE AND LEGEND OF WYATT EARP: 1955 was the year of the "adult western." Each of the networks offered at least one of this new breed of horse opera. ABC's major entry was *Wyatt Earp,* which sported Hugh O'Brian as the most dapper western lawman yet seen on television. Complete with flowered vest and string tie, Earp maintained law and order on his turf with the aid of two Buntline Specials—in adult westerns they shot to kill and, needless to say, the good guys seldom missed.

CHEYENNE: This one focused on the adventures of a taciturn, footloose frontier scout named Cheyenne Bodie. Clint Walker, who played the role with bare-chested vigor, proved to be as tough an hombre at the bargaining table as he was on the celluloid plains. He was constantly at loggerheads with his studio, Warner Bros., and his demands for a bigger piece of the action brought him a suspension in 1958, although he was eventually reinstated.

GUNSMOKE:

CBS found the most potent formula for success with its big 1955 western *Gunsmoke*. The chief ingredients were a six-foot-seven-inch hero, Dodge City's Marshal Matt Dillon (James Arness); an obsequious deputy named Chester Goode (Dennis Weaver), who walked with a limp, talked with a twang, and brewed a mean pot of coffee; a "cafe hostess" with a heart of gold and eyes for Matt—Miss Kitty (Amanda Blake); and that hoary staple of melodrama, the character who is always known as "Doc" (Milburn Stone). The show debuted with John Wayne's seal of approval (he introduced the first episode), quickly ended George Gobel's domination of Saturday-night ratings, and stayed on top for more than a decade, first as a half-hour series, then in a full-hour version.

Matt and Chester became national folk heroes. Children—and their fathers—all over the country imitated Chester drawling, "Mester Dellon . . ."

Kitty's "Be careful, Matt" also became an oft-repeated catchphrase.

(*Above*) FRONTIER: Worthington Miner, one of the golden boys of the Golden Age of television drama, produced NBC's 1955 series of half-hour western stories. Walter Coy (pictured with young Peter Votrian) was the narrator and occasional star of the series.

(*Below*) DICK POWELL'S ZANE GREY THEATER: This, like *Frontier,* was a western anthology series. Dick Powell narrated all the episodes and starred in some of them.

(*Above*) BROKEN ARROW: The Apache chieftain Cochise (Michael Ansara) and Indian agent Tom Jeffords (John Lupton) tried to find the path to peace in post-Civil War Arizona.

(*Below*) THE ADVENTURES OF JIM BOWIE: Scott Forbes played the dashing Indian fighter, hero of the Alamo, and inventor of the Bowie knife.

(Right) HAVE GUN, WILL TRAVEL: The never-ending search for a "new" type of hero resulted in 1957 in the appearance of a hired gun who called himself Paladin, smoked 58-cent cigars, quoted Keats and Shelley, collected chessmen, passed out calling cards reading "Wire Paladin, Hotel Carlton, San Francisco," and distastefully dispatched his adversaries with a Colt .44. As Paladin, Richard Boone swiftly completed his appointed rounds with a unique combination of epicurean zest, Spartan valor, and existential ennui.

(Bottom, right) WELLS FARGO: Dale Robertson, an Oklahoman with a shy smile, was the fastest left-handed gun in the West, in the role of Jim Hardie, Wells Fargo troubleshooter.

(Below) SUGARFOOT: All this well-meaning, good-natured lad wanted to do was keep his nose clean and become a lawyer, but wherever he went, people kept drawing guns on him. Will Hutchins had the title role in *Sugarfoot,* which alternated with *Cheyenne* for a while.

WAGON TRAIN:

No wagon trip west ever took longer than this high-budget series, which rolled on year after year, in sixty- and ninety-minute versions, until it got into a rut in the early sixties and left the air. It started in 1957 with Ward Bond as Major Seth Adams and Robert Horton as his scout, Flint McCullough. After Bond's death in 1961, John McIntire moved in as wagon master Chris Hale. Horton got tired of the show before most viewers did; he drifted off to Broadway and was superseded by Denny (Scott) Miller and Robert Fuller.

(Below) Wagon Train relied heavily on guest stars. Carolyn Jones joined Horton (left) and Bond in a 1957 episode.
(Left) James Whitmore turned up as an Indian.
(Right) Ann Sheridan **booked passage** with McIntire in 1962.

(*Above*) COLT .45: Natty Christopher Colt (Wayde Preston) was a gun salesman on a secret government mission. The blonde is Laurie Mitchell.

(*Below*) JEFFERSON DRUM: Jeff Richards portrayed an embattled newspaper editor.

(*Bottom*) LAWMAN: In 1958 John Russell and Peter Brown joined the continuing parade of westerns as Dan Troop, marshal of Laramie, and Johnny McKay, his deputy.

(*Top*) RESTLESS GUN: 1957 also found John Payne playing an itinerant cowpoke named Vint Bonner. Here he runs into a dangerous badman—Chuck Connors, who a season later would swap hats and become the upright star of his own western.

(*Above*) TRACKDOWN: Eight years before he found a series that was more to his liking *(I Spy),* Robert Culp starred as Texas Ranger Hoby Gilman.

(*Below*) TOMBSTONE TERRITORY: As Sheriff Clay Hollister, Pat Conway kept things reasonably orderly in Tombstone, "the town too tough to die."

(Above) WANTED—DEAD OR ALIVE: Nearly everybody had a gimmick in 1958. Steve McQueen, as bounty hunter Josh Randall, bagged his game with a .30-40 sawed-off carbine he called his "Mare's Laig."

(Below) THE RIFLEMAN: Chuck Connors, a Brooklyn boy who didn't quite make it with the Dodgers, hit the big time in this western, playing Lucas McCain, father of a motherless youngster (Johnny Crawford). Lucas was a virtuoso of the .44-40 Winchester carbine, which he twirled like a pistol. The mustachioed baddie in this scene is Dan Blocker (*Bonanza* did not start until a year later), and the third man is Mort Mills.

(Above) THE TEXAN: Rory Calhoun got along nicely with an orthodox six-shooter.

(Below) BAT MASTERSON: Of all the Dapper Dans of the West, none surpassed the sartorial magnificence or savoir faire of Bat Masterson, the gentleman marshal, played with cane, bowler, and strut by Gene Barry.

(Above) A lady gambler, Samantha Crawford (Diane Brewster), turned up frequently in the series. She could match Bret scheme for scheme, ploy for ploy.

(Below) Above all, the Mavericks were gambling men. Here Bart Maverick (Jack Kelly), Bret's brother, plays poker with his "Pappy" Beauregard Maverick (also played by James Garner). The kibitzer is Adam West, who made his mark years later as **Batman.**

MAVERICK: / **309**

He seldom rode a horse. He was slow on the draw. He was self-centered and untrustworthy. His intentions were less than honorable. What kind of western hero was this? A maverick—Bret Maverick, to be specific, played by James Garner. He moseyed onto television one Sunday night in 1957, and it took a while for viewers to realize that *Maverick*'s purpose was subversive—to undermine their respect for square-jawed, squareheaded cowboy Galahads and their square Code of the West. In fact, many viewers never caught on at all, which was the secret of the show's sizable success: it was possible to enjoy it either as western adventure or western spoof.

(Above) YANCY DERRINGER: Undiscouraged by *Maverick's* irreverence, the westerns kept coming in the late fifties. This one was, strictly speaking, a southeasterner—set in New Orleans. It starred Jock Mahoney as Yancy, a gentleman riverman who packed a tiny pistol in his hat. His Pawnee friend, Pahoo, was played by an actor named X Brands.

(Top, right) CIMARRON CITY: George Montgomery was a rugged cattle baron, Matt Rockford, and Audrey Totter played his girl.

(Right) RAWHIDE: A cattle drive was the plot device for this series, which enjoyed a longer run than most westerns. Clint Eastwood as Rowdy Yates (left) and Eric Fleming as Gil Favor were the stars (shown here with Kathleen Crowley).

(Bottom, right) BLACK SADDLE: Peter Breck (later of *The Big Valley*) played Clay Culhane, a gunfighter turned circuit lawyer; and Anna Lisa was Nora Travers, owner of the Marathon Hotel in Latigo, New Mexico.

(Below) SHOTGUN SLADE: Behind the whiskers is Ernie Kovacs, playing an old prospector in this episode. Scott Brady was Slade.

BONANZA

came along in 1959, and nobody paid much attention—at first. But when the show was moved to a new Sunday-night time slot, it caught fire and became television's top-rated show, year in and year out, through most of the mid-sixties. It was a family show in more ways than one. Its heroes were the members of the Cartwright clan, owners of a huge spread near Virginia City. Patriarchal, Bible-quoting Ben Cartwright (Lorne Greene) had **three** sons: serious-minded Adam (Pernell Roberts, who dropped out of *Bonanza* in 1965), cheerfully oafish Hoss (Dan Blocker), and impulsive Little Joe (Michael Landon). The plots contained less gunplay than horseplay and less action than wholesome drama with soap-opera overtones, the better to hook the entire family watching at home.

(Below) The young Cartwrights—Adam (seated), Hoss (behind him), and Little Joe (left)—were half-brothers. The tales of Ben's various marriages provided material for a number of scripts.

(Bottom, left) Dan Blocker as Hoss.

(Above) THE DEPUTY: Henry Fonda, no stranger to westerns, starred as Marshal Simon Fry. Allen Case was his gung-ho deputy, Clay McCord.

(Top, right) WICHITA TOWN: That same year (1959) another marshal-and-deputy team made its debut: Joel McCrea as Mike Dunbar and his son Jody as Ben Matheson.

(Right) LARAMIE: The cast included (left to right) Robert Fuller as Jess Harper, Bobby Crawford, Jr. as Andy Sherman, and Hoagy Carmichael as Jonesy—plus (not pictured) John Smith as Slim Sherman.

(Right) BRONCO: Ty Hardin was Warner Bros.' pawn in the studio's scheme to bring Clint Walker into line. *Bronco* was launched as part of *Cheyenne,* then had a brief fling of its own after Walker rejoined the fold.

(Bottom, right) JOHNNY RINGO: Johnny (Don Durant) was a reformed gunslinger. Karen Sharpe kept him from backsliding.

(Below) HOTEL DE PAREE: Perhaps the most gimmicky western of its day—on the hero's hatband were polished silver discs which blinded his adversaries. He was called Sundance, and Earl Holliman played the role, supported by Judi Meredith.

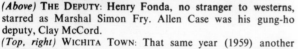

(Top, left) THE MAN FROM BLACKHAWK: The man was an insurance investigator who also was handy with his fists. Here he gets the better of Robert Bray, *Lassie's* future master.

(Top, right) THE REBEL: Nick Adams played an angry young Reb named Johnny Yuma.

(Left) GUNSLINGER: Impassive Tony Young was Cord, an undercover agent for the cavalry. Preston Foster was his commanding officer.

(Right) WHISPERING SMITH: This western escaped the notice of virtually everybody except a Congressional committee which singled it out as a particularly deplorable specimen of television violence. Its stars were Audie Murphy (right) and Guy Mitchell.

(Bottom, left) OVERLAND TRAIL: William Bendix as Kelly and Doug McClure as Flip superintended a stage line between Missouri and California.

(Bottom, right) THE TALL MAN: In this retelling of the story of Billy the Kid and Pat Garrett, Billy (Clu Gulager) became a mischievous but well-meaning anarchist and Garrett (Barry Sullivan) his tough but kindly guardian angel and occasional adversary.

(Below) TATE: The only thing that distinguished this short-lived 1960 summer series was the fact that Tate (David McLean) had only one good arm. The other, smashed in the war, was preserved in a rawhide-stitched black leather casing.

(Top, left) STONEY BURKE: The western adopted new guises in the sixties. Stoney (Jack Lord) was a rodeo champion, and the setting was contemporary. In this episode James Mason appeared in a bit role, as a derelict. Another rodeo western, *The Wide Country,* starring Earl Holliman and Andrew Prine, came along at the same time (1962).

(Left) EMPIRE: Another modern western, this one starred Richard Egan as Jim Redigo, foreman of a huge southwestern ranch owned by the Garret family (portrayed by Terry Moore, Anne Seymour, and Ryan O'Neal). After its first season the show was cut back from sixty minutes to thirty, its cast trimmed, and its title changed to *Redigo.*

(Above) THE VIRGINIAN: Television's first ninety-minute western had James Drury playing the nameless character Owen Wister had created and Gary Cooper had immortalized on the screen. Others in a large cast included Lee J. Cobb (who grumbled about the show from the outset and quit it in 1966), playing Judge Garth, and Doug McClure, in the role of Trampas.

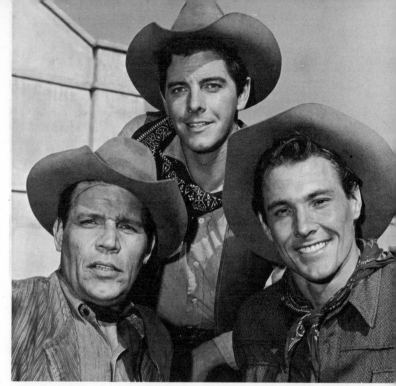

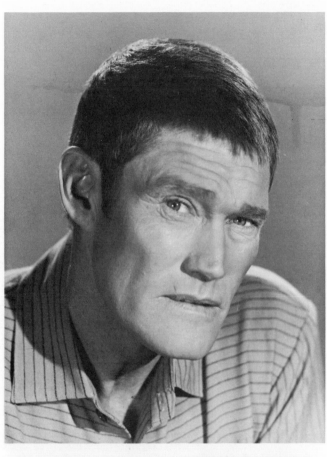

(Above) LAREDO: This 1965 version of a Texas Rangers saga played things more for laughs than for action. Neville Brand, Peter Brown, and William Smith (left to right) were a trio of rascally Rangers.

(Left) BRANDED: Chuck Connors got a new haircut and a new weapon—a broken sword—and returned to the western scene as a cashiered cavalry officer wrongly accused of cowardice who wanders through the West in search of the men who framed him.

 / 315

(Bottom, left) A MAN CALLED SHENANDOAH: As an amnesiac, Robert Horton was wandering too, and searching—for his identity.

(Below) THE WILD WILD WEST: A marriage of the western form with the extravagant content of the James Bond yarns, which had reached a peak of popularity in the mid-sixties, produced this gimmick-laden opus. Robert Conrad, as Jim West, was a swashbuckling secret agent for President Grant. Ross Martin was his pal Artemus Gordon.

Next Question

"IT IS NOT EVERY QUESTION that deserves an answer," wrote Publilius Syrus in 42 B.C. Some two thousand years later, television was to lend added weight to that observation, as a super-abundance of panel and quiz shows filled the ether with volley upon volley of questions.

Panel and quiz shows were a hangover from radio days, when the multitudes were entranced by such programs as "Double or Nothing," "The $64 Question," "Information Please," and "The Quiz Kids." Television seized on the concept hungrily, not only because of its successful track record, but also because this kind of programming could be produced at only a fraction of the cost of almost any other type of show. In time, most of the popular radio formats were adapted to television, and they were joined by hundreds of new variations. The channels were jammed with panelists and contestants eagerly trying to place the face, name the tune, or divine the price of a mink coat. Some of the shows, like *G.E. College Bowl* or *What in the World?*, made an effort to be educational as well as entertaining; almost all others were content to divert or amuse, rather than advance the cause of knowledge. Appearance and personality were major considerations in the selection of quiz contestants, and intellect was generally subordinated to beauty and charm when the panel was hired for a game show. Producers Mark Goodson and Bill Todman, the maharajahs of paneldom, were among the first to discover that the audience was probably more interested in the players than in the game. They assembled their panels with loving care, and their shrewdness is apparent in the fact that few loyal viewers of *What's My Line?* or *I've Got a Secret* can recall last week's lines or secrets, but most can remember Bennett Cerf's pun or the gown worn by Bess Myerson.

Logic decrees that quiz shows, as a programming device, should have become nothing more than a dim footnote in the history of television's first two decades. But logic (as well as ethics and good sense) took a bad beating in the late fifties when the quiz scandals rocked the foundations of the television industry. Although television was too big and too firmly entrenched to be shattered by the scandals, its reputation was permanently scarred. Yet, in the opinion of some observers, we have not seen the last of the big-money quiz.

Panel and quiz shows are something less than an art form, but they are not without their redeeming virtues. One must, for example, be appreciative of such moments as the time a game show emcee asked his panel to name a country beginning with the letter "G," and one contestant responded by writing G-A-P-A-N.

NEXT QUESTION/*Introduction*

WHAT'S MY LINE?

When this grandaddy of the panel shows went on the air in 1950, the panel included poet Louis Untermeyer, ex-Governor (of New Jersey) Harold Hoffman, Dr. Richard Hoffman, and Arlene Francis. Other early panelists were Hal Block (below, seated far right), Fred Allen, and Steve Allen. From 1951 until Dorothy Kilgallen's death in 1965, the roster of permanent panel members comprised Miss Kilgallen, Miss Francis, and publisher Bennett Cerf; former newscaster John Daly served as the show's moderator. While the format is a simple one (the panel tries to guess a guest's occupation), dozens of variations and near-copies of the program have come and gone without attaining any of the success or staying power of the original. This has led to the speculation that the personalities of the panelists, rather than the mechanics of the game, have been the determining factor in the longevity of *What's My Line?* The occupation of the show's first guest: hatcheck girl. Better remembered, perhaps, is the question that always popped up on the show: "Is it bigger than a bread box?"

(Above) I'VE GOT A SECRET: Like *What's My Line?*, this show was a product of the Goodson-Todman organization, a production company specializing in the packaging of panel programs. *Secret* was first broadcast in 1952; in the above photograph, taken on the show's sixth anniversary in 1958, the panelists included (left to right) Bill Cullen, Jayne Meadows, moderator Garry Moore, Henry Morgan, and Betsy Palmer.

(Below) TO TELL THE TRUTH: Another Goodson-Todman entry, this one made its debut in 1956. For a time it was on the air with both a daily daytime version and a weekly nighttime show. Many show-business personalities have appeared as panelists since *To Tell the Truth* was first broadcast, but the most recent group of permanent panel members has been Tom Poston, Kitty Carlisle, and Orson Bean, with Bud Collyer as the moderator.

(Below) NAME THAT TUNE: George deWitt was one of the show's emcees (others: Bill Cullen and Red Benson). The program debuted in 1954, and at one point presented as contestants *(bottom)* young actor Eddie Hodges and Marine Corps Major John Glenn. Years later, when *Name That Tune* was but a dim memory, Glenn's feats as an astronaut brought him a more enduring fame.

(Above) THIS IS YOUR LIFE: With Ralph Edwards as host, this show made its first appearance in 1952. Each week a surprised guest was called from the audience to sit in stunned and tearful grandeur as people and events from his past life were paraded before him. The program combined tribute with sentiment and nostalgia, and the mixture met with audience approval for almost a decade. Here, Edwards speaks with singer Lillian Roth.

(Below) WE THE PEOPLE: A video version of a radio favorite, the show was first seen in 1948. Dan Seymour was the host (with guest Celeste Holm). Seymour later left show business for a career in advertising and eventually was named president of one of the world's largest advertising agencies, J. Walter Thompson.

(Above) THE LAST WORD: One of the more sophisticated panel offerings, this show dealt with the vagaries of the English language. In 1959 the participants included (left to right) moderator Bergen Evans, Arthur Knight, June Havoc, and John Mason Brown.

(Left) G.E. COLLEGE BOWL: Two quartets of students acted as representatives of their schools in a duel of wits. The program was first seen in 1959 with Allen Ludden as the moderator; he was later succeeded by Robert Earle.

(Below) WHAT IN THE WORLD?: These panelists were presented with objects of archeological interest and asked to establish their origins. Shown here (left to right) are Drs. Carleton Coon, Margo Plass, and Alfred Kidder. The moderator is Dr. Froelich Rainey.

(Above) THE $64,000 QUESTION: Gino Prato, a New York shoe-maker who was one of the first big winners, stands in the isolation booth as Hal March asks the questions. The subject was opera.

(Below) THE $64,000 QUESTION: March with another contestant, Mrs. Mabel Morris.

(Top) THE $64,000 CHALLENGE: Many of the big winners on *Question* later appeared on this sister show. Above, Redmond O'Hanlon, a New York policeman whose subject was Shakespeare, and Myrt Power, a Georgia housewife whose specialty was baseball.

(Above) THE $64,000 CHALLENGE: Sonny Fox (later replaced by Ralph Story) asks the questions of actor Vincent Price (left) and jockey Billy Pearson. Their category was art.

THE QUIZ SCANDALS:

The era of the big-money quiz dawned on June 7, 1955, with the debut of *The $64,000 Question*. Several months later it was followed by *The $100,000 Big Surprise*, then by *The $64,000 Challenge*, and, finally, by *Twenty-One*. All of these shows operated on the premise that attractive contestants, struggling to win awesome amounts of cash, would capture the imagination and viewing loyalty of the audience. They did. The programs climbed to dizzying heights of popularity, and the nation sat entranced as the contestants, like human museum specimens, were locked in their isolation booths, there to ponder and perspire, writhe and weep. Winners became national heroes; losers had their grief assuaged with consolation prizes (on *The $64,000 Question* failure was rewarded with a new Cadillac). But in 1958, three years after it all began, the structure toppled and collapsed in a scandal-racked heap. First a former contestant on a show called *Dotto* stepped forward to announce he had evidence the program had been rigged; he was followed by Herbert Stempel, a *Twenty-One* contestant who described in detail how that show had been fixed. Networks, producers, and other former contestants all issued stout denials, but the truth finally emerged, after extensive probing by a district attorney, a grand jury, and a Congressional committee. Wholesale cheating had taken place, under the pretext that it was necessary to enhance the entertainment value of the shows. In the end, ten participants pleaded guilty to charges of perjury (they had lied to the grand jury), and a dozen other careers and reputations had been irreparably tarnished. Perhaps worst of all was the fact that many contestants, who had received no assistance and were guilty of no wrongdoing, would thereafter have to live under a cloud of suspicion. The big-money quizzes had indeed packed a wallop, but they left television with a black eye.

/ **323**

(Above) THE $100,000 BIG SURPRISE: Another dispenser of oodles of boodle, this show was first emceed by Jack Barry, then by Mike Wallace, shown here with Sue Oakland, guardian of the "Easy" questions, and Mary Gardiner, custodian of the "Hard" questions.
(Upper right) TWENTY-ONE: Emcee Jack Barry prepares to question Charles Van Doren (left) and Herbert Stempel.
(Right) TWENTY-ONE: Barry with Vivienne Nearing, a lawyer, who defeated Van Doren.

(*Top, left*) THE PRICE IS RIGHT: Contestants could win boats, cars, homes, jewelry, furs, and a hundred other miscellaneous items if they could guess the value of the item being offered. The show began as a daytime game, then graduated to a night-time period the following year (1957). Bill Cullen (shown with Beverly Bentley) was the emcee.

(*Above*) DR. I. Q.: "Give that man twenty silver dollars," the Doctor would shout after a correct answer had been given. When the show first came to television in 1953, James McLain was the mental banker, as he had been in the radio version during the forties.

(*Left*) BRAINS AND BRAWN: Fred Davis (left) and Jack Lescoulie were the co-hosts of a 1958 show in which two teams of brainy and brawny contestants matched skills for cash prizes.

(Below) TALENT SEARCH: A beardless Skitch Henderson was the host and accompanist in this 1950 audition for aspiring entertainers.

(Bottom) SONGS FOR SALE: Amateur songwriters brought their brainchildren to this television showcase, just as they had when it was a radio offering. It debuted in 1952 with Steve Allen as host; Jan Murray (shown with contestant George Handzik) later became host.

(Above) THIS IS SHOW BUSINESS: The panelists were (left to right) George S. Kaufman, Clifton Fadiman, and Sam Levenson. Guest performers displayed their talents and aired their problems to the panel. The program debuted in 1949, and had its most dramatic moment on December 21, 1952, when Kaufman, pondering the overcommercialization of Christmas, remarked, "Let's make this one program on which no one sings 'Silent Night.' " Hundreds of indignant letters resulted in his banishment from the show, although he was later reinstated.

/ **325**

(Below) JUKEBOX JURY: Peter Potter was the host who asked "Will it be a hit (bong!) or a miss (clunk!)?" The panel delivered its learned opinion of the songs in question. On this program they were (left to right) Page Cavanaugh, Lois Butler, Desi Arnaz, and host Potter. The show was first telecast nationally in 1953.

(Top) LEAVE IT TO THE GIRLS: First telecast in 1947, this show featured a battle of the sexes, and though each program presented a male "defender," the girls on the panel usually managed to deal the masculine ego some shattering blows. The panel had numerous members during the course of the show's run, but the three above, Maggi McNellis, Eloise McElhone, and Florence Pritchett, were most closely identified with the program.

(Above) DOWN YOU GO: An early word game first telecast from Chicago, this one introduced an erudite college professor named Bergen Evans. Shown here (left to right) are moderator Evans, Francis Coughlin, Toni Gilman, Robert Breen, and Carmelita Pope.

(Right) TWENTY QUESTIONS: The animal-vegetable-mineral game which had long been a radio mainstay arrived on television in 1954. The panel shown featured Herb Polesie, Fred Vandeventer, Florence Rinard, and guest Aldo Ray. Bill Slater was the man with the questions.

(*Top*) THE QUIZ KIDS: The precocious juvenile panel that amazed radio listeners for years came to television in 1952. The group above includes (left to right) Frankie Vander Ploeg, 7; Brenda Liebling, 7; Harvey Dytch, 8; Janet Ahern, 6; Vincent Granatelli, 7; quizmaster Joe Kelly. Clifton Fadiman later became host of the show.

(*Center*) JUVENILE JURY: Jack Barry was the moderator of this small-fry forum, which was first telecast in 1947. He is shown with a 1954 panel including (left to right) Joe Ward, Michelle Fogel, and Douglas Stewart.

(*Above*) LIFE BEGINS AT EIGHTY: At the other end of the spectrum was this panel of wisdom-dispensing oldsters, also moderated by Jack Barry. It was first broadcast in the late forties. The panel here includes (left to right) Fred Stein, Mrs. Georgiana Carhart, "Doc" Bowers, moderator Barry, Miss Isabelle Winlocke, and Rev. H. S. Hathaway.

(*Left*) BATTLE OF THE AGES: This early DuMont show was a contest pitting youngsters against a team of elderly people. Here, W. C. Handy, composer of "St. Louis Blues," performs on the premiere.

(Left) YOU BET YOUR LIFE: The one and only Groucho Marx was the star of this comedy quiz which was more comedy than quiz. First seen in 1950, it featured a secret word, a stuffed duck, some wacky contestants, and endless quips by the master.

(Below) IT PAYS TO BE IGNORANT: This panel played it for laughs, too: (left to right) Harry McNaughton, Lulu McConnell, George Shelton, and Tom Howard. The video version arrived in 1949.

(Bottom) PANTOMIME QUIZ: One of television's perennials since the late forties, this show was usually a summer replacement, but occasionally got a spot on fall schedules. The charade players on this series got their quota of laughs, but always played the game with ferocious intensity. In the 1951 photo shown, they are (left to right) Jackie Coogan, Vincent Price, host Mike Stokey, and Hans Conried.

(Above) WHO'S WHOSE?: Phil Baker, who in gentler days had emceed radio's "$64 Question," made his television debut in this 1951 game of who-is-married-to-whom. Robin Chandler was a member of the celebrity panel.

(Top, right) MASQUERADE PARTY: The makeup men disguised the guests and the panel tried to identify them on this show, first seen in 1952. An early panel comprised (from left to right) Phil Silvers, Buff Cobb, Ogden Nash, Ilka Chase, and emcee Peter Donald.

(Right) WHO SAID THAT?: Bob Trout (standing) was the "quote-master" of the panel show which first appeared in 1948. The object of the game was to identify the author of a quotation. John Cameron Swayze (far left) was the host, and some of the show's guests were (left to right) Senator Kenneth Wherry, H. V. Kaltenborn, and Vice President Alben Barkley.

(Bottom) WHO PAYS?: On this one (1959) the panel had to determine the contestants' celebrity employers. The panel members: Sir Cedric Hardwicke, emcee Mike Wallace, Celeste Holm, and Gene Klavan.

/ **331**

new *Lanolite Lipstick*

(Top, left) WHO'S THE BOSS ?: Standing (far right) are host Walter Kiernan and guests Joe Louis and Johnny, who always called for *his* boss. The show debuted in 1954.

(Left) WHERE WAS I?: This was an early photo quiz, with Peter Donald, Bill Cullen, and Nancy Guild.

(Bottom, left) WHAT'S GOING ON? Lee Bowman (left) was the host, and Kitty Carlisle and Hy Gardner were panelists. Other panelists, in distant areas, appeared via remote pickups.

(Above) PLACE THE FACE: Emcee Bill Cullen posed for this publicity photo. The show was first seen in 1953; contestants tried to identify faces of people from their past.

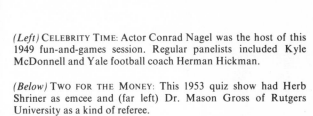

(Left) CELEBRITY TIME: Actor Conrad Nagel was the host of this 1949 fun-and-games session. Regular panelists included Kyle McDonnell and Yale football coach Herman Hickman.

(Below) TWO FOR THE MONEY: This 1953 quiz show had Herb Shriner as emcee and (far left) Dr. Mason Gross of Rutgers University as a kind of referee.

(Bottom) JUDGE FOR YOURSELF: Fred Allen made many television appearances, including a one-year stint, beginning in 1953, as host of this show. But he was never to recapture the glories of his radio days. One of his finest video contributions was the narration of "The Jazz Age" on *Project 20;* ironically, the program was telecast some nine months after his death, in 1956. He is shown here with a vocal group, The Skylarks.

While the Dishes Wait

DAYTIME TELEVISION IS DEDICATED to the proposition that all women were created to do housework and change diapers—and that while they are performing these chores (or avoiding them), there are two basic ways to attract their attention long enough to get the sponsors' messages across.

One way is the traditional one, proved ninety-nine and forty-four one-hundredths percent effective on radio: the soap opera. After a few false starts, the soap opera took hold in daytime television in 1951 and has dominated the ratings of afternoon shows ever since. The ratings for the 1965 season—which are typical of virtually every other season—show six soap operas among daytime's top ten programs: *As the World Turns* (the consistent daytime leader), followed by *The Secret Storm, Search for Tomorrow* (the oldest current soaper), *The Guiding Light, The Edge of Night,* and *Love of Life.*

But during a normal season some ten other daytime serials (as broadcasters prefer to call them) are also on the air. When one fails, it is almost invariably replaced by another. New title, new setting, new cast—but the same lugubrious problems: women without men, women with weakling husbands, women with lovers, women with ne'er-do-well children, women with designs on happily married men, women with nothing to live for. All of this turmoil and travail can be watched steadily, without respite, from eleven o'clock any weekday morning to four-thirty in the afternoon.

The other way television seeks to hook the housewife is by inviting her vicarious participation in fun and games. The game shows have been with us as long as television has, but in recent years they have proliferated to the point that there are as many of them on the air as soap operas and, if you are so inclined, you can watch them, with just a couple of half-hour breaks, for seven hours, one show after another, five days a week.

A third form of daytime programming has also become fashionable during the sixties—the reruns of defunct or current nighttime series. Most of them are comedy shows such as *I Love Lucy, The Andy Griffith Show, The Real McCoys,* and *The Dick Van Dyke Show,* but some dramatic series have also been tried. *Ben Casey,* for one, has been quite successful in daytime replays.

Where does all this leave the housewife who does not enjoy witnessing the agony of the soap-opera heroine or the ecstasy of the guessing-game champion? High and dry, except for the *Today* show and an occasional newscast or snatch of literate conversation on a talk show.

One morning in 1966, when a foreign-policy expert testified before the Senate Foreign Relations Committee, which was holding hearings on the war in Vietnam, a network decided against live coverage of the hearings. Women are not interested in watching that sort of thing, implied the executive who made the decision.

What *are* the women of America interested in watching? For whatever it's worth, television's answer to that question comes every week, Monday through Friday, from dawn until dark.

WHILE THE DISHES WAIT/*Introduction*

DENNIS JAMES

has been on television since 1938, and no other television product can make that claim. In that year he could be found in a five-by-ten room in DuMont's Madison Avenue headquarters, where the lights raised the temperature to 140 degrees. He was emceeing DuMont's experimental programs, which were beamed to the two or three hundred television sets then to be found in New York City. When the general public started buying sets a decade later, James came into his own. He was the announcer for DuMont's wrestling matches, and directed his patter toward the matrons in the audience. "Okay, mother," he would say, "that's a hammerlock." "Okay, mother" became his catchphrase, and mothers all over America were soon baking him cookies and knitting him argyles. When daytime television became a part of the lives of women all over the country, Dennis James was in the thick of it. His shows included *Turn to a Friend, The Name's the Same, High Finance, Cash and Carry, On Your Account, Club 60, Your First Impression, People Will Talk, Haggis Baggis, Judge for Yourself,* and many others, nighttime as well as daytime.

(Top, left) In 1959 he did *Haggis Baggis,* with Lillian Naud as the show's hostess.
(Top, right) For a while James was enmeshed in *High Finance.*
(Above) Nancy Wright joined him on his variety show, *Club 60.*
(Below) In the early fifties James was host of a popular program introducing new talent—*Chance of a Lifetime.*
(Bottom, left) He was still going strong in the sixties on *People Will Talk* and numerous other shows and commercials.

(Top) Double or Nothing's first anniversary, in 1953. (The girl is Joan Meinch.)
(Above, left) Parks on *Break the Bank,* which began in 1949.
(Above, right) On *Stop the Music.*
(Below) Balance Your Budget (with Lynn Connor).

"BERT PARKS,"

said television critic John Crosby, "has a smile you can read by." That smile and a superabundance of boyish exuberance have made him the most ubiquitous of all the daytime emcees and have also brought him numerous opportunities in nighttime shows, most conspicuously the annual role of master of ceremonies for the Miss America Pageant. His list of credits includes, in addition to those depicted here, *Masquerade Party, First Love, Yours for a Song, The Bert Parks Show, NBC Bandstand, The Big Payoff, Two in Love, Giant Step,* and *Hold That Note.* If any one man can be said to personify the spirit of daytime television's fun-and-games shows, that man is smiling Bert Parks.

(Above) Bid 'n' Buy.
(Below) On *County Fair* football star Frank Gifford tried to punch his way out of an eight-foot-long paper bag. He failed.

BEAT THE CLOCK: Bud Collyer is another member of the elite corps of game-show emcees whose services are always in demand. His *Beat the Clock* began in 1950 and was a nighttime show as well as daytime. *(Above)* Rev. Louis McGee, embracing his wife here, won $3,200 in a typical *Beat the Clock* stunt: without using his hands he maneuvered two toupees, which were suspended from the ceiling, so that they landed in a hat worn on his head. A beautiful blonde model known as Roxanne *(below)* became a television celebrity through her regular appearances as Collyer's *Beat the Clock* aide.

(Above) BRIDE AND GROOM: Couples got married on television in this early daytime series. Bob Paige (left) and Frank Parker (who replaced Byron Palmer) were the hosts.

(Below) THE BIG PAYOFF: Randy Merriman and Bess Myerson conducted this giveaway show. Here a Vermont housewife has just won a mink coat.

STRIKE IT RICH: Whoever could tell the saddest tale of woe was rewarded by emcee Warren Hull and by outside contributions through the show's "heart line." Mrs. Eleanor Kane, shown here with Hull, struck it rich for her five-year-old daughter, who was born deaf, dumb, and blind.

FEATHER YOUR NEST: Another Bud Collyer show, this one gave away home furnishings to winning contestants. Janis Carter assisted Collyer.

(Above) CONTEST CARNIVAL: Aspiring circus performers appeared in this 1953 daytime show. The permanent cast consisted of (left to right) Phil Sheridan, Gene Crane, Joanie Coale, and Harry Levan.

(Top, right) ON YOUR ACCOUNT: Win Elliot, who has emceed many shows, looked like this in 1954, when he was host of this show.

(Right) BREAKFAST IN HOLLYWOOD: Johnny Dugan starred in this one, which featured "Good Neighbor Awards" and a tribute to the oldest woman in the studio audience.

(Bottom, right) WELCOME TRAVELERS: Tommy Bartlett offered hospitality to passengers arriving in Chicago.

(Below) IT PAYS TO BE MARRIED: Wedded bliss was rewarded by Bill Goodwin (left).

DOLLAR A SECOND: *(Below)* Contestants had to undergo various humiliations to collect their dollars on this show, emceed by Jan Murray (shown above).

TRUTH OR CONSEQUENCES: The same was true of this adaptation of the old radio show. On television Jack Bailey and later Bob Barker (shown above) replaced Ralph Edwards as the show's gleeful Torquemada.

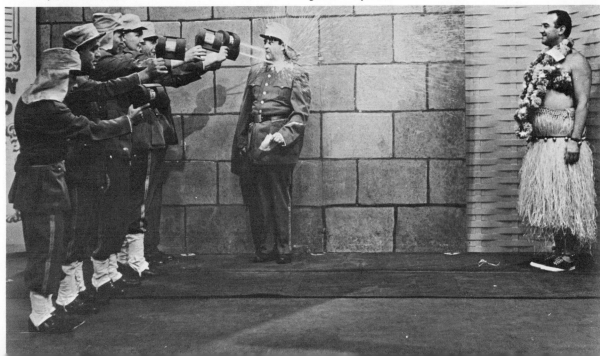

BIG GAME: Nighttime's big-money quizzes had smaller-scale counterparts on daytime television. Tom Kennedy was the star of this early-Saturday-evening quiz show.

342 /

KEEP IT IN THE FAMILY: In the late fifties dozens of new games, contests, and quizzes made their appearance on daytime television. *Keep It in the Family*, with Bill Nimmo, first appeared in 1957.

(Above) TIC TAC DOUGH: Jack Barry co-produced and emceed *Tic Tac Dough*, as well as the nighttime *Twenty-One*. Like many shows which started as daytime offerings, *Tic Tac Dough* eventually became a nighttime series too.

(Top, left) DOTTO: This show touched off the quiz scandals in 1958 when a contestant claimed that it was rigged. Jack Narz was the host.

(Left) DOUGH RE MI: Musical quizzes have always been a popular form of television entertainment. Gene Rayburn was in charge of this one.

(Bottom, left) MUSIC BINGO: Johnny Gilbert emceed this one.

(Below) TOP DOLLAR: Toby Reed was the host, and Bergen Evans (far right) verified the contestants' answers.

(*Above*) QUEEN FOR A DAY: Long a popular fixture of the daytime television scene, *Queen* was presented five afternoons a week, until it left the air in 1965 after several thousand performances. Women vied on each show to be chosen—on the basis of hard-luck stories—to be crowned Queen and showered with gifts by Jack Bailey (far left).

(*Above*) TREASURE HUNT: After *Dollar a Second* ran out of money, Jan Murray returned with another prize-laden series. Marian Stafford was the "Pirate Girl."

(*Below*) IT COULD BE YOU: Bill Leyden emceed this show in which home viewers, as well as those in the studio, could win **vacation trips.**

(*Below*) WHO DO YOU TRUST?: It started as *Do You Trust Your Wife?*, with Edgar Bergen. Johnny Carson eventually took it over. Later on, Woody Woodbury (shown here) became host of the show, which had been renamed *Who Do You Trust?*

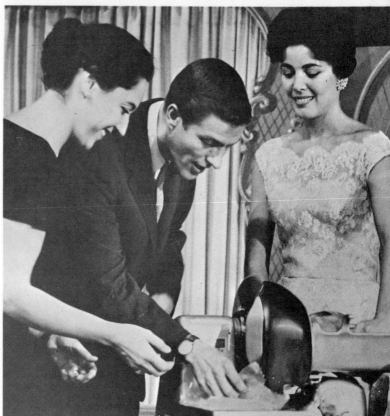

(Above) MOTHER'S DAY: Dick Van Dyke was the star of this daytime variety series in 1958. Dotty Mack (right) assisted him. Here Van Dyke shows a guest how to use a slicer.

(Left) PLAY YOUR HUNCH: In 1959 Merv Griffin was presiding over a show in which husband-and-wife teams competed in solving problems. Liz Gardner was Griffin's helper.

(Below) HOW DO YOU RATE?: Tom Reddy (center) tested contestants' skills and reactions in this 1958 entry.

(Above) LET'S MAKE A DEAL: Through the fifties and into the sixties, the fun-and-games shows kept coming, jamming the daytime airwaves. A television old-timer, Monte Hall, conducted this gambling show.

(Top, right) MAKE A FACE: Bob Clayton and Rita Mueller were in this one in 1962.

(Right) WHAT'S THIS SONG?: Win Martindale kept people guessing.

(Below, left) SPLIT PERSONALITY: NBC publicized the 1959–60 series by distributing this picture of its emcee, Tom Poston.

(Below, center) SEVEN KEYS: Jack Narz was the host.

(Below, right) SAY WHEN: Art James was the star.

346 /

(Above) SUPERMARKET SWEEP: 1965 brought a new type of television contest, the brainchild of David Susskind and his production staff—husbands raced around supermarkets to see who could grab the most groceries from the shelves. The emcee was Bill Malone. *Supermarket Sweep* was, thought some critics, a monument to greed and avarice.

(Below, left) THE OBJECT IS: Dick Clark, who had shaken up daytime television with his *American Bandstand* shows, was back in 1963 with a game.

(Below) CONCENTRATION: This became a long-running favorite of daytime viewers as did its host, Hugh Downs.

Soap Operas:

Radio, of course, is where the soap operas began—in 1932, with "Just Plain Bill." Television got around to them in 1947, when DuMont tried one called *A Woman to Remember,* which did not last long enough for anyone to remember *anything* about it.

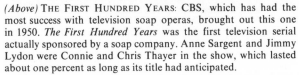

(Above) THE FIRST HUNDRED YEARS: CBS, which has had the most success with television soap operas, brought out this one in 1950. *The First Hundred Years* was the first television serial actually sponsored by a soap company. Anne Sargent and Jimmy Lydon were Connie and Chris Thayer in the show, which lasted about one percent as long as its title had anticipated.

(Left) SEARCH FOR TOMORROW: This was the first soap opera that hit real pay dirt. *Search* began in 1951 and is still running, with no end in sight. Here is the Barron family as it looked in the early days: Cliff Hall, Lynn Loring, Mary Stuart (still starring in the show), and Bess Johnson.

(*Above*) FOLLOW YOUR HEART: Sallie Brophy (left) and Nancy Sheridan were a Main Line debutante and her mother in this 1953 soap opera.

(*Below*) CONCERNING MISS MARLOWE: A soap-opera role has been just the beginning of the road for many actors and actresses. Efrem Zimbalist, Jr., for example, appeared opposite Louise Albritton in this serial before he went on to bigger things in Hollywood.

(*Above*) LOVE OF LIFE: Shortly after *Search for Tomorrow* was launched, *Love of Life* came along, and it too is still going strong. Here are Peggy McCay and Dennis Parnell in the early fifties.

(*Below*) HAWKINS FALLS: It was called a "television novel." Laif Flaigle (Win Stracke) and Millie (Ros Twohey) operated a home laundry in this 1953 episode.

(Above) THE BENNETTS: They were Paula Houston and Don Gibson.

(Top, right) WOMAN WITH A PAST: The woman was Constance Ford; the year, 1954.

(Right) A TIME TO LIVE: Another 1954 entry, with Pat Sully and Larry Kerr.

(Bottom, right) VALIANT LADY: Nancy Coleman played valiant Helen Emerson until she left the cast to do a Broadway show (Flora Campbell replaced her).

(Below) THREE STEPS TO HEAVEN: A small-town girl hit the big city in this 1953 starter. Phyllis Hill, Joe Brown, Jr., and Walter Brooke had the leads.

(*Above*) THE SECRET STORM: This one has been on the air since 1954, when Haila Stoddard was playing Pauline Harris.

(*Top, left*) MODERN ROMANCES: A new story unfolded each week, in five installments, narrated by Martha Scott.

(*Left*) ONE MAN'S FAMILY: Eva Marie Saint and Bert Lytell were in the cast when NBC brought this radio classic to television in 1949. This picture was shot in 1954, when the family included (from lower left, then up the stairs) Theodor von Eltz, Mary Adams, Russell Thorson, Anne Whitfield, Linda Leighton, and Martin Dean.

(*Below*) PORTIA FACES LIFE: In 1954 Fran Carlon (far left) played Portia. Around the table are Jean Gillespie, Ginger MacManus, Karl Swenson, and (back to camera) Charles Taylor.

(Above) THE BRIGHTER DAY: This is another soap opera that has kept going for more than a decade. At the beginning its cast comprised Lois Nettleton, Hal Holbrook, Bill Smith, and Mary Linn Beller.

(Top, right) GOLDEN WINDOWS: Grant Sullivan and Leila Martin persevered.

(Right) THE GREATEST GIFT: Philip Foster and Anne Burr both portrayed doctors in 1955.

(Bottom, right) DATE WITH LIFE: Each of the stories ran four to six weeks, then a completely new cast and plot took over. Barbara Britton starred with Bernard Grant in one 1955 segment.

(Below) KITTY FOYLE: Billy Redfield, Kathleen Murray, Ralph Dunne, and Ginger MacManus were involved in this one.

(*Above*) THE GUIDING LIGHT: It premiered in 1952 and hasn't run out of suds yet. By 1955 the personnel included Glenn Walken, Charita Bauer, and Lyle Sudrow.

(*Top, left*) WAY OF THE WORLD: These were disconnected daily dramas, rather than continuing serial episodes. Tom Tryon and Sarah Marshall appeared together in a 1955 chapter.

(*Left*) FROM THESE ROOTS: David Sanders and Ann Flood were engaged in 1958.

(*Below*) TODAY IS OURS: Patricia Benoit, Peter Lazer, Joyce Lear, and Patrick O'Neal had leading roles.

AS THE WORLD TURNS: This has become the *Bonanza* of daytime television—consistently the top-rated daytime program, week after week, year after year. Whatever women are looking for in their soap operas, *As the World Turns* seems to have it. It was put there by Irna Philips, whose success as creator and writer of this unique form of dramaturgy has earned her the title "Queen of the Soaps." One of the key roles in the show, Penny Hughes Baker, is played by Rosemary Prinz (pictured here). *As the World Turns* and *The Edge of Night,* which were unveiled the same day in 1956, were the first half-hour soap operas. Their success sparked a trend to thirty-minute daytime dramas.

354 /

THE EDGE OF NIGHT: This too has been an extremely popular serial. Its two central figures in the early days were played by John Larkin and Teal Ames, but both left the show in the early sixties to try their luck elsewhere. When Miss Ames was written out of the script—she was "killed" in an auto accident—shocked viewers deluged CBS with one of the largest floods of mail in the network's history. Larkin, who was replaced by another actor (Laurence Hugo), went to Hollywood, where he made a few movies and numerous television shows. He died in 1965.

(Above) YOUNG DOCTOR MALONE: Medical series were tried as daily half-hour serials in the 1960's, after *Ben Casey* and *Dr. Kildare* had proved their drawing power as hour-long nighttime dramas. This one starred (clockwise from upper left) John Connell, Freda Holloway, Augusta Dabney, and William Prince.

(Top, left) THE CLEAR HORIZON: The soap opera entered the Space Age with this 1962 effort, which was supposedly set at Cape Canaveral. (Actually it was made in Hollywood, as the movie capital broke New York's hold on soap-opera production.) Ed Kemmer and Phyllis Avery impersonated an air force captain and his wife.

(Left) MOMENT OF TRUTH: NBC, still attempting to break CBS's daytime monopoly, tried out a number of soap operas in the mid-sixties. This was one, with Douglas Watson and Louise King.

(Bottom, left) ANOTHER WORLD: This was another, with Susan Trustman, Michael Ryan, and Jacquie Courtney.

(Below) THE DOCTORS: Another medical saga, with James Pritchett (seated), Adam Kennedy, Ellen McRae, Elizabeth Hubbard, and Gerald O'Loughlin.

The Children's Hour

SEVERAL YEARS AGO, cereal manufacturers discovered the value of sugarcoating. Though mothers might prefer that their tykes start the day with a steaming bowl of oatmeal, most of the youngsters opted for the gaily-packaged, sugarcoated flakes and pellets. The kids generally won out, since mothers could console themselves with the fact that sugarcoated cereals were, after all, nourishing and healthful.

Producers of children's television programs were early converts to the philosophy of sugarcoating. Teachers, parents, and pressure groups insisted on at least a minimum of educational nourishment in children's programming, but the children wanted only to be entertained. Television learned to satisfy both, by providing entertainment leavened with occasional nuggets of information or education. Though such shows were few in number, they stilled the clamor of the protesters. And if critics pointed out that the overwhelming majority of children's programs were of the spun-sugar variety, television could always point to the educational stations, which served a constant diet of oatmeal.

Although most children's programs are uncomplicated in structure, it is usually difficult (for adults, at least) to decide why some are popular and others are not. There have been dozens of animal series, but none ever kindled the same kind of enthusiasm as *Lassie*. Puppets and marionettes have appeared by the score, but none ever approximated the hysterical reaction to *Howdy Doody*. Kindly old father figures have long dotted the television landscape, but none could ever match the long-running success of *Captain Kangaroo. Kukla, Fran and Ollie* and Shari Lewis could thrive on gentle whimsey, yet *The Three Stooges* could achieve equal prominence without ever being accused of subtlety. And who can define the secret ingredients that make an instant triumph of almost anything created by Walt Disney? Successful adult programs can often be subjected to some kind of logical analysis; the same kind of analysis, when applied to popular children's shows, trails off into phrases such as "a special kind of magic" or "that indefinable small-fry appeal."

Recent criticism of children's television has been aimed at commercials rather than program content. Though most of the high-pressure "get mommy to buy it for you" advertisements have disappeared, high-priced (up to $49.50) toys and war toys still turn up in the pre-Christmas ad campaigns. They invariably draw howls of outrage.

In 1966, a New York City survey disclosed that some three thousand children under the age of six were nightly viewers of *The Tonight Show* and the late movie. Why these tots watch television at midnight is yet to be explained, but perhaps, like many children's programs, it is a phenomenon that defies explanation.

THE CHILDREN'S HOUR/*Introduction*

CAPTAIN KANGAROO:

Bob Keeshan donned a uniform cap and a walrus mustache in 1955 when he became the Captain, and thus began a long reign as the dominant figure in preschool children's programming. Until that time most children's shows, with a few notable exceptions, had been loud, gaudy, and rather limited in creative imagination. (Keeshan himself had once served as Clarabell on the *Howdy Doody Show*.) *Captain Kangaroo* was an abrupt departure from the past. Its emphasis was on quiet conversation, gentle fantasy, and easy-to-swallow morsels of an educational nature. The program's acceptance and popularity seemed to grow with each passing year, as did the number of awards and citations from groups of parents, teachers, and educators.

KUKLA, FRAN AND OLLIE: Burr Tillstrom's puppets arrived on national television in 1949, although they had been seen locally (in Chicago) prior to that time. Fran Allison served as the human member of the troupe of Kuklapolitans, which also numbered among its members puppets named Buelah Witch, Dolores Dragon, Colonel Crackie, Madame Ooglepuss, and Fletcher Rabbit. Though the program was designed primarily as charming fantasy for children, its audience also included a considerable number of adult partisans.

MR. I. MAGINATION: Paul Tripp was the creator and principal performer on this show, which made its debut in 1949. Here he waits at the gates of Imagination Town, a magical place where any child's wishes would come true.

LASSIE:

Though there have been three major cast revisions since this show went on the air in 1955, its popularity as a children's adventure story never diminishes. The formula for the show has been a simple one: an intelligent and brave collie dog triumphs over evil and adversity. (A wag once insisted that all *Lassie* programs could be reduced to two lines of dialogue. Lassie: "Arf." Man: "I think she's trying to tell us something!") During the course of its run, Lassie's four families have been (bottom, right) George Cleveland as Gramps, Jan Clayton as Jeff's mother, and Tommy Rettig as Jeff; (center) Jon Shepodd and Cloris Leachman as the parents, Jon Provost as Timmy; (below) June Lockhart and Hugh Reilly as the parents, Jon Provost as Timmy; (top) Robert Bray as Ranger Corey Stuart.

WALT DISNEY'S

original contribution to television was *Disneyland,* which made its debut in 1954. It was a mixture of cartoons, nature films, action and adventure stories, and educational features, all stirred together by the hand of the master entertainer. The following year Disney introduced *The Mickey Mouse Club,* complete with club song and mouse-eared beanies.

/ 361

(Above) Jimmie Dodd leads the Mouseketeers on *The Mickey Mouse Club.*

(Left) Disney with Garco the robot, on a *Disneyland* episode entitled "Mars and Beyond."

(Below) Fess Parker as Davy Crockett on *Disneyland.*

(Above) CAPTAIN VIDEO: This was probably the first of the early space shows (1949) and undoubtedly influenced many of those that followed, especially in its use of far-out weaponry and Flash Gordon-type uniforms. Al Hodge played the intrepid Captain Video.

(Top, right) ROD BROWN OF THE ROCKET RANGERS: Cliff Robertson was the hero of this celestial action series which debuted in 1953.

(Right) CAPTAIN Z-RO: Roy Steffens wrote and played the lead in this early syndicated series. The Captain had the patent on a set of machines which enabled him to show up anywhere and at any time in history.

(Below) TOM CORBETT, SPACE CADET: This interplanetary adventure was set in the year 2355, with Frankie Thomas in the role of Corbett. It premiered in 1950.

(Above) ATOM SQUAD: This space opera, circa 1953, featured Bob Hastings (left) and Bob Courtleigh. In a typical episode the men of the Atom Squad foiled the villains who were trying to throw the earth out of orbit.

(Top, left) JET JACKSON, FLYING COMMANDO: At least that was what it was called in some markets; in other areas it was *Captain Midnight*. Featured were Sid Melton (left) and Richard Webb.

(Left) COMMANDO CODY: Judd Holdren played Cody, Sky Marshal of the Universe, in this series first seen in 1955. He is shown here with his assistant Joan (Aline Towne) as they prepare to battle a mad scientist.

(Bottom, left) SPACE PATROL: Ed Kemmer (top) was Commander Buzz Corry and Lyn Osborn was Cadet Happy in this science-fiction series shown in the early fifties.

(Below) ROCKY JONES, SPACE RANGER: Richard Crane was Rocky in another mixture of planets, rockets, and infernal machines.

(Above) THE FLINTSTONES: An early Hanna-Barbera show, this was a lampoon of the prehistoric scene. The futuristic counterpart of this series, *The Jetsons,* also had a successful television run.

(Top, right) YOGI BEAR: Another Hanna-Barbera creation, Yogi was "smarter than the average bear."

(Right) BEANY AND CECIL: Bob Clampett was the artist; he was also responsible for an earlier, non-cartoon version of Beany, the seasick serpent.

(Right, second from bottom) GERALD McBOING-BOING: The lad who used sound effects instead of speech had long been a motion picture favorite.

(Bottom, right) BUGS BUNNY: The rabbit outwitted all pursuers, pausing only to say, "What's up, Doc?"

(Below) THE BEATLES: This 1965 cartoon version of the mopheads was a consistent high scorer in the ratings.

(Bottom) ROCKY AND HIS FRIENDS: Jay Ward was the comedy mastermind behind this series, which delighted adults as well as youngsters. Shown (left to right) are Boris Badenov, Bullwinkle Moose, and Rocky.

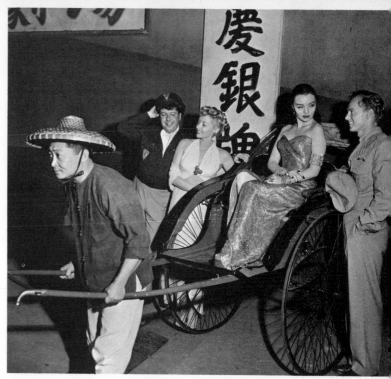

(Above) FLASH GORDON: This comic strip adapted for television featured Steve Holland as Flash.

(Below) SUPERMAN: He was able to leap tall buildings in a single bound. This syndicated version of the famous comic strip first appeared in 1950. Featured in the cast were (left to right) Jack Larson as Jimmy, John Hamilton as editor Perry White, Noel Neill as Lois Lane, and George Reeves as the Man of Steel.

(Above) TERRY AND THE PIRATES: This comics feature, originated by Milton Caniff, arrived on television in the early fifties. Featured were William Tracy (far left) as Hotshot Charlie, Gloria Saunders (in the rickshaw) as the Dragon Lady, and John Baer (far right) as Terry.

(Above) THE SINGING LADY: Ireene Wicker, who had starred in this program during its radio days, brought it to television in 1949.

(Top, right) VERSATILE VARIETIES: The storyteller and hostess was Lady Iris Mountbatten (first cousin to Viscount Louis Mountbatten and third cousin to King George VI). The show was seen in the early fifties.

(Right) SMILIN' ED'S GANG: Genial Ed McConnell was the spinner of tales on this show, first telecast in 1954.

(Right, second from bottom) MAGIC COTTAGE: Pat Meikle was starred on this early children's program shown on the DuMont network.

(Bottom, right) UNCLE JOHNNY COONS: Johnny Coons was the star and solo performer on this show, which featured tall tales, old-time movies, and odd hats.

(Below) ANDY'S GANG: In 1957 Andy Devine replaced Smilin' Ed. He is shown with Nino Marcel, who played Gunga Ram, an elephant boy.

HOWDY DOODY

was first telecast in 1947 and remained on the air until 1960. The show was a loud and lively entertainment effort, and although it made no pretense of being anything else, parents sometimes complained that the program had no redeeming educational value. Buffalo Bob Smith was the creator and host of the show, assisted by a succession of clowns named Clarabell. Since children who attended the telecasts often appeared on camera, the demand for tickets was overwhelming, and the waiting list a long one. At one time, it was said, expectant mothers would write to request tickets for their unborn children.

(Left) The original Howdy Doody as the audience saw him in the first six weeks of the television show, before his contours were changed.

(Below) With youngsters in the "peanut gallery" behind them, Bob Smith, Howdy, and Clarabell celebrate the show's tenth anniversary.

(Above) SHARI LEWIS: First seen on *Hi, Mom* in 1957, Miss Lewis and her puppets (Lamb Chop and Charlie Horse) later appeared on the *Shari Lewis Show*. A versatile entertainer, Miss Lewis is an accomplished singer and dancer as well as a ventriloquist.

(Top, right) JUDY SPLINTERS: Shirley Dinsdale was the puppeteer on this Hollywood-based kiddie program. It was seen in the late forties and early fifties and was twice awarded an Emmy.

(Right) JIMMY NELSON AND DANNY O'DAY: This twosome made many appearances on early television, including a stint as commercial salesmen on Milton Berle's *Texaco Star Theater*.

(Below) LUCKY PUP: Puppeteers Hope and Morey Bunin operated Pinhead and Foodini, the stars of the show. The program was on the air in 1948 and remained a children's favorite for many years.

(*Above*) ROOTIE KAZOOTIE: Todd Russell and his lineup of puppets, including (left to right) Rootie Kazootie, El Squeako Mouse, Gala Poochie, and Polka Dottie, were the stars of this show, which debuted in 1950.

(*Left*) JOHNNY JUPITER: Wright King played a general-store clerk who invented interplanetary television, thus sparking his friendship with a puppet named Johnny Jupiter.

(*Bottom, left*) CHILDREN'S CORNER: Josie Carey was the only live member of the performing troupe on this 1955 show.

(*Below*) FUNNY BONERS: This was a children's stunt show, which featured ventriloquist Jimmy Weldon and a talkative duck, Webster Webfoot.

(Above) FLIPPER: A dolphin is the hero of this adventure series, which debuted in 1964. The human cast supporting Flipper included Brian Kelly, Tommy Norden, and Luke Halpin.

(Right) RIN TIN TIN: The action took place in Fort Apache and the stars were Rin Tin Tin (a magnificent German Shepherd) and Rusty (played by ten-year-old Lee Aaker). The series was first telecast in 1954.

(Below) FURY: In these tales of a boy and his horse, the boy was Bobby Diamond, the horse Fury, and the cast included Peter Graves (far left) and William Fawcett (far right).

(Above) NATIONAL VELVET: These tales of a girl (shown here with a rabbit) and her horse came along in 1960. Lori Martin starred as Velvet Brown, the role that brought motion-picture fame to Elizabeth Taylor; the horse was King.

(Right) DAKTARI: The girl is Cheryl Miller, and the cross-eyed lion is Clarence in this jungle story which debuted in 1966.

(Below) MY FRIEND FLICKA: Another boy (Johnny Washbrook) and another horse (Flicka) were featured in this series based on the book by Mary O'Hara. The show was first aired in 1957 and also featured Gene Evans (far left) and Anita Louise.

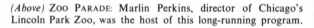

(Above) ZOO PARADE: Marlin Perkins, director of Chicago's Lincoln Park Zoo, was the host of this long-running program.

(Right) MR. WIZARD: One of the first (and best) of the educational shows for youngsters had Don Herbert (left) as Mr. Wizard, the science instructor; his young assistant was Bruce Lindgren.

(Bottom, right) EXPLORING: Dr. Albert Hibbs was the guide on these educational forays.

(Below) WHAT'S NEW: This series is presented by the National Educational Television network. In this episode, exploring the history of the riverboat, Charles Murphy (left) played Captain Dan and Rouen Caboche was Jimmy.

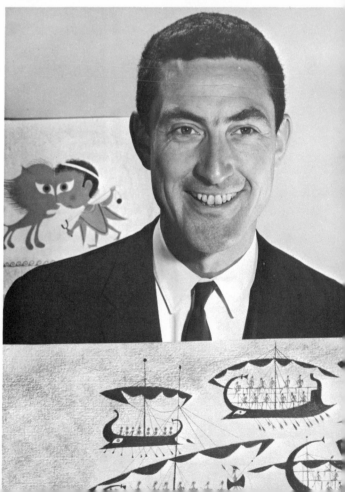

(*Above*) WINKY DINK AND YOU: Jack Barry was the host of a program which began in 1953 and encouraged children's at-home participation.

(*Right*) DING DONG SCHOOL: Designed for preschoolers, this show featured the conversation and instruction of Miss Frances (Dr. Frances Horwich). It was first telecast in 1952.

(*Bottom, right*) DISCOVERY: Virginia Gibson and Frank Buxton are the co-hosts on these educational adventures for children. Below, they take a trip to the Foo Hsing Theater.

(*Below*) LET'S TAKE A TRIP: Sonny Fox was the guide on this series of excursions to all parts of the world. His two companions were Ginger McManus (left) and Brian "Pud" Flanagan. The show was a 1955 entry. When it ended, Fox became host of *Wonderama*, a popular children's show in New York City.

(Above) DENNIS THE MENACE: Jay North was the mischievous Dennis (shown here with George Cisar) in the television version of Hank Ketcham's cartoon.

(Below) CAPTAIN GALLANT OF THE FOREIGN LEGION: Former Olympic star Buster Crabbe and his son Cuffy were the featured performers in this series, which made its first appearance in 1955.

(Bottom) SGT. PRESTON OF THE YUKON: As the Mountie in the Yukon, Richard Simmons was accompanied by his horse Rex and his dog Yukon King in this show which debuted in 1955.

(Top) LITTLE RASCALS: The old "Our Gang" movie shorts became a syndicated television package with a new title. They also became a smash hit all over again. Yes, that's Jackie Cooper (third from left).

(Above) SKY KING: Sky King (Kirby Grant) was television's first flying cowboy. He is shown here with his niece Penny (Gloria Winters).

(Below) THE THREE STOOGES: They were (left to right) Joe De Rita, Moe Howard, and Larry Fine, and their television appearances revived an act that had long been a favorite of young moviegoers.

(Above) ON YOUR MARK: Sonny Fox was host of a children's series which appeared first in 1961.

(Below) PIP THE PIPER: The residents of Pipertown included (left to right) The Leader (Lucian Kaminsky), Pip (Jack Spear), and Miss Merry Note (Phyllis Spear).

(Bottom) KIDS AND COMPANY: Cartoonist Ham Fisher (creator of "Joe Palooka") and Johnny Olsen were hosts on this early DuMont series.

(Top) CHOOSE UP SIDES: This was a fun-and-games show for the small fry, emceed by Gene Rayburn (getting into the spirit of things, at right).

(Above) THE UNCLE AL SHOW: Music, stories, and puppets were featured on this show, which was first seen in 1958. The cast included (left to right) Wanda Lewis, Uncle Al Lewis, Larry Smith, and Janet Greene.

(Below) GUMBY: Gumby was the tiny plastic clay hero of this 1957 show, and he was joined by Bobby Nicholson in the "Fun Spot."

(Above) BIG TOP: Jack Sterling (left) was the ringmaster of "the biggest circus show on television." Ed McMahon, later to become Johnny Carson's straight man and announcer, served as a clown (right) on the show, which debuted in 1950.

(Left, top) INTERNATIONAL SHOWTIME: Featured were circus acts from around the world, with Don Ameche as the host.

(Left) THE MAGIC CLOWN: Tricks, games, and prizes were the specialities of a prestidigitator named Zovella, who played the Clown in this show, which ran from 1949 to 1954.

(Bottom, left) SUPER CIRCUS: One of the earliest circus extravaganzas (1949), this one boasted Claude Kirchner (rear) as the ringmaster, Mary Hartline as a spectacular bandleader, and clowns Scampy, Cliffy, and Nicky.

(Below, center) CIRCUS BOY: Mickey Braddock starred in the adventures of Corky, a boy adopted by a circus troupe at the turn of the century. The series was first presented in 1956.

(Below, right) CIRCUS TIME: Another 1956 show, this one featured circus acts, with ventriloquist Paul Winchell and his dummy Jerry Mahoney as the hosts.

SOUPY SALES:
He started with a local show in Detroit *(Soupy's On)*, graduated to a network program, and finally landed in New York, where he launched a daily local show that was syndicated widely. Soupy's specialties are the pie in the face (at least one a show, sometimes dozens); outrageous riddles, puns, and old jokes; and conversations with his animal friends (here, he is caressed by Black Tooth, "the kindest dog in the country"). He has always been a favorite of the youngsters, but recently he has also become "in" with the hipster set.

The Real World

DURING THE FIRST *See It Now* telecast, in 1951, Edward R. Murrow showed a view of the Atlantic Ocean, then one of the Pacific, both on live television. "We are impressed," said Murrow, "by a medium in which a man sitting in his living room has been able for the first time to look at two oceans at once."

In the years that followed, looking at two oceans has become child's play. Viewers have been able to see virtually everything that lies between those seas and beyond them. Television has brought the whole world into our living rooms.

For most of us television has become the primary source of news and information about our world. Daily newscasts give us the headlines and some sidelights. Documentary films take us to every corner of the globe and show us what is behind the headlines.

We have all become eyewitnesses to history. Whereas we used to read about current events described in the past tense, we can now watch many of them taking place. We are spectators at political conventions, United Nations debates, civil-rights confrontations, Congressional hearings, news conferences, spaceship launchings and recoveries.

From television we learn about the arts and sciences, take educational courses, receive religious instruction, and watch every conceivable type of sports event—and some that are inconceivable.

The leaders of our nation and the rest of the world are no longer just disembodied radio voices or shadows glimpsed briefly in movie newsreels or still photographs. We see them as they are. Through television they visit us in our homes, talk to us, try to persuade us, and sometimes try to fool us. Often they reveal more of themselves than they would like.

We have been transported to China, India, Vietnam, Berlin, Paris, Leopoldville, Santo Domingo, Bogalusa; we have been inside the White House, the Kremlin, the Vatican, the Louvre, mental hospitals, bookie joints, football locker rooms; we have viewed current wars and reviewed past ones; we have journeyed back through time into the worlds and minds of Leonardo, Van Gogh, Beethoven, Columbus, Lincoln, Shakespeare, Mark Twain, and Jesus Christ; we have seen sights we never knew existed, observed the people who control our destinies, and listened to wise men and fools exchange ideas.

No place on earth is farther away than the nearest television set. No human being is immune to the penetrating scrutiny of the television camera. Television's powers of enlightenment are limitless, and it is still learning how to use them. By bringing the real world into our homes, television is subtly but profoundly altering the shape of that world.

There are still millions of people in this broad land of ours who have never seen the Atlantic and Pacific Oceans except on their television screens. But they have seen things even more wondrous on those screens—places and people, beauty and horror, hope and despair, crises and trivia—the essence of life in the twentieth century. We too are impressed.

THE REAL WORLD/*Introduction*

(*Above*) JOHN CAMERON SWAYZE: He moved from radio to television in 1948, to telecast that summer's Presidential conventions. That autumn he started a daily newscast, *Camel News Caravan,* which was an early-evening NBC fixture until 1956, when *The Huntley-Brinkley Report* dislodged it. Swayze continued to use his opening phrase, "And a good evening to you," and his closing line, "Glad we could get together," in later stints as panel-show host and commercial announcer.

(*Below*) DOUGLAS EDWARDS: He was the first major radio newscaster to switch to television, making the transition in 1947. In August of 1948 he began a daily early-evening newscast on CBS, *Douglas Edwards with the News,* which remained on the air until 1962, when Walter Cronkite displaced Edwards.

(*Above*) DREW PEARSON: The controversial Washington columnist appeared on television in the early days. His *Washington Merry-Go-Round,* featuring "predictions of things to come," was a twice-a-week DuMont show.

(*Below*) WALTER WINCHELL: Another combative columnist, Winchell tried just about everything on television, but as the medium progressed he seemed to become a quaint anachronism. In 1952 he conducted a television version of his highly opinionated radio news show ("Good evening, Mr. and Mrs. North America, and all the ships at sea . . ."). He left the air in 1955, after a dispute with Robert Kintner, then president of ABC, but was back a year later with a short-lived variety series. In 1957 it was *The Walter Winchell File,* a melodrama series he narrated, and in 1960 he tried the variety format again. His last major assignment on television was as the unseen narrator of *The Untouchables.*

EDWARD R. MURROW

led television news out of infancy and into maturity, ushering it from the confines of the newsroom into the whole wide world. When he died in 1965, Murrow's longtime associate Fred W. Friendly said, "His standards will continue to be those by which we measure ourselves." They are the standards Murrow set with his pioneering *See It Now* series, which enriched the lives and improved the minds of millions of Americans from 1951 to 1958. *See It Now* was television's first news-documentary series, combining film footage and live commentary to tell its news stories—creating a form which has been used ever since by television documentarians. After *See It Now* was canceled in 1958, Murrow, disgusted with television's "decadence and escapism," appeared much less frequently on the medium. He left it completely in 1961 to become head of the United States Information Agency. His portentous voice, furrowed brow, and uplifted left hand with its ever-present cigarette will always be remembered, as will his opening "This . . . is the news" and closing "Good-night, and good luck." But Murrow once expressed a wish to be remembered in a different context. In his most famous *See It Now* program, on April 6, 1954, Murrow attacked Senator Joseph McCarthy. ("This is no time for men who oppose Senator McCarthy's methods to keep silent," he said.) CBS gave McCarthy air time to reply, and McCarthy used it for a personal attack on Murrow's integrity. It was then that Murrow said, "When the record is finally written, as it will be one day, it will answer the question who has helped the Communist cause and who has served his country better, Senator McCarthy or I. I would like to be remembered by the answer to that question." And so he is.

(Above) Person to Person, in which Murrow "visited" celebrities' homes electronically, began in 1953. (An offshoot of this was a filmed, continent-hopping discussion series, *Small World,* which Murrow did in 1958 and 1959.)

(Right) Murrow appeared in a few episodes of *CBS Reports.* This is a scene from the first *CBS Reports* program—"Biography of a Missile," in 1959.

(Below) Throughout his television career Murrow teamed with Fred Friendly, who produced *See It Now* and *CBS Reports* and ultimately was named president of CBS News (he resigned in 1966 after a bitter battle with the front office).

(*Above*) He interviewed many world leaders, among them David Ben-Gurion in Israel in 1956.

(*Top, left*) In 1956, on *Person to Person,* the Duchess of Windsor played jacks, while the Duke looked on noncommittally.

(*Bottom, left*) For *See It Now's* "This is Korea . . . Xmas '52" Murrow went to the battlefront.

(*Below*) *See It Now* liked to focus on one small aspect of a larger issue, to bring it into sharper focus. In 1955 Murrow covered a school-board election in Jefferson County, Colorado.

HUNTLEY AND BRINKLEY:

"One is solemn, the other twinkly," rhymed "Newsweek" after these two news commentators had become one of television's biggest attractions and had broken CBS's traditional hold on the news-watching audience. The solemn one is Chet Huntley (left), a newsman in the Murrow mold. The twinkly one—actually, "wry" is the adjective most often applied to him—is David Brinkley. After years of obscurity (Huntley had worked, without notice, for both ABC and CBS; Brinkley had been with NBC since 1943), they were teamed up for the 1956 Presidential convention, and two television-news stars were born. Viewers found their easygoing palaver a refreshing change from the sobersided commentary which characterized CBS's news shows (and NBC's earlier efforts too). NBC was so pleased with the result that the pairing was made permanent. *The Huntley-Brinkley Report* began in the fall of 1956 and was expanded from fifteen minutes daily to thirty in 1963.

WALTER CRONKITE:

Unable to compete with Huntley and Brinkley on their own terms, CBS turned to a solid, hard-working journalist, Walter Cronkite. What he lacks in color, he makes up for in thoroughness, resourcefulness, and knowledgability. He is CBS's "anchor man"—the man who can sit at the center of an unpredictable, fast-breaking, complex news event (a convention, an election night, a space mission) and hold everything together, hour after hour, without wilting and without boring his audience. In 1962 he was placed in direct competition with Huntley and Brinkley five nights a week (as well as at special events), when he was tapped to conduct his network's early-evening newscasts. He has held his own nicely. Since joining CBS in 1950, Cronkite has also served as narrator of *You Are There, The Twentieth Century, Eyewitness to History,* and numerous *CBS Reports* programs and other news specials.

(*Above*) ROBERT TROUT: Some of radio's old-timers have managed the transition to television with ease. This urbane veteran, who joined CBS in 1932, is one of them.

(*Above*) ERIC SEVAREID: He has become television's foremost pundit—indeed, virtually the only one—in a medium which frowns on expressions of opinion by its newsmen.

(*Below*) LISA HOWARD: Women too have found a place in television news. Lisa Howard, who quit an acting career to become a newswoman, scored several notable scoops, including exclusive interviews with Khrushchev and Castro, before her death in 1965. Other women who have succeeded in television newscasting include United Nations expert Pauline Frederick and Washington correspondent Nancy Hanschman Dickerson.

(*Below*) FRANK MCGEE: Although many of television's journalists are converted radio reporters or newspapermen, the medium has also bred a substantial number of skilled craftsmen of its own. One of the most prominent is Frank McGee, who started his news career in television and rapidly moved to the top of his profession.

KEFAUVER CRIME COMMITTEE HEARINGS: Television's most electrifying moments have come during those telecasts—like the conventions and debates—through which viewers have been able to watch history being made right before their eyes. An early instance was the Kefauver Committee hearings into crime in America, telecast live during 1951. The broadcasts made television stars of such diverse figures as Senator Estes Kefauver, Senator Charles Tobey, Rudolph Halley, Virginia Hill, and Frank Costello. Costello's face was never shown—he insisted on this degree of privacy—but his hands performed an unforgettable television ballet as his testimony progressed. The hearings also introduced many people to the contents of the Fifth Amendment to the Constitution; it was invoked repeatedly by witnesses.

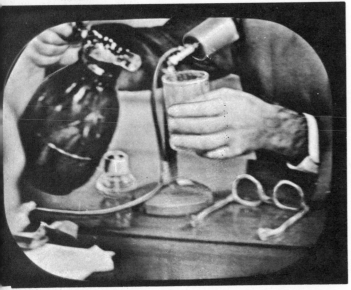

(Above) ARMY-MCCARTHY HEARINGS: In addition to providing news and drama, telecasts of live events can give the audience decisive insights into the minds and characters of the dramatis personae of those events. A classic example is the Army-McCarthy Hearings of 1954, which gave many viewers their first good look at the shadowy figure who was stirring up a stormy controversy all across the nation—Senator Joseph McCarthy. What they learned about McCarthy during the hearings eventually brought about his downfall. Many analysts believe that the turning point in McCarthy's career was the moment when, in view of a watching nation, Joseph N. Welch, the mild-mannered Boston lawyer, turned on McCarthy and cried out, "Have you no sense of decency, sir? At long last, have you left no sense of decency?" An abundance of fascinating supporting players performed with McCarthy and Welch, Roy Cohn, G. David Schine, chief counsel Ray Jenkins, Senators John McClellan, Karl Mundt, and Stuart Symington, Secretary of the Army Robert T. B. Stevens, and many others.

(Below) QUEEN ELIZABETH'S CORONATION: In 1953 the networks raced to be first on the air with BBC kinescopes, jetted across the Atlantic, of the coronation of Britain's new monarch.

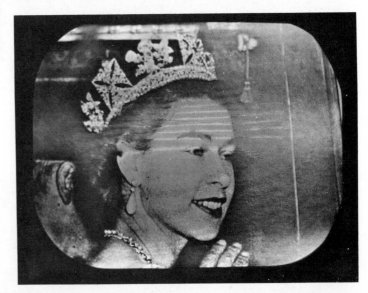

(Above) CHURCHILL FUNERAL: Communications satellites added a new dimension to live coverage. In January, 1965, as the world mourned the death of Sir Winston Churchill, portions of the funeral ceremonies were relayed from London via satellite.

(Below) PAPAL VISIT: Later that year Pope Paul VI came to New York for a day, to address the United Nations, and television cameras followed him every step of the way. Here, near the close of his visit, he presides over a mass at Yankee Stadium.

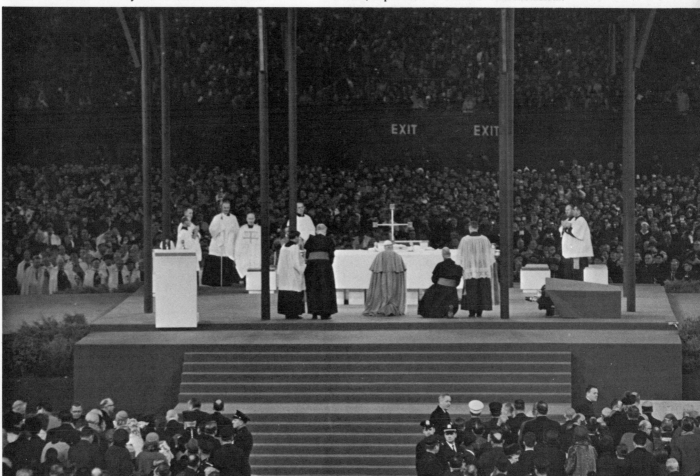

That quadrennial madness, the Presidential convention, in all of its pageantry and buffoonery, has been shown to a fascinated electorate since 1948, when a small band of television novices brought the sights and sounds of that year's political conclaves to set owners. As the years passed, television itself played a larger and larger role in the conventions. The events on the floor were

(Left) Ed Murrow, Walter Cronkite, and Lowell Thomas participated in CBS's coverage of the 1952, 1956, and 1960 conventions.

(Above) MEET THE PRESS: Television's best-known and longest-running interview series started in 1947. This was a 1951 program, with Senator Joseph McCarthy as the guest. Martha Rountree was *Meet the Press's* moderator at that time; Ned Brooks replaced her later. Lawrence E. Spivak is the show's permanent panelist, producer, and most relentless inquisitor.

(Below) FACE THE NATION: Premiering in 1954, this was CBS's answer to NBC's *Meet the Press*. Here Dave Beck, then president of the Teamsters Union, is grilled.

(Above) AMERICA'S TOWN MEETING: This was one of television's earliest discussion shows, moderated first by George V. Denny, then, beginning in 1952, by John Daly (pictured here). Daly, one of television's pioneer newsmen, arrived on the scene in 1949. For twelve years he, almost literally, *was* ABC News. He conducted a nightly newscast, covered conventions and other special events, narrated documentaries, and, from 1953 to 1961, ran the news department as an ABC vice president. In 1961 the network began to place more emphasis on news, the department was reorganized, and Daly resigned.

timed to take advantage of the presence of the television audience. Reporters and cameramen swarmed over the convention halls, decked out in Martianesque electronic equipment, buttonholing delegates, elbowing each other, and turning the conventions into a razzle-dazzle television show, complete with heroes and villains, stars and character actors, matinee idols and clowns.

(Right) David Brinkley (left) and Chet Huntley put new life into NBC's convention coverage in 1956 and continued as a team in 1960 and 1964. They are shown here at the Los Angeles Sports Arena just before the Democratic convention began in 1960.

(Right) OPEN END: Producer David Susskind was not sure what he was getting into when he became a television performer in 1958. His first *Open End* show was a floundering account, with remote-camera pickups, of the Broadway opening of "The World of Suzy Wong." The next week Susskind experimented with a different format—a kaffeeklatsch. It proved a winning formula, and Susskind stuck with it, presiding over round-table discussions which lasted for hours (in later years for just one hour). Occasionally Susskind has tried going it alone with just one guest—most infamously in 1960, when he found himself eyeball to eyeball with Nikita Khrushchev. The embarrassingly inept interview degenerated into a debate and an exchange of insults.

(Right) MIKE WALLACE INTERVIEWS: Until Wallace came along in the mid-fifties, interview shows tended to be innocuous exchanges of questions and answers. Wallace changed all that, first on a local New York show called *Nightbeat*, then (and with less success) on a weekly ABC show. Wallace's questions were candid, sharp, and sometimes rude. They elicited answers that were often startling and almost invariably revealing. The Wallace show eventually died, but his hard-hitting approach was adopted by other television interviewers.

THE GREAT DEBATES:

During the 1960 Presidential campaign the two candidates, Democrat John F. Kennedy and Republican Richard M. Nixon, competed for votes in a series of four debates, telecast to the nation by all three networks. These scenes are from the first "Great Debate" (moderated by Howard K. Smith), which some analysts believe turned the political tide in Kennedy's favor. Nixon, in a light suit, badly lit, without makeup, and perspiring under the hot lights, did not make the forceful impression his supporters had hoped for. Kennedy, on the other hand, seemed more at ease and projected exactly the image that his partisans wished to convey. Nixon learned from his mistakes and performed much more impressively in the later debates, but it is generally conceded that the first debate lost him some votes which he never regained. Whatever the effect of the debates on that particular election, there is no doubt that they have had a profound impact on the conduct of later political campaigns. Televised debates between candidates for local and state offices have become commonplace, and nominees are chosen today with an eye toward the impression they can be expected to make on television.

(Above) NEWS CONFERENCES: Before television came along, Presidential press conferences were disembodied events reported in the third person in the newspapers. President Eisenhower changed that when he permitted his conferences to be filmed and shown later on television. President Kennedy carried things a step further and invited live coverage of his conferences. Here he is during one of them.

(Below) CUBAN CRISIS: Critical events in one of the most perilous episodes in world history were played out on television. The night of October 22, 1962, President Kennedy took to the air to tell the nation about the danger of Soviet missiles in Cuba and what he intended to do about it.

(Below) STEVENSON'S CHALLENGE: During the missile crisis, viewers saw United Nations Ambassador Adlai Stevenson challenge Valerian Zorin, the Soviet delegate, to deny the presence of the missiles in Cuba. This was one of many historic United Nations episodes which have been telecast.

(Above) In front of the White House Jacqueline Kennedy, Caroline, and John, Jr. waited for a car to take them to the Capitol rotunda, where the late President lay in state.

(Right) Just minutes earlier Lee Harvey Oswald had been shot by Jack Ruby, in full view of the television audience.

THE ASSASSINATION OF PRESIDENT KENNEDY: The horrifying news . . . the forlorn hope . . . the chilling confirmation of the President's death . . . a bouquet of roses . . . the last films of a smiling, waving young man, full of life . . . the first pictures of a morose, defiant young man charged with murder . . . a coffin . . . a blood-stained pink suit . . . a new President . . . an incredible murder in a police station . . . the face of a young widow . . . muffled drums . . . a riderless horse . . . a piteous kiss . . . an endless line of mourners . . . a cardinal droning . . . a child's salute . . . the folding of a flag . . . an eternal flame. The events and the emotions of those awful four days in November, 1963, have become an ineradicable part of the memories of millions of viewers. For four days there was nothing on television but the pictures and sounds of the aftermath of the assassination of John F. Kennedy. The American people sat—stunned, heartsick, and fascinated—in front of their television sets, watching the harrowing drama unfold. It was an almost unendurable experience, but one hundred and ninety million Americans endured it, then began to live again.

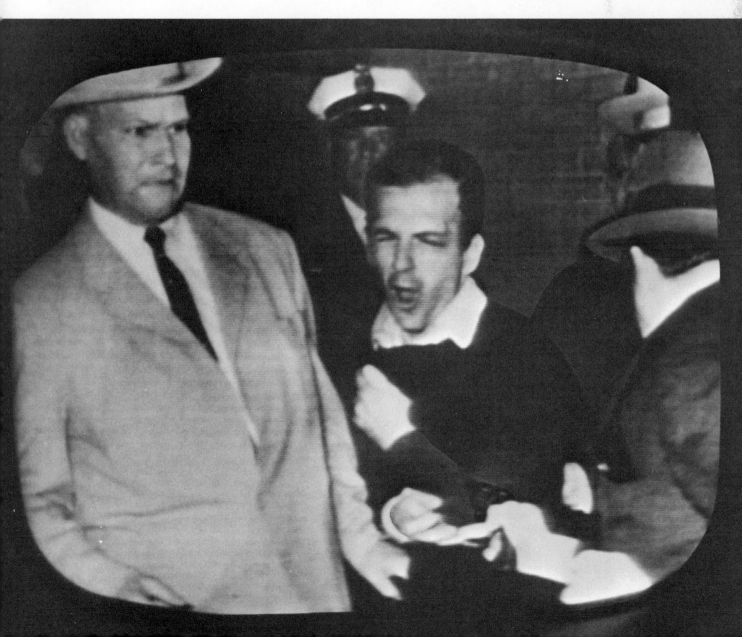

(Above) THE AMERICAN REVOLUTION OF '63: Civil rights became a burning issue during the sixties, and a large portion of the output of television's news departments dealt with the problems of the American Negro. In 1963 NBC devoted three hours of a September evening to an in-depth study of "The American Revolution of '63."

(Below) KKK—THE INVISIBLE EMPIRE: CBS Reports examined the Ku Klux Klan in 1965. The program was produced by the late David Lowe, who had also been responsible for "Harvest of Shame" (about migrant workers) and several other highly acclaimed documentaries.

(Below) HISTORY OF THE NEGRO PEOPLE: A broader approach was taken by this National Educational Television series, which explained the plight of 1965's Negro by recounting earlier history and describing the life of Negroes in other countries. This scene is from an episode filmed in Brazil.

394 /

(Right) THE BATTLE OF NEWBURGH: Other national problems were also brought to viewers' attention by television. This *NBC White Paper* focused on Newburgh, New York, where the city manager had provoked a national controversy by denying welfare payments to families like this one.

(Center, right) SIXTEEN IN WEBSTER GROVES: This 1966 news special turned up some disturbing facts about suburban teen-agers.

(Bottom, right) A REAL CASE OF MURDER: This 1961 *CBS Reports* program looked into the case of a Brooklyn boy who had been convicted of a murder he had not committed. Here the youth, Peter Manceri, and his parents talk with the show's producer, Jay McMullen.

(Below) DAVID BRINKLEY'S JOURNAL: In 1961 Brinkley began a weekly "TV column" in which he covered anything from Cocoa Beach to British Guiana, from James Hoffa to Antonino Rocca, from cowboys to highway-department scandals. The show was in the *See It Now* tradition, but Brinkley's sardonic touch and the work of producer Ted Yates gave it a flavor all its own. Like *See It Now* its ratings were low, sponsors were hard to find, and it lost its spot in the weekly schedule in 1963.

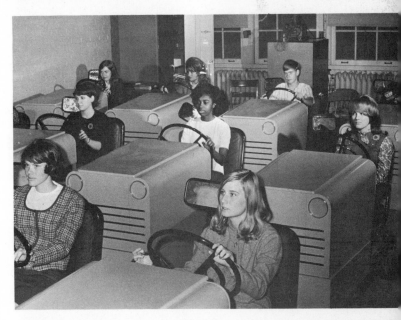

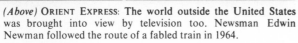

(Above) ORIENT EXPRESS: **The world outside the United States was brought into view by television too. Newsman Edwin Newman followed the route of a fabled train in 1964.**

(Top, right) BACK TO BHOWANI: Here a production crew films novelist John Masters narrating a program about one section of Africa. This was part of ABC's *Close-Up* series, which debuted in 1960 and provided several notable documentaries, including "Walk in My Shoes" and "Yanqui, No," which used hand-held cameras to produce remarkably vivid film portraits.

(Center, right) TOKYO THROUGH DIFFERENT EYES: This scene in a Japanese night spot was part of a 1964 news special.

(Right) LEGACY: The life of a German farmer was the subject of one show in this 1965–66 NET series which traced the roots of our civilization.

(Above) EXPEDITION: Several different real-life adventure series were telecast in the late fifties and early sixties. Colonel John Craig (right) was host of this globe-trotting 1961–62 show. Here he interviews Commander George P. Steele, a submarine skipper.

(Left) BOLD JOURNEY: Jack Douglas presented this series in the late fifties.

(Bottom, left) HIGH ADVENTURE: This New Guinea scene was part of the opening episode of a Lowell Thomas series which began in 1957.

(Below) THE STATELY GHOSTS OF ENGLAND: A different sort of adventure—a tongue-in-cheek ghost hunt—starred Margaret Rutherford in 1965.

(Below) KHRUSHCHEV IN BERLIN: The Cold War—and some hot ones—received a great deal of attention from the television news departments. One of many programs on the always-tense Berlin situation was this *NBC White Paper,* which concentrated on Khrushchev's role in Berlin developments.

(Right) THE TUNNEL: Another NBC documentary described the escape of fifty-nine men, women, and children from East Berlin. Apprehensive about the show, the U.S. State Department caused its postponement. It was eventually shown in December of 1962. Piers Anderton, the show's narrator, was photographed at the West Berlin end of the tunnel through which the refugees made their escape.

(Center, right) REVOLUTION IN THE DOMINICAN REPUBLIC: The networks displayed enterprise and skill in their reports of this 1965 crisis—they contradicted some of the statements which had been issued by Washington officials.

(Bottom, right) WAR IN VIETNAM: It required all the ingenuity, dedication, and courage television could muster to keep viewers informed about this incredibly complex war and its political ramifications. In the first stages television coverage was confined almost exclusively to the battlefield itself and, despite enormous difficulties, correspondents like Morley Safer (left) turned in magnificent performances. On one occasion Safer provoked the wrath of the Defense Department by filming and describing the burning of a South Vietnamese village by United States Marines. As the war progressed, and opposition to it became more demonstrative, television also began to come to grips with the difficult political issues surrounding United States involvement in Vietnam.

(*Right*) WIDE WIDE WORLD: Dave Garroway was the host of a highly original series which appeared in 1955 and ran for ninety minutes on Sunday afternoons. *Wide Wide World* presented live pickups from various parts of North America (it eventually went to film as well, for overseas sequences) to provide diverse views of whatever subject *Wide Wide World* was interested in during a given week. The topic might be youth or middle age, the coming of spring or preparations for Christmas, or music, or doctors, or America's heritage. Before the rest of television caught up with *Wide Wide World* and the show lost its uniqueness, it had demonstrated, more graphically than any previous program, that television could truly become a window on the world.

(*Below*) THE POPULATION EXPLOSION: Overpopulation, the source of so many of the world's ills, was analyzed in a sobering 1959 documentary, much of which was filmed in India. "The Population Explosion" was the second of the *CBS Reports* programs.

(Left) A CONVERSATION WITH HERBERT HOOVER: Television brought the public closer to its leaders than it had ever been before. This was just one of many intimate glimpses of Presidents and former Presidents which television afforded its audience. In the 1955 program Hoover conversed with newsman Ray Henle in the Hoover Library at Stanford University.

(Center, left) DECISION: THE CONFLICTS OF HARRY S TRUMAN: The networks turned down this series, but it was shown on dozens of local stations beginning in 1964. It covered the historical events of Truman's years in Washington, including (as shown here) his stunning upset victory over Thomas E. Dewey in 1948.

(Bottom, left) THE CRISIS IN PRESIDENTIAL SUCCESSION: President Eisenhower appeared frequently on television during his term in the White House and afterward. In this 1964 *CBS Reports* show he suggested changes in Presidential-succession procedures. The interviewer is Eric Sevareid.

(Below) MEET THE VEEP: Truman's Vice President, Alben W. Barkley, had his own fifteen-minute talk series, beginning in 1953. On the shows he chatted with Earl Godwin (left).

(Above) ADLAI STEVENSON REPORTS: The man Eisenhower defeated had a television series for a while before he became Ambassador to the United Nations. His conversational companion was Arnold Michaelis (right).

(Below) LYNDON JOHNSON'S TEXAS: President Johnson conducted a tour of his Texas ranch, of the house where he was born, and of the surrounding countryside, in "The Hill Country: Lyndon Johnson's Texas," telecast in the spring of 1966.

(Below) WHITE HOUSE TOUR: Mrs. John F. Kennedy proved a charming and informative guide in 1962, when she invited the television audience to see the White House and its treasures. **The program was shown on all three networks.**

(Above) A CONVERSATION WITH JAWAHARLAL NEHRU: **Leaders** of other nations as well as our own were interviewed on television. In 1955 Nehru talked with Chester Bowles as part of a series of programs featuring conversations with "elder wise men."

(Above) TRUJILLO: PORTRAIT OF A DICTATOR: **The late strong** man of the Dominican Republic was questioned by Bill Leonard (left) on *CBS Reports* in 1960.

(Below) THE TWENTIETH CENTURY: In addition to recounting the history of our times, this series occasionally went abroad for interviews with men like Spain's Franco (shown here in 1963, with *The Twentieth Century*'s host, Walter Cronkite). The series began in 1957, and for several years thereafter was the only weekly program of its kind on the air.

(Below) AMERICAN WHITE PAPER: UNITED STATES FOREIGN POLICY: In 1965 NBC presented a three-and-one-half-hour review and analysis of United States foreign policy. It contained interviews with many foreign leaders, including Egypt's Nasser **(the newsman is Dean Brelis, right).**

VICTORY AT SEA
recounted the history of United States naval operations during World War II. The series of films made its debut in 1952, was repeated in later years (it even played on Japanese television in 1961), won numerous prizes for its creators, and set the style for countless historical documentaries which followed. It consisted of film footage of the war, painstakingly collected and edited into twenty-six half-hour films. The producer was the late Henry Salomon, who later organized and spearheaded the *Project 20* unit which produced so many memorable historical chronicles. Richard Rodgers composed the background score, and Leonard Graves narrated.

(Left) THE TWISTED CROSS: One of the earliest *Project 20* productions was this account of the rise and fall of Hitler, first telecast in 1956, and narrated by Alexander Scourby. The story was told through captured German news film, which contained scenes such as this one of Joseph Goebbels addressing a Nazi street-corner rally.

(Center, left) WINSTON CHURCHILL—THE VALIANT YEARS: In 1961 Churchill was the subject of a weekly documentary series. Much of its narration consisted of Churchill's own words, spoken by Richard Burton. Here, during a visit to Canada, Churchill meets with Franklin D. Roosevelt and MacKenzie King.

(Bottom, left) D-DAY PLUS 20: Still another view of World War II was presented in 1964, when Eisenhower returned to Normandy to recall the invasion which had taken place there twenty years earlier. His companion was Walter Cronkite, who narrated this *CBS Reports* film.

(Below) YOU ARE THERE: An entirely different sort of historical series, also narrated by Cronkite, was on the air in earlier years, beginning in 1953. *You Are There* sent news correspondents back through time to report on dramatic re-creations of pivotal events. This was the assassination of Julius Caesar (played by Russ Conway).

(*Above*) THE KREMLIN: This 1963 documentary utilized footage shot at the Kremlin, plus flags, flames, shadows, and other dramatic effects to reconstruct events that had taken place inside the Kremlin's walls. The Soviet government protested against some aspects of the film.

(*Below*) CARL SANDBURG—LINCOLN'S PRAIRIE YEARS: Sandburg described Lincoln's youth to Howard K. Smith (left) in this 1962 *CBS Reports* program.

(*Above*) THE REAL WEST: Gary Cooper, who in the movies had helped perpetuate myths of the Old West, debunked them as the narrator of this documentary, which showed how things *really* were. The *Project 20* special was filmed in 1961, shortly before Cooper's death.

(Left) BISHOP FULTON J. SHEEN: Religious programming has taken many forms. One was *Life Is Worth Living,* weekly sermons delivered by Bishop Sheen, beginning in 1953. For a while the program was scheduled opposite Milton Berle's immensely popular show. Berle, who called himself "Uncle Miltie" and was sponsored by Texaco, liked to joke—mischievously but respectfully—about his competition, dubbing Bishop Sheen "Uncle Fultie" and using gags like, "We both work for the same boss—Sky Chief." Bishop Sheen enjoyed the ribbing.

(Bottom, left) REV. BILLY GRAHAM: A number of the evangelist's "crusades" have been telecast, starting in 1953.

(Below) DR. NORMAN VINCENT PEALE: *What's Your Trouble?* was the title of the weekly series in which the best-selling pastor advocated positive thinking.

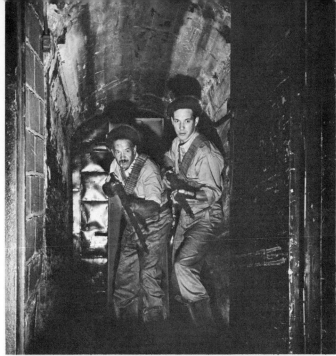

(*Above*) LAMP UNTO MY FEET: This is television's oldest surviving religious series, dating back to 1948. In one show Siobhan McKenna and Fritz Weaver read a translation of Paul Claudel's "La Chemin de la Croix."

(*Top, left*) LOOK UP AND LIVE: In 1954 this series joined *Lamp unto My Feet* in CBS's Sunday-morning lineup. This is a 1957 episode, a drama starring Frank Silvera and Mario Alcalde as Loyalist sentries during the Spanish Civil War.

(*Left*) FRONTIERS OF FAITH: NBC's counterpart of *Lamp* and *Look* is this Sunday-morning half hour, which is shared by Protestants *(Frontiers of Faith)*, Catholics *(The Catholic Hour)*, and Jews *(The Eternal Light)*. It began in 1951, and the next year dramatized excerpts from "The Diary of Anne Frank," starring Abby Bonine (left) and Adelaide Klein.

(*Bottom, left*) THIS IS THE LIFE: Various denominations make film series for showing by local stations. This is a typical one, produced by The Lutheran Church–Missouri Synod.

(*Below*) CROSSROADS: These were weekly documentary dramas about clergymen and their work, telecast beginning in 1955. In this episode Chuck Connors (left) portrayed Philadelphia Athletics pitcher Lou Brissie, here talking to John Goddard. Needless to say, religious programs, even those with sports figures, have seldom attracted as large an audience as do real sports events shown on television.

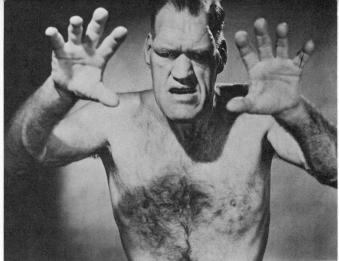

(*Below*) The Zebra Kid weighed in at 375 pounds.

(*Top, right*) The Swedish Angel eschewed frills and relied on pure menace for the success of his act.

(*Bottom, right*) The Smith Brothers were a "tag team," wrestling together against other twosomes.

(*Page 409, top, left*) Gorgeous George's tonsorial and sartorial elegance made him television's most talked-about wrestling attraction.

(*Page 409, bottom, left*) Antonino Rocca has earned more money from wrestling than any other performer.

WRESTLING

was the sport that captured the fancy of the earliest television watchers. It was perfect for television's primitive equipment in those early days—it took place indoors, within a small area, with only two participants for the cameras to focus on. Some viewers took the bouts seriously; others, aware that the matches were about as spontaneous and unrehearsed as a Balanchine ballet, still found them entertaining. Everyone enjoyed rooting for the virtuous good guys, booing the black-hearted bad guys, and watching the antics of such fanatical ringside characters as Hatpin Mary. The man who did the most to popularize wrestling on television was DuMont's man at ringside, Dennis James (top left). He came equipped with dog biscuits, walnut shells, and pieces of wood, which he would crack into the microphone whenever a wrestler applied a bone-crushing hold. He also had balloons, which he rubbed to simulate groans. And when a grappler was sent flying across the ring, James would play a cadenza on a harmonica. Most of the fun, however, was inside the ring, where the wrestlers vied to outdo each other in the outlandishness of their costumes, hairdos, and histrionics.

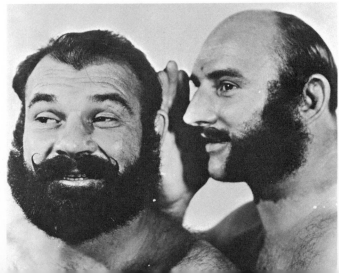

(Above) BOWLING: Like wrestling, bowling has always been a natural for television because camera coverage is so simple. In the mid-fifties it became an immensely popular television spectator sport. This is Don Carter, a bowler with an unorthodox style who dominated the game for years.

(Below) ROLLER DERBY: This is a sport nobody knew existed until television discovered it. Teams of men and women scoot around indoor tracks, attempting to overtake their opponents and bashing anyone who gets in their way. Beyond that, roller derby defies description. Though millions have watched it and have made folk heroes out of such eight-wheeled wonders as Tuffy Brasuhn, it is no easy task to find anyone who can tell you what the point of roller derby is or how it is scored.

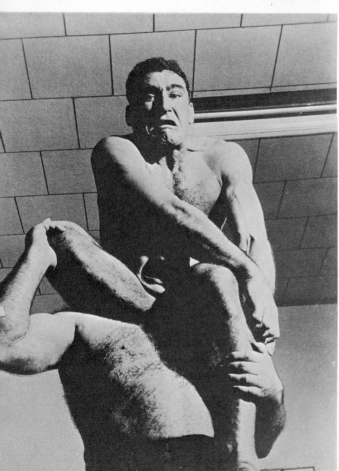

Horse Racing:

National coverage has largely been confined to telecasts of the Triple Crown events and, infrequently, other races of exceptional interest. In addition, regional hookups bring the Saturday features at major tracks to viewers in several sections of the country. In the sixties, the growth of interest in harness racing has been accompanied by expanded coverage of trotting and pacing races by big-city stations.

(Above) Fred Capossela has called most of the races telecast from New York and Florida tracks.

(Below) Clem McCarthy, radio's most illustrious racing broadcaster, was at the microphone for some early turf telecasts. Here he is pictured with Sammy Renick, jockey turned racing analyst.

BOXING

became a twice-a-week tradition in homes all over America. Wednesday and Friday were fight nights on the networks, and housewives became resigned to relinquishing control of the television set at ten o'clock (ET) on those evenings. Local and regional boxing telecasts proliferated too. Television brought viewers the greatest fighters of their times—Ray Robinson, Rocky Marciano, Willie Pep, Archie Moore, and countless others. It also created new ring heroes—Chuck Davey, Irish Bob Murphy, Harry (Kid) Mathews, Roland La Starza, Chico Vejar, Tommy (Hurricane) Jackson—most of whom, when last seen, were stretched horizontally across the television screen. As the fifties passed and boxing entered the sixties, it was gradually losing its television audience. The fighters who had become favorites with viewers were departing from the scene; fatalities inside the ring and scandals outside were tarnishing the sport's image; and boxers and promoters were discovering the economic advantages of closed-circuit television beamed into theaters. Soon there was just one weekly network boxing show. Then there were none.

(Above) Many championship bouts were telecast, including this 1951 welterweight clash in which Kid Gavilan (facing camera), whose "bolo punch" excited viewers, won a fifteen-round decision over Johnny Bratton.
(Page 410, top, right) Russ Hodges called the Wednesday-night fights.
(Page 410, bottom, right) Jimmy Powers was the voice of the Friday-night fights.
(Top, left) Bill the Bartender (Bill Nimmo) was a familiar figure between rounds on Wednesday nights in the early 1950's.
(Bottom, left) Jack Drees took over the Wednesday-night fights in the late fifties. Dr. Joyce Brothers, a psychologist who had displayed her boxing knowledge on *The $64,000 Question,* was on hand for some of the bouts.
(Below) On Saturday nights Don Dunphy, for years radio's top fight announcer, telecast *The Fight of the Week,* which began in 1960.

GOLF

can be found all over television on weekend afternoons, even though it seldom attracts very large viewing audiences. Sponsors theorize that the minority audience which does tune in contains enough purchasing power to make the telecasts worth their while. As a result various big-money tournaments and weekly filmed series have been created expressly for television, augmenting coverage of such traditional events as the Masters Tournament, the U.S. Open, and the P.G.A. Championship.

(Above) Gene Sarazen, a former golfing great, turned sportscaster for *Shell's Wonderful World of Golf*, a weekly series filmed all over the globe.

(Top, left) Arnold Palmer dominated tournament golf for years and won admirers at home and on the course who were dubbed "Arnie's army."

(Bottom, left) Slammin' Sammy Snead, the long-ball hitter with the exemplary swing, was a favorite of viewers in television's early years.

(Below) Jimmy Demaret forsook the tournament trail for the microphone—he described the play in the weekly *All-Star Golf*.

BASEBALL

monopolizes daytime television for at least four days every October, when the World Series is telecast nationwide. Other national games include the annual All-Star contest, plus various weekend network series. But most games are shown on a local or regional basis, at the discretion of the individual teams, many of which limit telecasts severely in hopes of luring more fans to the ball park.

(Above) This joyous mob scene took place during the first World Series ever telecast—the 1947 Series between the Yankees and Dodgers, which was beamed to four cities: New York, Philadelphia, Washington, and Schenectady. When this photo was snapped, pinch hitter Cookie Lavagetto (hatless, center, facing camera) had just doubled off the Ebbets Field wall with two out in the ninth, to spoil Bill Bevens' no-hitter and win the game for the Dodgers, 3–2.

/ **413**

(Left) Joe Garagiola injected a greater degree of humor, expertise, and irreverence into baseball commentary than had previous sportscasters. After knocking around for several years, he settled down in 1965 as play-by-play man for the Yankees.

(Bottom, left) Leo Durocher and Lindsey Nelson were NBC's microphone team for a while, before Durocher returned to coaching and managing and Nelson became the voice of the Mets.

(Below) Dizzy Dean (left) and Buddy Blattner broadcast CBS's *Game of the Week* for several seasons.

FOOTBALL—

specifically professional football—grew into television's most successful sports attraction. College football has always found an enthusiastic audience for its Saturday games and for dozens of annual bowl games (many of which were invented just for television), but the professional game has far surpassed it—and every other sport—as a television drawing card. Rights to televise the National Football League's games (and, to a lesser extent, the upstart American League's tilts) were the objects of fierce bidding battles between the networks, with prices soaring to unprecedented heights every time the television contract was put on the auction block. During the sixties the National Football League enjoyed prosperity beyond its most optimistic expectations, profiting not only from the lucrative television deals but also from packed houses during home games, as the stadiums were filled with fans whose interest in the sport had been stimulated by the telecasts. Home games were blacked out, and if no tickets were available, fans would travel more than a hundred miles to taverns and motels outside the blackout limits to watch the games on television.

414 /

(Left) Cleveland Browns star Jimmy Brown, here charging through the Philadelphia Eagles line, became pro-football's greatest running back, smashing all previous records for ground gaining.

(Top) Norman Sper and His Football Forecasts was shown by many local stations in the early fifties.

(Above) Herman Hickman, coach turned sportscaster, did a postgame show for a while.

(Below) Red Grange and Lindsey Nelson teamed up for the NBC *Game of the Week* beginning in 1955.

(*Above, left*) TED HUSING: In the early days radio's top hands, Husing among them, moved over to television and handled many different sportscasting chores.

(*Above, right*) BILL STERN: A contemporary of Husing, Stern was at the microphone for many of the biggest sports events.

(*Below, left*) RED BARBER: Before switching to television, Barber was generally recognized as radio's finest baseball commentator.

(*Below, right*) HARRY WISMER: He too was a successful radio broadcaster, but during the television era he became better known for his escapades as owner of the New York Titans football team.

(*Above, left*) MARTY GLICKMAN: A former track star, his radio and television specialty was basketball play-by-play.

(*Above, right*) MEL ALLEN: For years Allen was television's best-known and best-paid sportscaster, as "The Voice of the Yankees" and commentator for many other events, including (as shown here) *Jackpot Bowling* in 1959.

(*Below, left*) TOMMY HARMON: The Michigan All-American has been seen frequently as a sportscaster.

(*Below, right*) BUD PALMER: He is representative of a new breed of sportscaster—younger, less florid, more knowledgable—who unseated most of the old-timers and brought more depth to the coverage of athletic events. In addition to Palmer, men like Chris Schenkel, Jim McKay, Paul Christman, Curt Gowdy, Jim Simpson, Jack Whittaker, and Frank Gifford became television's streamlined versions of radio's Sterns, Husings, and Wismers.

LANDY-BANNISTER RACE: One of television's most thrilling moments was supplied by these two men—John Landy of Australia (left) and Roger Bannister of England, the world's first two under-four-minutes milers, whose match race was telecast from Vancouver in 1954. Bannister won, just barely, in 3:58.8.

OLYMPIC GAMES: Since 1956 the quadrennial Games have been seen on television, usually in the form of filmed or taped highlights, rushed to the United States from overseas. This is the finish of a sprint during the 1964 Olympic Games in Tokyo.

(Above) WINTER OLYMPICS: The winter phase of the Olympics achieved new prominence through television coverage. Skiing, ski jumping, figure skating, and ice hockey won many new adherents after viewers became familiar with the events through television. This ski jumper was caught in flight during the 1960 Winter Olympics in Squaw Valley, California.

(Right) CHAMPIONSHIP BRIDGE: Bridge got its own weekly show, starring Charles Goren (standing), in 1959. But bridge is just one of dozens of minor sports, pastimes, and competitions which have found a spot on television. The viewers' appetite for sports appears to be insatiable, and the three networks have sent production crews all over the world in search of events that can be used in their weekly omnibus sports series. *ABC's Wide World of Sports* usually is a step ahead of its competitors, but you never can tell what outlandish "sport" will turn up on any of the networks' Saturday and Sunday programs. Barrel-jumping, bocce, auto-wrecking derbies, sky-diving, Eiffel Tower-climbing, rattlesnake-hunting, Polynesian spear-throwing—these are just a few of the competitions which have been recorded by the cameras as television sports coverage has become increasingly comprehensive and skillful in recent years.

(Left) CONTINENTAL CLASSROOM: It did not take broadcasters or educators long to realize that this marvelous medium of television offered unparalleled opportunities for mass education. In 1957 WCBS-TV, New York, tried an experiment—at six-thirty in the morning, five days a week, it offered a course in comparative literature. It became apparent after the first broadcast that *Sunrise Semester,* as the program was called, had found a sizable audience, even at six-thirty A.M. That first day bookstores all over the city reported that all their copies of Stendhal's "The Red and the Black," the book under discussion on *Sunrise Semester,* had been gobbled up. The next year NBC joined the educational movement, with a nationwide telecourse series, *Continental Classroom.* One of its teachers was Dr. Peter Odegard (shown here, in 1962), a political scientist. *Sunrise Semester* eventually went network too, in 1963.

(Bottom, left) EDUCATIONAL TELEVISION: Educational stations all over the country have for years offered courses for children and adults, in school and out, for credit or just for education's sake. This is Dr. Persia Campbell conducting a "You, the Consumer" course over WNDT-TV, New York's educational outlet.

(Below) DR. FRANK BAXTER: Television's most celebrated professor is this bald, bespectacled scholar, whose Shakespeare lectures in the early fifties drew an astonishingly enthusiastic response from viewers all over America. Dr. Baxter subsequently presided over the *Bell Science Series,* which presented a number of instructional programs; this one, "Gateways to the Mind," explained the human senses.

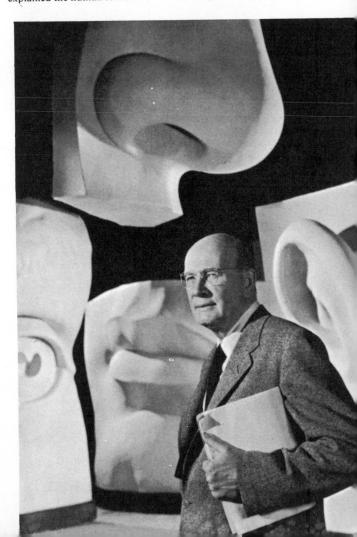

(Above) A TRIBUTE TO GRANDMA MOSES: Art and artists have been exposed to viewers in a number of ways. One was a visit to Grandma Moses, a 1955 *Wide Wide World* sequence. *See It Now* also paid a call on Grandma Moses.

(Top, left) VINCENT VAN GOGH: A SELF-PORTRAIT: Van Gogh's paintings, his words (read by Lee J. Cobb from the artist's letters to his brother Theo), and films of the scenes he painted were blended artfully by producer Lou Hazam to create a prize-winning documentary in 1962.

/ **419**

(Left) THE LOUVRE: In 1964 the great Parisian palace and museum was the subject of a documentary, narrated by Charles Boyer. The program concentrated more on the building and its history than on the masterpieces it houses, though many paintings and sculptures were shown on television for the first time.

(Bottom, left) HENRY MOORE: MAN OF FORM: The English sculptor sat for a television portrait in 1965. Here, in his studio at Much Hadham, Moore chats with newsman Charles Collingwood.

(Below) U.S.A.: ARTISTS: Andy Warhol, Pop Art's most publicized practitioner, was displayed in a 1966 NET documentary.

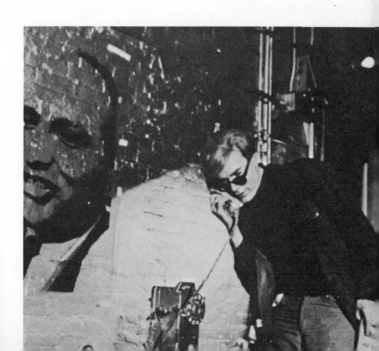

(Above) WANDA LANDOWSKA AT HOME: Men and women of music have received attention from the news departments too. Mme. Landowska talked with an interviewer and played the harpsichord in this 1953 telecast, which set the style for the "elder wise men" series that ran under several titles before settling on *Wisdom*.

(Top, left) CASALS AT 88: The great cellist played and talked with Isaac Stern (right) during this 1965 documentary.

(Center, left) MAN WITH A VIOLIN: ISAAC STERN: A few days later Stern himself became the subject of a *Twentieth Century* profile.

(Left) SINATRA: A man who purveyed a different sort of music, Frank Sinatra, was scrutinized in another 1965 documentary.

(Above) THE WORLD OF IDEAS: Dr. Charles Frankel, chairman of Columbia University's philosophy department, launched a cerebral discussion series in 1958.

(Below) HEMINGWAY: In 1961 *Du Pont Show of the Week* offered a biography of the novelist.

(Bottom) ACCENT: Poet John Ciardi was the host of a far-ranging weekly cultural series in 1962. This was an episode called "The Children and the Poet."

(Top) KEY TO THE AGES: Dr. Theodore Low conducted this cultural series in 1955.

(Above) THE ROOTS OF FREEDOM: "In Defense of Rome," starring James Mason in 1964, was the third in a series of cultural specials tracing the origins of Western civilization.

(Below) ESSAY ON BRIDGES: A more abstract form of television journalism appeared in the mid-sixties. This program was a film montage of impressions of bridges, written by Andrew Rooney and narrated by Harry Reasoner.

(Above) DR. SPOCK: The world's most celebrated pediatrician, Dr. Benjamin Spock, dispensed advice to parents in his 1955–56 program.

(Right) THE NATURE OF THINGS: Dr. Roy K. Marshall, an astronomer, presented one of the most popular early science series. Here, with William Van Pfefferle, fire chief of Camden, New Jersey, he demonstrates a "walkie-lookie" transmitting station.

(Bottom, right) THE SEARCH: Research projects at American universities were described in a series which had its premiere in 1954. The birth of a baby was shown on the air during a broadcast explaining the work of Yale University's Child Study Center. Charles Romine was the program's host.

(Below) ADVENTURE: The American Museum of Natural History in New York was the locale of this science series which arrived in 1953, with Charles Collingwood as host.

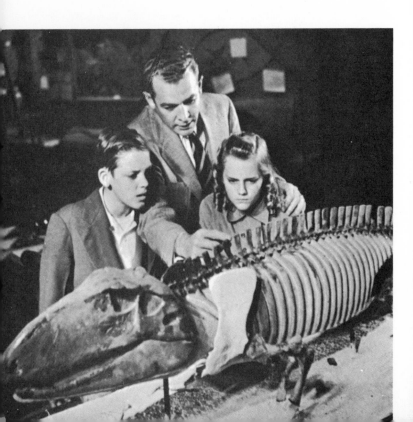

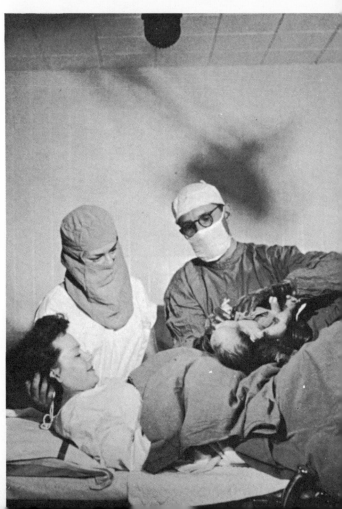

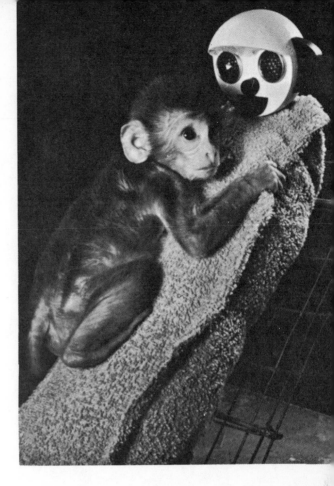

(Above) OUT OF DARKNESS: This extraordinary study of mental illness has become a television classic. First shown in 1956, it was produced and written by Albert Wasserman and narrated by Orson Welles. The program followed this woman, Doris L., through the various phases of her illness and treatment.

(Top, right) CONQUEST: Scientific breakthroughs were revealed in this series, which began in 1957. Monkeys were observed during research into the meaning of "mother love."

(Below) THE MYSTERY OF STONEHENGE: The mystery was solved in a 1965 documentary which, in a suspenseful on-camera demonstration, proved the validity of a new theory about the ancient Druid ruins: Stonehenge was a primitive but highly ingenious astronomical observatory.

PROJECT: MAN IN SPACE: As the sixties dawned, the world had entered the Space Age, and television was there to record man's first journeys into the unknown. This 1960 documentary contained Soviet films showing cosmonauts being trained. It was produced by David Wolper, who became the leading independent (non-network) supplier of television documentaries.

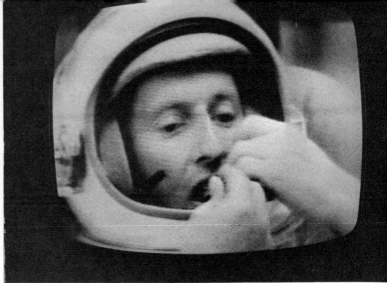

SPACE SHOTS

received intensive coverage from all three networks. They set up shop at Cape Canaveral (later renamed Cape Kennedy) and the Houston control center and followed our astronauts as closely as was permitted, from pre-launch preparations, through the countdown, launch, flight, re-entry and recovery, to the post-mission developments. As the astronauts progressed from Alan Shepard's first brief flight to John Glenn's orbital milestone, to two-man flights, to "walks" in space, to docking maneuvers and on to ever more amazing accomplishments, the viewing public rode with them, cheered their successes and heaved a collective sigh of relief when they returned safely to earth.

/ **425**

This series of four pictures (above and left) was shot during television coverage of the Gemini II mission in March of 1965: *(Above)* a simulation of one of the astronauts (they were actually Virgil Grissom and John Young), twenty-one minutes before blastoff; *(top, left)* blastoff; *(left)* a few seconds later; and *(bottom, left)* two minutes later.
(Below) When Gemini VII had its day several months later, television pictures were transmitted from the recovery ship for the first time.

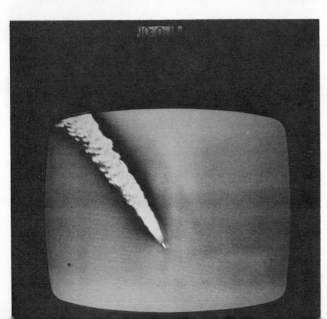

An engineer works with a model of Telstar in 1962.

(Right) The first signals which Telstar I relayed between America and Europe went through this receiving and transmitting station near Andover, Maine.

COMMUNICATIONS SATELLITES,
another product of space research and development, opened up exciting new prospects for television. The big breakthrough came on July 10, 1962, when Telstar I was put into orbit high above the earth and successfully transmitted television pictures from one continent to another. Telstar was soon followed by Relay I, Syncom I (the first synchronous satellite), and then more advanced versions of Telstar, Relay, and Syncom. In April, 1965, satellite communications moved beyond their first experimental stage and were made available for commercial use when Comsat's first satellite, Early Bird, was placed into orbit and offered to anyone who wanted to use it for transatlantic transmissions. By bouncing signals off satellites, television had overcome the barrier of the earth's horizon. The medium's own horizons were now unlimited, since every point on earth could be connected with every other point through live television. And the inhabitants of our planet wondered what new marvels lay ahead —and what they could expect to see on their television screens in the years to come. / **427**

THE END

Index

Fleming, Eric, 310
"Flight," 210
"Flint and Fire," 206
Flintstones, The, 364
Flipper, 370
Flood, Ann, 353
Floor Show, 112
Flynn, Joe, 145
Foch, Nina, 191, 208, 214
Fogel, Michelle, 327
Foley, Red, 106
Follow the Sun, 278
Follow Your Heart, 349
Fonda, Henry, 182, 183,
    214, 292, 312
Fontaine, Joan, 280
Fontanne, Lynn, 217
Fonteyn, Margot, 168, 169
Football, 414
Foote, Horton, 190, 194, 222
Foran, Mary, 150
Forbes, Scott, 304
Ford, Constance, 202, 350
Ford, Ernie, 71, 112, 114
Ford, Paul, 143
Ford, Ross, 156
Ford, Tennessee Ernie, 71,
    112, 114
Ford Festival, The, 64
Ford 50th Anniversary Show,
    119, 165
Ford Show, The, 71
Ford Star Jubilee, 101, 170,
    216, 217
Ford Star Revue, The, 97
Ford Startime, 98, 116, 181, 227
Ford Theatre, 235
Foreign Assignment, 273
Foreign Intrigue, 273
Forsythe, John, 136, 157, 198, 226
"For Whom the Bell Tolls," 223
Foster, Phil, 85
Foster, Philip, 352
Foster, Preston, 286, 313
Fountain, Pete, 115
Four Just Men, The, 273
Four Peanuts, The, 68
Four Star Playhouse, 234
Four Star Revue, 31, 40
Fox, Sonny, 322, 373, 375
Foy, Eddie, Jr., 155, 174
Francescatti, Zino, 118
"Frances Langford Presents," 179
Franchot, Richard, 202
Francis, Anne, 231, 289
Francis, Arlene, 58–59, 318, 330
Franciscus, James, 252, 260, 301
Franco, Francisco, 402
Frankel, Charles, 421
Frankenheimer, John, 190, 222,
    223, 227
"Frank Sinatra
    —A Man and His Music," 98
Franz, Eduard, 251
Fraser, Elisabeth, 143

Frawley, William, 125, 134
Freberg, Stan, 44
Frederick, Pauline, 385
Fredericks, Dean, 283
Fred Waring Show, The, 112
French Chef, The, 70
Frenkel, Liber, 68
Friday Night Fights, The, 410, 411
Friendly, Fred W., 381, 382
Froman, Jane, 100
From These Roots, 353
Frontier, 304
Frontier Circus, 284
Frontiers of Faith, 407
Front Page Detective, 272
Front Row Center, 215
Frost, David, 49
F Troop, 39, 145
Fugitive, The, 267, 290
Fuller, Robert, 306, 312
Funny Boners, 369
Funny Manns, 34
Funt, Allen, 74
Furness, Betty, 62
Fury, 370

G

Gabor, Eva, 181, 191
Gabor, Zsa Zsa, 82
Gallagher, Helen, 183
Gallant Men, The, 283
Gallop, Frank, 90
Gam, Rita, 65, 225
Gardiner, Mary, 323
Gardner, Ed, 150
Gardner, Erle Stanley, 245
Gardner, Hy, 85, 332
Gardner, Liz, 345
Garfield, John, 225
Gargan, William, 258
Garland, Beverly, 249, 266
Garland, Judy, 74, 88, 101, 172
Garner, James, 309
Garrett, Mike, 282
Garrett, Pat, 313
Garroway at Large, 34, 75, 76
Garroway, Dave, 75–76, 77,
    99, 167, 399
Garry Moore Show, The, 60, 61
Garson, Greer, 233
Gates, Maxine, 272
"Gateways to the Mind," 418
Gavilan, Kid, 411
Gavin, John, 283
Gazzara, Ben, 225, 280, 289
Gear, Luella, 138
G.E. College Bowl, 316, 321
Gene Autry Show, The, 295
"Gene Kelly Show, The," 180
General Electric Guest House, 119
General Electric Theater, 238
"General Foods
    25th Anniversary Show," 167

Genevieve, 84
Gennaro, Peter, 108
George, Anthony, 280
George Gobel Show, The, 46
"George Has a Birthday," 211
*George Sanders
    Mystery Theatre,* 236
*Georgia Gibbs'
    Million Record Show,* 99
Gerald McBoing-Boing, 364
Gering, Dick, 139
Gershwin, George, 170
Gethers, Steven, 210
Get Smart!, 161
Ghostley, Alice, 173
Gibbs, Georgia, 99
Gibson, Don, 350
Gibson, Hoot, 292
Gibson, John, 204
Gibson, Virginia, 108, 146, 373
Gidget, 135
Gielgud, John, 181, 225
Gifford, Frank, 337, 415
Gilbert, Billy, 172
Gilbert, Johnny, 343
Gilbert, Paul, 152
Gilbert, Ruth, 14
Gilbert, Sir William, 174, 179, 186
Gilbert and Sullivan, 174, 179, 186
Gilford, Jack, 253
Gillespie, Jean, 351
Gilligan's Island, 150
Gilman, Toni, 326
Ging, Jack, 250
Gingold, Hermione, 82, 191
Girl About Town, 95
Girl Talk, 62
Gish, Lillian, 216
Glamour-Go-Round, 67
Gleason, Jackie, 15–17, 90,
    113, 130, 182, 222
Gleason, Jimmy, 266
Glenn, John, 320, 425
Glickman, Marty, 415
Glynis, 155
Gobel, George, 46, 102, 181, 303
Goddard, John, 407
Goddard, Mark, 288
Godfrey, Arthur, 16, 56–57, 67,
    100, 102, 107
Godfrey, Kathy, 67
Godwin, Earl, 400
Goebbels, Joseph, 404
Goldbergs, The, 122, 131
Golden Windows, 352
Goldstein, Ruby, 52
Golf, 412
Gomer Pyle, USMC, 145
Gomez, Thomas, 216, 220
Goodman, Benny, 120, 181
Goodman, Dody, 84
Goodman, Lee, 52
Good Morning!, 78
Goodson, Mark, 317, 319
Goodson-Todman, 319

"Good Times," 168, 169
Goodwin, Bill, 340
Goodyear Playhouse, 194–97, 198
"Good Years, The," 183
Gordon, Gale, 142, 157
Goren, Charles, 417
Gorgeous George, 111, 408
Gormé, Eydie, 81
Gosfield, Maurice, 143
Gotell, Walter, 258
Gould, Sid, 329
Goulding, Ray, 40
Goulet, Robert, 105
Gowdy, Curt, 415
Grable, Betty, 217
Grady, Don, 134
Graham, Billy, 406
Graham, Virginia, 62
Granatelli, Vincent, 327
Grand Ole Opry, 106
Grange, Red, 414
Granger, Farley, 206, 216, 226
Grant, Bernard, 352
Grant, Harvey, 127
Grant, Kirby, 374
Grant, Lee, 197
Grauer, Ben, 271
Graves, Leonard, 403
Graves, Peter, 370
Gray, Billy, 129
Gray, Donald, 260
Gray, Joel, 172
Grayco, Helen, 113
Graziano, Rocky, 37, 42
Great Debates, The, 390
Greatest Gift, The, 352
Greatest Show on Earth, The, 280
Great Gildersleeve, The, 153
"Great Sebastians, The," 217
Great Talent Hunt, The, 329
Greaza, Walter, 266
Green, Adolph, 177, 182
Green, Martyn, 172
Green, Mitzi, 146
Greene, Angela, 153
Greene, Janet, 375
Greene, Lorne, 191, 217, 240, 311
Greene, Richard, 284
"Green Pastures," 190, 212
Greenwood, Joan, 213
Gregory, Dick, 78
Gregory, James, 264
Gregory, Paul, 216
Grey, Zane, 304
"Greybeards and Witches," 211
Grier, Roosevelt, 121
Griffin, Merv, 85, 100, 345
Griffith, Andy, 144, 160, 207
Griffith, Hugh, 253
Grimes, Tammy, 182
Grindl, 140
Grissom, Virgil, 425
Gross, Mason, 333
Grove, Betty Ann, 100
Guardino, Harry, 252

Guestward Ho!, 133, 158
Guiding Light, The, 334, 353
Guild, Nancy, 332
Guinness, Alec, 227
Gulager, Clu, 313
Gumby, 375
Gunslinger, 313
Gunsmoke, 293, 303
*Guy Lombardo's
   Diamond Jubilee,* 114
Gwynne, Fred, 148, 160

H

Hackett, Bobby, 97
Hackett, Buddy, 151
Hadley, Nancy, 157
Hadley, Reed, 261, 266
Hagen, Jean, 128
Haggis Baggis, 336
Hagman, Larry, 148
Hale, Alan, Jr., 287
Hale, Barbara, 245
Hale, Chanin, 22
Hale, Nancy, 301
Haleloke, 57
Haley, Jack, 40, 97
Hall, Cliff, 348
Hall, Jon, 288
Hall, Monte, 346
Halley, Rudolph, 386
Halliday, Heller, 215
Hallmark Hall of Fame, 174, 176, 212–13, 228
Halls of Ivy, The, 142
Halop, Florence, 156
Halpin, Luke, 207, 370
Hamer, Rusty, 128
Hamilton, Joe, 184
Hamilton, John, 365
Hamilton, Margaret, 183
Hamilton, Neil, 65
Hamilton, Robert, 68
Hamilton Trio, The, 18
"Hamlet," 228, 229
Hammerstein, Oscar, 2nd, 52, 165, 167, 173
Hammond, Peter, 285
Handy, W. C., 327
Handyman, 70
Handzik, George, 325
Haney, Carol, 171
Hank, 142
Hanna, William, 364
Hanna-Barbera, 364
"Hans Brinker or
   The Silver Skates," 176
Hanschman, Nancy, 385
"Hansel and Gretel," 176
Happy, 135
Harbor Command, 261
Harbourmaster, 286
Hardin, Ty, 312
Harding, Ann, 231
Hardwicke, Sir Cedric, 142, 175, 216, 231, 331

Hardy, Patricia, 233
Harland, Robert, 266
Harmon, Tommy, 415
Harper, Ron, 266
Harrigan & Son, 153
Harrington, Pat, Jr., 81
Harris, Jonathan, 275
Harris, Julie, 195, 206, 212, 213, 226
Harris, Robert H., 131
Harris, Rosemary, 225
Harris, Stacy, 262
Harrison, Rex, 182, 215
Harry's Girls, 146
Hart, Moss, 330
Hart, William S., 292
Hartline, Mary, 376
Hartman, Paul, 130, 199
"Harvest of Shame," 394
"Harvey," 225
Haskell, Jack, 76, 83
Hasso, Signe, 202
Hastings, Bob, 363
Hatfield, Hurd, 65, 231, 253
Hathaway, H. A., 327
Hathaways, The, 133
Hatpin Mary, 408
Have Gun, Will Travel, 305
Havoc, June, 154, 174, 321
Hawaiian Eye, 278
Hawkins, Jack, 216, 273
Hawkins, Jimmy, 297
Hawkins Falls, 349
Hayakawa, Sessue, 23, 203
Hayden, Russell, 300
Hayden, Sterling, 222
Hayes, Bill, 174
Hayes, Gabby, 297
Hayes, Helen, 193, 204, 214, 215, 231
Hayes, Richard, 83
Haymes, Dick, 171
Haynes, Hilda, 212
Hayward, Leland, 165, 182, 183
Hayward, Louis, 275
Hazam, Lou, 419
Hazel, 140
Heatherton, Joey, 90
Heaven for Betsy, 137
Hecht, Ben, 217
Heckart, Eileen, 196
Hedison, David, 274, 287
Heggen, Thomas, 145
"Heidi," 168, 169
Heidt, Horace, 113
Heifetz, Jascha, 89
"Heiress, The," 226
"Helen Morgan Story,
   The," 220, 221
Hellinger, Mark, 209, 260
Hellman, Lillian, 212
Hemingway, Ernest, 219, 223, 421
Hemion, Dwight, 187
Henderson, Kelo, 300
Henderson, Marcia, 151

Murphy, Audie, 106, 313
Murphy, Charles, 372
Murphy, Irish Bob, 411
Murray, Arthur, 109
Murray, Don, 191, 197, 212, 215
Murray, Jan, 325, 341, 344
Murray, Kathleen, 352
Murray, Kathryn, 109
Murray, Ken, 27, 111
Murrow, Edward R., 165, 378,
    381–83, 384, 388
Music Bingo, 343
"Music of Gershwin, The," 170
*Music Shop Starring
    Buddy Bregman, The,* 114
"Music with Mary Martin," 179
Myers, Carmel, 63
Myerson, Bess, 317, 330, 338
My Favorite Husband, 137
My Favorite Martian, 148
My Favorite Story, 236
My Friend Flicka, 371
My Friend Irma, 154
"My Heart's in
    the Highlands," 192
My Living Doll, 149
"My Lost Saints," 196
My Mother, the Car, 149
"My Name Is Barbra," 187
My Son Jeep, 136
"Mystery of Stonehenge,
    The," 423
My Three Sons, 134

N

Nabors, Jim, 145
Nader, George, 259, 288
Nagel, Conrad, 333
Naish, J. Carrol, 133, 158, 235, 268
Naked City, 260
Name's the Same, The, 330, 336
Name That Tune, 320
Narz, Jack, 343, 346
Nash, N. Richard, 194
Nash, Ogden, 169, 177, 331
Nasser, Gamal Abdel, 402
National Velvet, 371
Nature of Things, The, 422
Natwick, Mildred, 253
Naud, Lillian, 336
Navy Log, 282
NBC Bandstand, 337
NBC Comedy Hour, The, 44
NBC Opera Company, 164, 168,
    169, 170
NBC White Paper, 395, 398
Nearing, Vivienne, 323
Nehru, Jawaharlal, 402
Neill, Noel, 365
Neiman, Irving Gaynor, 222
Nelson, Barry, 137, 275
Nelson, David, 132
Nelson, Harriet, 132
Nelson, Jimmy, 14, 368

Nelson, John, 325
Nelson, Lindsey, 413, 414
Nelson, Lori, 155
Nelson, Ozzie, 132
Nelson, Penny, 325
Nelson, Ralph, 173, 217, 220
Nelson, Ricky, 132
Nesbitt, John, 65
Nettleton, Lois, 352
Neville, John, 229
Neville, Oliver, 229
*New Adventures of
    Martin Kane, The,* 258
New Breed, The, 266
Newhart, Bob, 47
Newman, Edwin, 396
Newman, Paul, 168, 169, 210
Newman, Phyllis, 49
Newmar, Julie, 149
New Stu Erwin Show, The, 130
Newton, Robert, 285
New York City Ballet, The, 177
Nichols, Mike, 176, 179, 182,
    184, 218, 329
Nichols, Red, 118
Nichols and May, 176, 179,
    182, 218
Nicholson, Bobby, 375
Nickell, Paul, 198, 214
Nielsen, Leslie, 195, 209, 266
Nigh, Jane, 272
Nightbeat, 389
"Night to Remember, A,"
    190, 203
Nimmo, Bill, 342, 411
Nitti, Frank, 223
Niven, David, 234, 289
Nixon, Richard, 82, 390
"Noah and the Flood," 119
Noah's Ark, 248
Nolan, Kathy, 135, 144
Nolan, Lloyd, 191, 258
Nomkeena, Keena, 299
Norby, 133
Norden, Tommy, 370
*Norman Sper and His Football
    Forecasts,* 414
Norris, Jan, 150
Norris, Kathi, 67
North, Jay, 374
Northwest Passage, 285
Norton, Cliff, 20, 34, 76
Noteworthies, The, 107
No Time for Sergeants, 144
"No Time for Sergeants," 207
Novak, Nina, 118
Novins, Stuart, 389
No Warning, 241
Nunn, Alice, 150
"Nur Ein Tag," 254
Nureyev, Rudolph, 163
Nurses, The, 251
"Nutcracker, The," 177
Nye, Louis, 81
Nype, Russell, 168, 169

O

Oakland, Sue, 323
Oakley, Annie, 175, 297
Object Is, The, 347
O'Brian, Hugh, 179, 182, 302
O'Brien, Edmond, 247
O'Brien, Erin, 99
O'Brien, Louise, 77
O'Brien, Pat, 153, 215
O'Brien, Patrick, 68
O'Connell, Helen, 114
O'Connor, Donald, 38, 176
"October Story," 195
Odegard, Peter, 418
Odetta, 180
O'Donnell, Cathy, 211
Oedipus, 218
Official Detective, 264
O'Hanlon, Redmond, 322
O'Hara, Mary, 371
O. Henry Playhouse, 233
O'Herlihy, Dan, 235
Oh! Susanna, 154
Oh, Those Bells!, 157
O'Keefe, Dennis, 134
"Old Glory:
    Benito Cereno, The," 254
"Old Man," 222
Oldsmobile Music Theatre, 231
Oldsmobile Show, The, 97
"Old Tasselfoot," 196
Olivier, Laurence, 227, 229
O'Loughlin, Gerald, 355
Olsen, Johnny, 375
Olsen, Merlin, 121
Olsen, Ole, 40
Olsen and Johnson, 40
Olson, Nancy, 170
"Olympics Telethon," 164
Omnibus, 117, 179, 203, 218, 219
"Once upon an Eastertime," 167
O'Neal, Patrick, 139, 353
O'Neal, Ryan, 314
O'Neal, William, 175
$100,000 Big Surprise, The, 323
O'Neill, Eugene, 202, 215
One Man's Family, 351
"One Touch of Venus," 168, 169
On the Boardwalk, 112
On Trial!, 245
On Your Account, 336, 340
On Your Mark, 375
On Your Way, 67
Opatoshu, David, 217
Open End, 389
"Orient Express," 396
*Original Amateur Hour,
    The,* 50, 68
Osborn, Lyn, 363
"Oscar Awards," 188
O'Shea, Michael, 153
O.S.S., 274
Oswald, Lee Harvey, 392, 393
Our American Heritage, 231

/ **445**

INDEX